A POPULISM OF THE SPIRIT
– FURTHER ESSAYS IN POLITICS AND UNIVERSAL ETHICS

Shimon Cowen

Published in 2022 by Connor Court Publishing Pty Ltd

Copyright © Shimon Cowen 2022

All rights reserved. No part of this book may be reproduced or transmitted in any form or by any means, electronic or mechanical, including photo copying, recording or by any information storage and retrieval system, without prior permission in writing from the publisher.

Connor Court Publishing Pty Ltd
PO Box 7257
Redland Bay QLD 4165
sales@connorcourt.com
www.connorcourt.com

Printed in Australia

ISBN: 9781922815293

Cover image: Detail of "Sparks of Kedusha, Breaking Light" by Chaim Bill Meyer

Image Permissions: Reproduced by permission of the artist.

Praise for the predecessor volume to
A Populism of the Spirit – Further Essays in Politics and Universal Ethics

A Populism of the Spirit – Further Essays in Politics and Universal Ethics is a sequel to – appearing around a decade after – Shimon Cowen's *Politics and Universal Ethics*. From transcripts of the bipartisan launches of *Politics and Universal Ethics* by members of all six State legislatures in Australia:

"In this book Dr Cowen argues powerfully, drawing on a wide range of research, that it is to our society's peril if we ignore the objective values or universal ethics which have moored society for thousands of years."
Mr Peter Abetz (Liberal), Member of the Legislative Assembly, Parliament of Western Australia

"There is a temptation ... to believe that everything is negotiable and everything is contestable. This is a temptation which Rabbi Cowen's book suggest we shouldn't yield to. Rabbi Cowen makes it very clear that communities are founded upon a fundamental truth with which we must not meddle. Even if we disagree upon matters in terms of emphasis to a degree, there are certain truths which…are in fact are universal, they are not for negotiation or adulteration …. I think it's a book ... that all legislators should read."
Hon Michelle Roberts (Labor), Parliament of Western Australia

"I think that's what this book is about – the foundation of making good judgments in government for the whole of society and not just a largely noisy minority that we often get presented and lobbied with."
Hon Leesa Vlahos (Labor), Parliamentary Secretary to the Premier, Parliament of South Australia

"Rabbi Cowen's book highlights universal ethics, objective values as a platform for conversation ... People of good will will come to different conclusions of good through that conversation, but affirming shared values ... in political and policy debate, is vital for this Parliament, this State and this nation."
Hon Stephen Wade (Liberal), Shadow Attorney General, Parliament of South Australia

"Dr Cowen stands as one of a small group of men and women…who have sought to apply their intellect, their faith and reason to articulate a vision of a better world, grounded importantly in spiritual literacy … The work of Dr Cowen can speak into each of [...the over 80 legislatures] around the Western world and into each of [… their contemporary] debates … in some regard to those transcendent and enduring values that have guided western civilization for 3000 years and related civilizations during that time."
Murray Thompson (Liberal), Parliament of Victoria

"This book is outstanding in terms of outlining what is involved in objective and universal ethics and moral standards in political practice."
Hon Christine Campbell (Labor), Parliament of Victoria

"[T]he whole question of universal ethics covered so well by the … book, is one that should concern all of us in public life … [U]niversal ethics … answers to the search of a humanity that always endeavours to give itself rules for both personal and communitarian life. These universal ethics are the fundamental values for our common humanity. Rabbi Cowen has made a great contribution to that discussion, to that search".
Hon Luke Foley (Labor), Leader of the Opposition, Legislative Council, Parliament of New South Wales

"I hope the book is taken seriously and that it can in future times be looked back upon as a volume which challenged some of the assumptions which are being made within politics today and which will cause men and women of conviction to be honestly able to re-examine their consciences, re-examine their party platform and to strive for a better world for human beings based on this notion of the universal ethic, which … should bind us together".
Mr Michael Ferguson (Liberal), Shadow Minister for Education and Skills, Parliament of Tasmania

TO MY MOTHER,
LADY ANNA COWEN
OF BLESSED MEMORY

CONTENTS

Preface and Acknowledgments 9

Part 1: The New Challenge to Universal Ethics 15
1   The Repression of Religious Freedom 17
2   The Recovery of the Human Spirit in Politics 37

Part 2: More Questions for Universal Ethics 53
3   **Conflict and Higher Moral Authority** 55

    Conflict Resolution: an Ethical Supplementation of the Harvard Negotiation Project 55

    Jonathan Pollard: to Whom is Loyalty Due? 73

4   **The Basis for a Commonly Recognized Universal Ethics in the World Religious Cultures** 87

5   Universal Ethics and the United Nations 107

Part 3: Political Applications of Universal Ethics 126
6   **Education and Spiritual Literacy** 127

    An Education in a Shared Ethic 128

    Why should a Kid pay for a Ride on a Train? An Argument for a Spiritual Education 145

    The Spiritual Component in School Curriculum   *Submission to the National Curriculum Review (2014)* 157

    The National Curriculum of 2021 as an Instrument of Secularization 166

    Aging and Spirituality 169

7   **The Assault on Conscience and Religious Freedom** 175

    Abortion and the Coercion of Conscience 176

    The Consequences and Cost of Moral Capitulation 188

    Psychotherapy and Religious Freedom: the Trial of JONAH 194

    Access to Therapy and Religious Freedom 203

8 Sexuality and Human Identity 207
   Changes in Family Law before Same-sex Marriage 208
   Heterosexuality and Human Identity 216
   Transgenderism and the Dissolution of Identity 222
9 Issues of Justice 233
   Universal Ethics and the Constitution 234
   The Courts and Universal Ethics 241
   Drugs and the Culture of Personal Responsibility 247
10 Recovering the Sanctity of Life 255
   Compassion for the Whole Person 256
   What Life is and Why Killing is Wrong 258
   The Nihilism in Euthanasia 263
   The Contagion of Euthanasia 265
11 Universal Ethics in Economic Life 273
   Universal Ethics and Economic Life 273
12 The Environment 283
   Religiously Conscious and Secularizing Environmentalism 283

Part 4: Manifestoes 301
13 There is more than this... 303
   Four Lectures in Advance of the Victorian State Elections 2014 303
   Introduction. Reestablishing the Political Moral Centre 303
   First Lecture. Culture, the Divine and Happiness 307
   Second Lecture. Homosexuality: what does Sex have to do with G-d? 319
   Third Lecture. Life: Whose is It? 329
   Fourth Lecture. Compassion and its Corruption 337
14 A Populism of the Spirit 347

Preface and Acknowledgments

This book — *A Populism of the Spirit – Further Essays in Politics and Universal Ethics* — is a sequel to a book I wrote more than a decade ago called *Politics and Universal Ethics*. It collects essays written over the intervening years largely in response to legislative and ideological movements which clash with universal ethics. The "universal ethics", to which both books refer, are the core, shared values at the root of the great world faiths and cultures, known as the Noahide laws. They are so named for Noah, the survivor of the biblical Flood, with whose descendants — all humanity — civilization was renewed on the basis of this ethical code.

In 1991, the United States Congress endorsed the Noahide Laws as the "bedrock of society from the dawn of civilization". *The Theory and Practice of Universal Ethics — the Noahide Laws*, an extensive treatment of the Noahide laws which I published several years ago, carries further endorsements of the Noahide laws, as foundational to society, by the President of the European Union, the Head of an Islamic State, King Mohammed VI of Morocco and a Governor General of Australia. Jewish, Christian, Muslim and Buddhist scholars have all affirmed a basic resonance with the Noahide laws and a Jewish-Hindu summit affirmed common acceptance of a Supreme Being. This Supreme Being instructed the Noahide laws, a basic compass of universal morality.

The deepest opposition to universal ethics in Western societies today comes from an ideology that has captured much of the spectrum of politics. In *Politics and Universal Ethics* I described it as "hedonistic materialism". It acknowledges neither the great G-d of creation nor the small "G-d" in the human being, namely, the soul or conscience. It believes that the human being is *defined and compelled* by drives or emotions and perceptions and is accordingly fulfilled only through the actualization of those emotional drives and perceptions. The faith tradition, which is largely unified around belief in a Creator and the universal ethics commanded by the Creator, maintains, on the other hand, that the human being is *free* from compulsion by drives and perceptions. It maintains that the human being has a soul or conscience, which inwardly resonates with the Creator and with universal ethics. Human freedom derives from the fact that the human being, to use the terms of the great psychologist Viktor Frankl, is *both* a "psychophysical organism" with emotive drives and perceptions *and equally* the bearer of a conscience which can transcend the psychophysical self. Freedom consists in the choice either to submit to jostling and often morphing interests within the lower, psychophysical self, or to *transcend* interests altogether — to consult conscience. In the act of self-transcendence, the human exposes the soul or conscience and makes it sovereign within him or herself. With this accomplished sovereignty of conscience, a person then comes back to review the physical and psychological interests which clamour for actualization. On the basis of the knowledge of the soul, universal ethics, the human decides which of these emotions or drives and perceptions to accept, which to reject and which to modify. I have discussed the psychological concept of human freedom and the moral structure of human personality made possible by conscience in another book. It translates and introduces relevant writings of Viktor Frankl and is entitled *The Rediscovery of the Human — Psychological Writings of Viktor E. Frankl on the Human in the Image of the Divine.*

The particular crisis of our time is that those who believe that the human being is not free, have now taken steps legislatively, judicially and through social policy, to make sure that the human being will not be free. Accordingly, the first part of this volume, on the new challenge to universal ethics, documents the actual repression of the faith tradition and its expression of universal ethics. It also sets out the legislation which could restore religious freedom. It is followed by a chapter devoted the "The Recovery of the Human Spirit in Politics", a series of vignettes portraying qualities of the human spirit for all those who have forgotten, or flagged in their recognition of, it and want to know what it is that must be recovered and live again in political life.

The second part of this volume parallels the second part of its predecessor *Politics and Universal Ethics* on theoretical questions in universal ithics. In the first volume, this section explored in a chapter on "'Right' and 'Left' in Universal Ethics", how the diverse political temperaments of "Right" and "Left" can theoretically both operate within the perimeter of universal ethics. It also discussed the question of "Eternal Law and Human Legislation", namely, how within the framework of Divinely given universal principles, there is scope for human ("positive") law reflecting cultural and historical particularity and needs. This volume discusses further theoretical questions in three chapters (3-5). The first explores how universal ethics can contribute to the settling of conflict — conflicting interests of opposed persons or groups; and conflicts of loyalty, where the State, for example, is at variance with universal ethics. The second examines the potentials within the great world faith cultures for transcendence towards the same Creator, which opens them to the conscious formation of a global culture of universal ethics. The third essay in this section critiques, from the standpoint of universal ethics, a foundational document of the United Nations, The Universal Declaration of Human Rights, in terms of its goals of universality, drawing common allegiance and motivating international cooperation.

The third part of this book continues, as did the third part of *Politics and Universal Ethics*, with applications of universal ethics to actual political questions. This part divides into seven chapters, grouping essays which relate to the concerns of the seven Noahide laws: belief itself ("spiritual literacy"), the respect and protection of belief, human sexuality, justice, killing and theft (economic ethics) and the proper treatment of the environment.

The final part of this book, entitled "Manifestoes", contains pieces which were written with an eye to political action required to restore universal ethics. Chapter 13 contains four lectures collectively titled "There is more than this...", which were delivered prior to a state election and were subsequently disseminated amongst politicians in an attempt to arouse awareness of universal ethics. The final chapter (14), "A Populism of the Spirit" again searches for the roots of potential political change in popular resonance with universal ethics. The book largely addresses social and political events in Australia, but its comments are generalizable to Western society at large.

This book is thus compounded of individual essays and writings. They have been thematically knitted together in its overall structure and specifically within the individual chapters, each of which has a short introduction. Since they were written as individual essays in response to a host of circumstances, there are some minor overlaps and repetitions. Notwithstanding this, I trust that each piece contributes a distinct thought. Many of them have undergone further rewriting and editing since their first publication.

I am very grateful to the publisher Anthony Cappello of Connor Court Publishing for living up to a now somewhat eclipsed ideal of publishing: allowing ideas to be heard, even if they do not flow with the tide of mass sentiment. Ms Gerlinde Turchin has my thanks for her proofreading of the manuscript. The painting on the cover is by the Australian artist Chaim Bill Meyer and is entitled "Sparks of *Kedusha* ['Holiness'], Breaking Light". It is my hope that the light of the human spirit will indeed break through the darkness of the present time and, with the Creator's help, redeem the potentials (the "sparks") of holiness in humanity, nature and society into a world actually and wholly redolent of the Divine.

The following are the original places of publication of the individual essays. "The Repression of Religious Freedom" was published first as "The Repression of Religious Freedom in Australia and the Federal Legislation Needed to Restore it" in *the Journal of Judaism and Civilization*, Vol. 15. It subsequently appeared in *Quadrant Magazine*, January-February, 2022. Chapter 2, "The Recovery of the Human Spirit in Politics", is a melange of pieces, somewhat reworked, some of which were first printed in the first chapter of the Journal *Interface,* Double Biennial Issue, Volumes 4 and 5, 2011-2012 and in the first chapter of the second Double Biennial Issue, Volumes 6 and 7, 2013-2014. These volumes were also entitled *Contemporary Politics and Social Policy through the Lens of Traditional Faith and Universal Ethics*. Both the essays "Conflict Resolution: an Ethical Supplementation of the Harvard Negotiation Project" and "Jonathan Pollard: to Whom is Loyalty Due?", included in Chapter 3, were originally published in the Double Biennial Issue of *Interface*, Volumes 6 and 7, 2013-2014. Mr Eliezer Kornhauser was the sponsor of the research of the first of these pieces. The essay in Chapter 4 "The Basis for a Commonly Recognized Universal Ethics in the World Religious Cultures" was originally published as "Transcendence, the World Religions and the Noahide Laws" in the *Journal of Judaism and Civilization*, 13, 2018. "Universal Ethics and the United Nations: *An Examination of the United Nations' "Universal Declaration of Human Rights"*, placed in Chapter 6, was originally published as "What needs Rectification in the Universal Declaration of Human Rights" in the *Journal of Judaism and Civilization*, Vol. 14, 2019. "An Education in a Shared Ethic - *Common Values of Judaism, Christianity and Islam*" was originally funded by the Australian Federal Attorney General as a free-standing publication and was subsequently reprinted in the Double Biennial Issue of *Interface*, Volumes 4 and 5, 2011-2012. The second essay in Chapter 6, "Why should a Kid pay for a Ride on a Train? An Argument for a Spiritual Education" was published in the Double Biennial Issue of *Interface*, Volumes 6 and 7, 2013-2014 with the title "Why should a Kid pay for a Ride on a Train? An Argument for Religion in Education". The third piece in Chapter 6, "The Spiritual Component in School Curriculum - *Submission to the National Curriculum Review (2014)*" was first published the Double Biennial Issue of *Interface*, Volumes 4 and 5, 2011-2012. The final piece in Chapter 6, "The National Curriculum of 2021 as an Instrument of Secularization" has not previously been published. "Abortion and the Coercion of Conscience" and "The Consequences and Cost of Moral Capitulation", found here in Chapter 7 were both published in the Double Biennial Issue of *Interface*, Volumes 4 and 5, 2011-2012. "Psychotherapy and Religious Freedom: the Trial of JONAH" and "Access to Therapy and Religious Freedom", also included in Chapter 7, were first published in the *Journal of Judaism and Civilization*, Volume 14, 2019. "Changes in Family Law before Same-sex Marriage" originally titled as "Family Law and the Biblical Concept of Marriage", included here in Chapter 8, was first published in the Double Biennial Issue of *Interface*, Volumes 4 and 5, 2011-2012. "Heterosexuality and Human Identity" was first published in Michael Stokes and David Daintree (Eds), *Dangerous Ideas*, Redlands Bay: Connor Court Publishing, 2017. "Transgenderism and the Dissolution of Identity" was first published in *News Weekly*, May 19, 2018. The essays in Chapter 9, "Universal Ethics and the Constitution *Searching the Constitution for Limits on Abortion....*" and "The Courts and Universal Ethics: A *Conversation with a former Chief Justice*" were both first published in *Quadrant*, March 2015. The final essay in that Chapter, "Drugs and the Culture of Personal Responsibility" was first published in *News Weekly*, December 2, 2017, as "Drugs and Society". The sources of the four essays, included in Chapter 10 are as follows. The essay, "The Coercion of Conscience" was first published the Double Biennial Issue of *Interface*, Volumes 4 and 5, 2011-2012. "What Life is and Why Killing is Wrong – *A Victorian Bill for 'Assisted Dying'*". "The Nihilism in Euthanasia" (published originally in the *Australian Jewish News*, 2017) and "The Contagion of Euthanasia" (first published in *Public Discourse* 11 September, 2017) were all subsequently published in the Double Biennial Issue of *Interface*, Volumes 6 and 7, 2013-2014. In Chapter 11, the essay "Universal Ethics and Economic Life" is here published for the first time. The essay printed in Chapter 12 as "Religiously Conscious and Secularizing Environmentalism" was first published in the *Journal of Judaism and Civilization*, Vol. 15, 2021. The lectures comprised in Chapter 13 under the title "There is more than this..." were published previously in the *Journal of Judaism and Civilization*, Vol. 10, 2014. The final essay in Chapter 14, "A Populism of the Spirit" was first published in *Hakira*, Vol. 22 (Spring 2017).

PART 1: THE NEW CHALLENGE TO UNIVERSAL ETHICS

Chapter 1

The Repression of Religious Freedom

Over ten years ago I published a book entitled *Politics and Universal Ethics*. It began with a chapter on the rising sceptre of an ideology, pitted against traditional faith with its compass of universal values, which have been the foundation of civilization. The new ideology was not simply secular, but *secularizing*: it wanted to "remove" the great G-d from the universe and the "small" G-d — the human soul with its resonance with the Divine moral compass — from the human being. It was a materialistic ideology, opposed to the spiritual. But its materialism was also deeply hedonistic, that is to say, oriented to physical and psychological gratification. It pursued the quest for pleasure and the flight from pain, uninhibited by the review of conscience, anchored in traditional faith, that decides what pleasures may legitimately be indulged and what pain may legitimately be escaped.

I called this new ideology "hedonistic materialism" and shortened it to "Hedonomat" alluding to another variant of a materialistic world view, which had dominated much of the world for almost a century. That was "Diamat", short for "dialectical materialism", the official doctrine of the communist world, half of which vanished with the collapse of the USSR and its European satellites. Just as "Diamat" was the ideology of one form of tyranny, so too, in recent years, "Hedonomat", the dominant ideology of the "liberal" West, has been culturally and legislatively installed with tyrannous features. The tyranny is experienced particularly by its identified enemy, traditional faith, which, contrary to it, upholds the human spirit and enduring ethical principles of an eternal Creator. Hedonistic materialism, primarily through legislation and policy, has acted to crush religious freedom. It does this globally. The focus of this paper is how it does so in Australia, and what may be done to restore religious freedom.

This paper seeks to document (a) the dimensions of religious freedom, (b) the actual legislative and policy measures that have been directed against them, (c) the social and political culture — of unfiltered and corrupted emotions, disabled critical intellect and removal of freedoms — which support this program, and finally (d) what must be legislated in a Federal Religious Freedom Bill to restore and guarantee religious freedom in Australia.

The dimensions of religious freedom

Religious freedom pertains to the rights granted to (1) the *faith community* to preserve its own existence, and to do so (a) *inwardly*, in its freedom to teach and model its beliefs and so educate successive generations of the faith community and (b) *outwardly*, through its free participation in the life and politics of the wider society, in order to safeguard its existence within society and to advocate, like any other group, for its values. Religious freedom then pertains to rights granted to (2) the religious *individual* to live in accordance with conscience, whether in respect of (a) one's own *private* life or (b) in public *interactions* with the rest of society. Religious freedom pertains finally (3) to the right to preservation of the integrity of the family, whereby the bonds and educative role of *parents with their children* are not infringed. These five headings are now discussed in turn.

Religious freedom of the faith community in its inner life

Faith communities are traditions with long lineages. From the making known of the one Creator by Abraham came out Judaism, Christianity and Islam. The message of a supreme Deity, as discussed in Chapter 4, came also to the great Eastern religions, Hinduism and Buddhism. The adherents of these five faiths constitute some three quarters of the world's population. Even before Abraham, there was a common ancestor and earlier root of the world faiths in the biblical figure of Noah.

Associated with Noah, the ancestor of humanity after the biblical Flood, are seven Divinely communicated "Noahide Laws". They form a common core and root of the world faiths, a universal moral compass. These ethical laws or principles consist of belief in and respect for the Creator, sexual morality, justice, the prohibitions of theft and killing and the teaching of a proper regard for animal and non-animal nature. The different world faiths may have developed differently, but this common ethical teaching at their root constitutes the universal moral compass they have imparted to civilization. Not only does this universal moral compass arise from an *historical* tradition. So also the aware human soul resonates with it.

The belief in an eternal Creator and in the eternal moral compass given by the Creator is sustained in the individual faith traditions by the experience of faith and the transmission of its teachings from generation to generation. This transmission occurs with the family, prayer community and the educational institutions of the faith community. Without the freedom to maintain this educational transmission of faith and its ethical teaching, prayer and religious practice and the integral ethos of its institutions, the very existence of the faith community is threatened.

Religious freedom of the faith community within society.

Faith exists both "outside" and "inside" politics. It is "outside" politics as an encompassing framework — the living memory — of the enduring values, which establish civilized society. However, it is also "inside" politics as a participant in the political process, like any other group, protecting its existence and advocating for its values. This dual relationship of the faith community and politics is recognized in section 116 of the Australian Constitution:

> The Commonwealth shall not make any law for establishing any religion, or for imposing any religious observance, or

for prohibiting the free exercise of any religion, and no religious test shall be required as a qualification for any office or public trust under the Commonwealth.

On the one hand, this provision decouples politics from faith: religion does not limit a free play of groups and interests in the society. Office holders *do not have to belong* to a faith group and certainly not to any *particular* faith group. On the other hand, it removes State control from faith, guaranteeing the "free exercise of any religion", *including its participation and manifestation of its values in politics and public life, which may not be fettered by the State*. Religion deserves respect and protection as the historical background and foundation of our society, as the phrase of the Preamble to the Constitution, "humbly relying on the blessing of Almighty G-d", states. And it is certainly entitled, *no less than any group in society*, freely to participate in politics, stating and defending its values and needs.

Freedom of conscience in the private life of the individual

Fundamental to the faith tradition is the concept that the human being must live one's own private life according to conscience. What does this mean? A person has a body, which is a source of impulses, needs and emotions; the person also has a mind which is a source of varying perceptions. Standing above both bodily and mental dimensions, however, is the human conscience. The religious name for conscience is the soul. By virtue of conscience or soul the human being is capable of *self-transcendence* and self-examination. That means that the soul or conscience enables one to stand above, and distance oneself from, one's own impulses and perceptions, and to judge whether or not, and with what modifications, to act upon them. The human being, in whom soul or conscience is active and sovereign, asks not "what do I want", but ethically "what is wanted of me".

It may seem strange to ask, what kind of a freedom has to be guaranteed by the State to allow the individual to to lead one's own *private* life according to conscience? Yet it is not strange, and contemporary society and politics have brought to light an example of the need for the State to guarantee precisely this freedom. This is in the realm of the access to therapeutic help for a religious individual, whose psychological issues make it difficult for one to live according to one's conscience. Thus, a person with a gambling addiction or kleptomania needs access to therapeutic help in order to live according to a conscience, the beliefs of which are against gambling and stealing. The same applies to a person with psychological impulses and perceptions which incline one to homosexuality or gender dysphoria, neither of which one's own religious conscience may accept, and one seeks therapeutic help to overcome them. It is only the individual — and no political edict — that can determine whether one should change one's own character and personality. This is a matter of freedom of conscience. The religious individual, not the State, will decide whether or not he or she is "broken" and in need of "repair", with therapeutic assistance, in free private exercise of conscience.

Freedom of conscience in the public life of the individual

In order in daily life to manifest one's faith, the individual must be permitted to carry out his or her social involvements with integrity of conscience. Thus, where, for example, an act of killing — be it in a routine "abortion on demand" or in an act of euthanasia or "physician assisted suicide" — violates the religious conscience of a doctor or paramedic, he or she must free to stand aside. Moreover, freedom of conscience must be granted not only in relation to direct involvement in the repugnant act, but also in relation to indirect or complicitous involvement in the act such as in a doctor having to refer an individual to another doctor, known to have no objection to the act, such as an abortion, to which the first doctor objects.

Similarly, at a further remove, an individual should not be compelled to perform a service which facilitates an activity which his or her faith deems morally repugnant. There is a great difference between showing respect for a homosexual as a person, and having to cater a homosexual marriage, to which, as an act, one is religiously opposed; or between showing respect for a prostitute as a human being, and having to rent one's property for a brothel, where one's faith morally rejects the activity of prostitution.

The integrity of the family and the parent-child relationship.

Central to the faith tradition is the integrity of the family and the parent-child relationship. The traditional family is a biological unit. A husband and wife find the expression of their union in their biological offspring; and the child finds in its parents its source. These bonds of biological identity also have a spiritual dimension and continuity: faith is transmitted from generation to generation, parents to children, through the family unit. Religious schooling is an agency of, and the prayer and religious community a vital adjunct to, the parents in this generational transmission of faith. The protection of the bonds of the family is thus integral to religious freedom and religious existence. This is recognized in several treaties to which Australia is a signatory. In Article 7(1) of the United Nations Covenant on the Rights of the Child (1989) there is affirmed the right of the child *"to know and be cared for by his or her parents"*. Article 23 (6) of the Universal Declaration of Human Rights states that *"Parents have a prior right to choose the kind of education that shall be given to their children"*. Article 18 (4) of the International Covenant on Civil and Political Rights requires *"respect for the liberty of parents … to ensure the religious and moral education of their children in conformity with their own convictions"*.

Legislative and policy programs to repress religious freedom

We now identify legislative and policy programs in Australia which undermine each of these five domains of religious freedom.

Legislation to undermine the inner life of faith communities

One feature of The Victorian Change or Suppression (Conversion) Practices Prohibition Act 2021 is its specification of beliefs which a faith community may not transmit and recommend to its members or children. Specifically, it prohibits — with the sanction of imprisonment (up to ten years) and fines — parents, schools and ministers of religion form teaching religious values and beliefs concerning sexuality. It makes the bizarre "concession" that one may make mention of such beliefs, provided one does not recommend to adherents or children that they live by these beliefs. It has an associated apparatus for reporting on, and punishing, families, schools and congregation in which the transmission and recommendation of these beliefs occur. This is the most egregiously anti-religious legislation in Australian history and is recognized internationally as setting a "benchmark" in the rigour of its pursuit to crush the transmission of those religious beliefs opposed by its architects.

At the time of writing, the Victorian Government has signalled its intention to amend the Victorian Equal Opportunity Act (2010) to remove key religious exemptions to discrimination law in employment in religious schools or organizations (now passed into law). In short, it intends to force religious schools to hire or keep in their employment staff, whose manifest life style and values conflict with the religious values the institution seeks to teach and model to its students. This attempt to make religious schools contradict their own ethos coalesces with the Change or Suppression Act, which dictates what religious schools may not teach. Together, they seek to invade the inner sancta of the faith community. The result is the removal of the freedom of the faith community to maintain its existence by breaking the inner transmission of its beliefs and values.

Legislation to undermine the outer life of faith groups in society

The Victorian Government has announced its attention to amend the *Racial and Religious Tolerance Act 2001* to (1) include, amongst the topics of punishable "vilification", reference to sexual and gender orientation; (2) to alter the threshold for punishment from the existing criterion of "inciting hatred against, serious contempt for, or revulsion or severe ridicule" to being "*likely* to incite…"; and (3) to set up a reporting and investigative apparatus to hunt out all such infringements. What this means simply is that public statements by faith groups in relation to their beliefs about sexual morality now come within the punishable category of "vilification". An objection that an expressed belief or value would be "likely" to offend, even though no offense has occurred, nor was intended, is sufficient to punish the religious group which expressed it; and to intimidate it into silence before it opens its mouth. Its result is to limit the freedom of religious groups to participate in public, political discussion.

The rights, which protect the existence of a faith group in society, go beyond their ability to participate in the political process. They extend to societal facilitation of fulfilment of its basic needs. Religious instruction is a basic need for the children of religious families. The International Covenant on Civil and Political Rights, Article 30, states that a child may not "be denied the right...to profess and practise his or her own religion...". This requires the allowance of a minimum of special religious education for the children of parents, who cannot afford to send their children to a private religious school, and who instead study in State schools. Yet, in Victoria, the one hour of optional special religious instruction that had been available to children in State Schools, was removed from classroom hours by a political decision. Instead, children were given the (effective) disincentive of coming before school or receiving the class during lunchtime. At the same time, the State Government presented its "compensation" for this through a new core curriculum subject which relativized the world religions amongst one another and with secular humanism.

A more recent bill (Education and Training Reform Amendment (School Employment) Bill 2020) has been introduced into the Victorian Parliament to ensure that Chaplains in State Schools be employed on the basis of the Equal Opportunity Act. Thereby, chaplains are placed in a category of workers with children, for whom religious beliefs may not be a factor in terms of which to discriminate in their employment. The tragicomic result of this legislation is no chaplains or "atheistic" chaplains for religious students in Government schools. This is not the expression of a secular State, but of a *secularizing* State which seeks to purge all provision for religious teaching, practice and expression from public institutions.

It may here be further noted, that the Victorian Government also resolved to remove the opening prayers from the Parliamentary sittings. No one had been compelled to pray. But it was an opportunity for those who wished, to do so. But the existence of a religious symbol, from amongst all other symbols in the Parliament, is eliminated.

Legislation against freedom of conscience in private life

The Change or Suppression (Conversion) Practices Prohibition Act, which strikes at a number of domains of religious freedom, is directed primarily against conscience in the private life of an individual. This law, as noted, makes it a criminal offence for a therapist, when freely approached by a religious individual with help for unwanted same-sex attraction or gender dysphoria, to provide that therapy. It represents a direct attack on two tenets of religious belief (1) that a human being is inwardly free and capable of living in accordance with conscience and (2) it negates and criminalizes norms of the faith tradition. It enforces its view that the human is *not* free to live in accordance with conscience, and makes sure that the individual will not be free to do so. It imprisons the individual in his or her own psyche and the therapist, who answers that individual's request for help, with an actual gaol sentence.

Legislation against freedom of conscience in public life

The Victorian Abortion Law Reform Act of 2008 introduced abortion on demand for foetuses up to 24 weeks. In religious law, an abortion performed not to save the mother's life or upon other extremely rare grounds, may be deemed murder. The Act provided that a doctor who on grounds of conscience did not want to perform such an abortion was exempt from doing so. *However*, it required the doctor with the conscientious objection, on pain of professional discipline and implied possible disbarment from the profession, to *refer* the patient to another doctor, known to have no objection to performing the abortion. In other words, it compelled the doctor with a religious objection to be *complicit* with, by facilitating, the religiously prohibited act of killing. In underworld terminology, this is the same as being forced to give the name and contact details of a "hitman" who will take out a "contract" to kill another. If not killing, it is forced complicity with it.

Similarly, though to lesser degree of severity but also a violation of religious freedom, there is the threat that the Federal Sex Discrimination Amendment (Sexual Orientation, Gender Identity and Intersex Status) Act 2013 may be used to force individuals to supply their services or venues for an activity which their religion prohibits. This is coercion to *support* an act which the individual on religious grounds finds repugnant. As discussed and to repeat, the refusal to support repugnant acts is different to discrimination against persons. One should not discriminate in the provision of goods and services to a homosexual person, but one may refuse to endorse an *act*, which religious belief forbids, such as the *act* of a same-sex wedding. One may not discriminate against a person who is a prostitute, though one should be free, on the basis of religious conscience, to refuse to rent a venue for the purposes of prostitution, which *activity* religious belief forbids. Now that the Victorian Parliament has legalized prostitution, this becomes an important issue.

Policy and legislation infringing the parent-child relationship

As noted in the first section, an essential religious freedom is that of parents to raise children in their own values. This too has been negated by policies and legislation. The first of these violations is a sex-education program imposed on all children in State Schools in Victoria, for example, by the so-called "Safe Schools Program". This a program which exposes children at a naturally impressionable age to a host of sexual lifestyles, many of which are contrary to religious belief and practice. In so doing it detaches children from the values of their parents and suggests to them sexual lifestyles contrary to parental, religious values. The teaching of "gender fluidity" under the "Safe Schools" program sexualizes, and so exploits and manipulates, children at the most susceptible point of their development. Under the normal guidance of their parents, children grow overwhelmingly into their traditional roles. At the age of 12, some 26% of children have a naturally fluid sexual identity.[1] In the general population some 2-3% of the population have homosexual behaviours. What this program does is to prey upon the 24%, who with normal socialization and parental education, would grow into traditional roles. It draws children away from parental values.

Until recently, private and religious schools were exempt from the State imposed "Safe Schools" program. Only the children of religious families, which could *not* afford a private religious schooling for their children, were vulnerable to this interference with parental guidance. Now, however, in Victoria with the Change or Suppression Act, the State interferes with criminal sanctions to seek out and punish *private* religious schools (along with parents and ministers of religion) who seek to impart religious norms of sexual behaviour to their children and students. The State's separation of children from parental values thus now operates in both Victorian State and private schools. It is proposed that a parent who counsels his or her child in traditional sexual ethics will be guilty of "family violence".

The child is not normally considered to be a free and responsible agent in society and is protected from itself by not being permitted to a drive a car, drink alcohol and so forth. Government policy in Victoria has made an exception to this. Under the Change or Suppression Act, the expressed desire of a child to "transition" from one sex to another may only be affirmed. Any therapeutic investigation of causes leading the child to this dysphoria is prohibited and punishable. Should the parents resist the administration of "puberty blockers", as a step towards the

---

[1] See S. D. Cowen, *Homosexuality, Marriage and Society*, Redland Bay: Connor Court, 2016, pp. 85 ff.

transitioning, the child is granted through Government policy a unique "mature minor" status to act wholly independently of its parents. The Victorian Change or Suppression Act which punishes the parents, who obtain therapeutic counsel for their child with gender dysphoria, takes for its jurisdiction the whole world. The parent, who takes his or her child anywhere on the earth's surface for this psychological assistance, awaits gaol upon return to Victoria. The Australian Royal College of Psychiatrists and the Australian Medical Association have warned against the dangers of solely "affirmative" gender transitioning and the importance of psychological investigation, but this has not availed to impede the detachment of children from parents.

A further observation. We have noted the stipulation by the United Nations Covenant on the Rights of the Child of the right to identity, "to know and be cared for by his or her parents". Legislation to provide artificial reproductive services for non-biological parents *creates* orphans: it brings children into the world, not to be raised by their biological parents. This is, and has been experienced by many persons, whose existence was "commissioned" through artificial and donor reproduction as, a profound loss of the right to identity.

The culture of the repression of religious freedom
Distorted emotions

The culture supporting the legislation and policy to repress religious freedom is opposed to the concept of the human soul with its compass of universal values. It is this self-transcending conscience with its objective moral compass that is nurtured by the faith tradition. It is the task of conscience to evaluate and measure emotions, perceptions and world-views by reference to that moral compass. Accordingly, the emotions which spontaneously well up within oneself, or are borne through media or mass sentiment, need to be subjected to the review of conscience to examine whether they correspond to authentic norms. Conscience refines and arights feeling, thought and attitude. Without the standard of conscience, they are subject to corruption.

The word used in the last ten years and more to drive legislative changes, and to repress the religious views which critique them, is "compassion". Over and over again, we have heard how all of these programs express "compassion" and how those who oppose them are "cruel". Yet the "paradox" — and we shall see that it is really not a paradox — is that the movement borne along by this ostensible "compassion" has turned into a movement of unprecedented cruelty, harshness and repression. In return for being "likely" to offend with their beliefs, and for teaching them to their children, the religious are to be gaoled and fined. Their homes, schools, and institutions of prayer are to be invaded, monitored and subject to informer reporting. In the public square the expression of their values is to be gagged by "vilification" laws.

The cruelty of this "compassion" extends not only to their targeted enemies, individuals and communities of faith. It extends above all to the persons whom their "compassion" was meant to benefit. To reiterate one example, the inducement, without and against parental permission, of young children, who are regarded as non-responsible minors in all other respects, to undergo irreversible modifications and sterilization of their bodies, is a cruelty which has now awoken the concern of medical and psychiatric associations in Australia. These "transitioning" children are being drawn by legislation and policy into a cohort of the highest incidence of suicide.

The reason why the "compassion" behind this legislation and policy has capsized into such cruelty and harshness is that it was from the outset a corrupted emotion of compassion — no compassion at all. It was based on the suppression of the moral compass which would have corrected it from the outset.

The mobbing of intellect

As noted, the moral compass of conscience, nurtured by faith, ensures not only that the emotions should be properly informed and honed. It ensures also that the mind functions as it is meant to, as a dispassionate, independent, self-examining and critical faculty. With the submergence of the spiritual in society has come the collapse of reasoned and balanced discussion and analysis. The great newspapers, once characterized by journalistic independence, balance and a quest for objectivity, are no longer interested in debate. They have become organs of propaganda for one-sided world-views. The universities, which were meant to be the home of critical intellect, have "cancelled" free discussion, producing students who cannot think critically, but are martialled by ideological teachers. Their graduates in turn reproduce the same "group-think" in the professions they enter. Professional associations — of psychologists, doctors and lawyers to name some — are ideologically regimented, threatening independently thinking and dissenting members with professional deregistration or disbarment.

Nowhere was the mobbing of intellect and the cancellation of debate seen more than in the lead-up to the Parliamentary decision to introduce and pass the Victorian Change or Suppression (Conversion) Practices Prohibition Act 2021. The Act addressed the access to therapy by individuals, whether for themselves or their children, for unwanted same-sex attraction and gender dysphoria. A document prepared by a radicalized University department and several activist organizations presented a series of ghoulish reports of bizarre therapies, which no one — including religious persons — would endorse. The intention was to stymie all therapy for unwanted same-sex attraction or gender dysphoria with the caricature label of "barbaric quackery", which became a catch-cry that brooked no examination or qualification. The Parliament refused to consider copious evidence of successful and non-coercive therapies which individuals had sought and with which they were happy. The warnings of harm to individuals and children in prohibition of all therapeutic investigation of trauma and other factors in patients seeking this help for themselves and their children were disregarded. Major mainstream media ran campaigns, deliberately repressing conflicting evidence. In short, the legislation was based on a falsehood and a libel. This mobbing of intellect and negation of its faculty of critical review has resulted in the most punitively ramifying and repressive law against religious freedom in Australian history and in the contemporary Western world.

The disregard for freedom and the culture of control

Religious freedom and freedom in general are related. This is because freedom is measured and created not by the ability to choose which interests, tastes or desires to pursue. I do not manifest my freedom in being able to decide whether I will eat a strawberry or a chocolate ice-cream, whether I will follow this "want" or that "want", whether I shall allow this idea or that idea to appeal to me. In all of these cases I am deciding about *which* "want" I shall allow to *drive* me.

The real meaning of freedom, as the great psychologist Viktor Frankl would say, is to stand above "drivenness". That means, in contraposition to *my* sense of my wishes, desires, interests, angles on life, I can transcend to a vantage point, where I ask not "what do I want?", but rather, "what is wanted of me?" In other words, it is that I have the possibility of saying "no" — to the impulses and perceptions and catch-cry ideologies which attempt to drive me — because these conflict with a higher moral compass. This self-transcending higher purpose and truth is represented by conscience, and conscience is sustained by the faith tradition. The secularizing culture of hedonistic materialism, which has unravelled so many human institutions and basic societal values is not interested in self-distancing or self-examination. Nothing stands in the way of its unmediated and unreflected impulse, perception and attitude. It is intrinsically unfree because it has repressed its own power of self-transcendence and self-reflection, which makes the human being free. And it reproduces its own unfreedom in society by repressing, cancelling and punishing all who argue with it. Nowhere does it act with greater aggression than against the faith tradition, which teaches the freedom that arises from the possession and invocation of conscience.

Societies which acknowledge religious freedom are free societies;

those which repress religious freedom become comprehensively unfree. The longest and most restrictive "lockdown" under the Corona virus in the entire world occurred in the administrative region with the worst record of violation of religious freedom in the democratic "West": in the Australian State of Victoria. Freedom, and particularly freedom of prayer, was not a part of the concept of "life" which the Victorian Government sought to preserve through the curfews and house-arrest of citizens for a series of lockdowns over some twenty-one months. For two years running, to name one example, Jewish people in Victoria were not allowed, under any conditions, to gather to pray on the holiest day of their year, Yom Kippur. This was the thinking of a deeply materialistic political culture which could not grasp prayer as a source of deliverance (in conjunction with practical measures) from the very crisis, in which it found itself. The less it respects faith and prayer, the tighter its controls become as it struggles alone to "manage" life and nature. Not as a much reviled political leader, who *does* believe in a Creator, said: "these are times for more prayer, not less."

The legislation required to protect religious freedoms

In the following, some basic requirements for a Federal Law to protect religious freedom are set out. They are organized according to the categories of religious freedom in the first section and meet the abuses of these aspects of religious freedom, which were set out in the second section.

The inner life of the faith community within society

1. There shall be no dictation (and certainly not with fines and gaol) of which religious beliefs families, religious schools and congregations may teach their members. This is to implement throughout Australia the guarantee of the Australian Constitution in section 116 of "the free exercise of any religion".

    Presently violated by the Victorian Change or Suppression (Conversion) Practices Prohibition Act

2021

2. There may be no restriction of the right of religious institutions to select any or all of their staff, with reference to criteria consistent with the beliefs, values and ethos of the institutions.

Presently threatened by an intended amendment to the Victorian Equal Opportunity Act. [This law has been passed, since the time of writing].

The outer life of the faith community within society.

1. There shall be no curtailment or prohibition of the expression of religious beliefs and views in the political sphere. This is consistent with Article 18 (1) of the Universal Declaration of Human Rights: "Everyone shall have the right to freedom of thought, conscience and religion. This right shall include freedom to have or to adopt a religion or belief of his choice, and freedom, either individually or in community with others and in public or private, to *manifest* his religion or belief in worship, observance, practice and teaching."

Presently threatened by a proposed amendment to the Victorian Racial and Religious Tolerance Act to prohibit expression of certain beliefs as "vilification".

2. There may not be withheld the entitlement of students in State schools to opportunities for religious instruction and for chaplaincy. This is in accordance with the United Nations Convention on the Rights of the Child, specifically in Article 14 "States Parties shall respect the right of the child to freedom of thought, conscience and religion"; and in Article 30 "In those States in which ... religious ... minorities exist, a child belonging to such a minority ... shall not be denied the right, in

community with other members of his or her group … to profess and practise his or her own religion…" Presently violated by exclusion of Special Religious Instruction from Victorian State School Classroom hours.

Religious freedom of conscience in the private life of the individual

1. No individual may be denied access to medical or psychological care or procedure required by his or her religious beliefs and practice.

Presently violated by the Victorian Change or Suppression (Conversion) Practices Prohibition Act 2021 criminalizing access to therapy for unwanted same-sex attraction and gender dysphoria.

Religious freedom of conscience in the public life of the individual

1. No individual may be compelled to provide goods or services for an act which contravenes his or her religious conscience. This includes, for example,

(a) doctors and medical staff, who may not be compelled to carry out a form of killing prohibited by their faith, such as abortion on demand, or any form of complicity with that act of killing (such as compulsion to produce referral to another doctor known to have no objection).

Presently violated by the Victorian Abortion Law Reform Act 2008, which forces doctors to refer.

(b) the provision of services for an act prohibited by an individual's religious beliefs, for example, to rent a venue for prostitution, or to cater for a marriage, prohibited by one's religion. This needs to be made clear in relation to the Federal Sex Discrimination Amendment (Sexual Orientation, Gender Identity and Intersex Status) Act 2013

The integrity of the parent-child relationship

1. The rights of parents to raise children in their own values shall be respected, in accordance with Article 26(3) of the Universal Declaration of Human Rights: *"Parents have a prior right to choose the kind of education that shall be given to their children"*. And so also Article 18 (4) of the International Covenant on Civil and Political Rights: "The States Parties to the present Covenant undertake to have respect for the liberty of parents and, when applicable, legal guardians to ensure the religious and moral education of their children in conformity with their own convictions".

This will entail that there be

(a) no imposition upon children in schools of sex-education program which violates the religious principles of their parents

Currently violated by "Safe Schools" programs

(b) no granting to minors of independence from their parents' consent in undertaking psychological or medical treatment

Currently violated, in Victoria, by Schools' ability to accord "mature minor" status to children for undertaking sexual transitioning independent of their parents' consent.

(c) no interference with the counselling of children provided or organized by parents for their children

Currently violated by: Victorian Change or Suppression (Conversion) Practices Prohibition Act 2021.

Chapter 2

The Recovery of the Human Spirit in Politics

This chapter is a mélange of pieces which adumbrate answers to the questions, what the human spirit is and how it can and should manifest itself in politics. The first piece, "The Return of the Human Spirit" has to do with *identifying* and *regaining* the human spirit — the conscience or soul — which the contemporary culture of hedonistic materialism represses. It has to do with self-transcendence, whereupon the soul's moral compass can be accessed and become the sovereign adjudicator within the person and culture.

The second piece "The Light of the Human Spirit" deals with *qualities* of the human spirit proceeding from a reflection on the Scriptural phrase "The lamp of the Creator is the human spirit". The metaphor of light (the lamp") alludes to the *transcendent* and *unchanging* quality of the spirit.. It alludes also to the *transformative* power of the spirit — a light which is able to dispel darkness.

The third piece, the "Commonality of the Human Spirit" speaks about the *universality* and *objectivity* of the human spirit, which is brought out in the cross-cultural resonance of the universal ethics of the human spirit.

The final piece, "The Human Spirit in Action", talks about the hallmark features of human spirit as it negotiates the turbulent waters of politics in particular. These features are idealism, commitment to deed, acknowledgement of error as part of the process of self-improvement, honesty and a regard for others' essential humanity, even where one rejects their conduct and values.

The Return of the Human Spirit

We live in times in which a culture prevails that views the human being as being driven by experienced physical and psychological needs and desires; as being virtually unconditionally entitled to the gratification of those experienced needs and desires; and deems the inhibition of the fulfilment of those felt needs and desires as pain, which should be escaped at virtually any cost. The flight towards personal gratification has brought with it the dissolution of traditional sexual morality and the structures of family and marriage which framed it. The flight from pain, burden and responsibility has brought with it regimes of mass killing, notably abortion on demand, "assisted suicide" and euthanasia. These are only some, but perhaps the signal, features of the "Zeitgeist" — the spirit of the times — of what I have called "hedonistic materialism".[2]

There are three hallmark features of the current cultural ethos and its ideological rationale. The first is that the human being is grasped as a pool of fluid drives. More significant than *what* "I want" is *that* "I want", and virtually nothing should be allowed to impede this sovereign, subjective "wanting". There is no inner independent or objective power of moral review. The second is that this host of desires, expressing purported human "freedom" and "autonomy", is uninterested in the way these are to be reconciled with stable, orderly and harmonious social institutions. They are essentially chaotic, indifferent to consequences: they will not listen to, or hear, an opposing voice. They cannot subject themselves to critique or claims of others. Thirdly, they justify the headlong gratification of desire and indifference to social consequences, by a doctrine of "compassion". This compassion is tautological: it is compassion upon the "pain", which results from withholding "pleasure". There is no review of the validity of indulging that pleasure, but full validation of the "pain" which results from withholding that pleasure.

The "compassion" invoked to permit the unqualified flight

---

[2] See S. D. Cowen, *Politics and Universal Ethics*, Ballan: Connor Court Publishing 2011, Chapter 1.

towards pleasure and from pain, is, needless to say, a false compassion. It is a law unto itself, not a law of conscience. But it is sanctimonious, imperious and vainglorious as it moves to silence and coerce all those who would oppose it. One is reminded that the most advanced — compassionate — laws *perhaps ever* enacted for the protection of animals from pain, where enacted by Hitler, the symbol of mass murder and destruction. His "compassion" was willful and pagan, wholly uninstructed by the moral template of conscience and the religious tradition which nurtures and informs conscience.

All of this occurs because the human being is grasped solely as a psychophysical being, whose impulses are subject to no moral review or critique. The religious tradition, however, knows that the human being in addition to the psychophysical dimension possesses a soul or conscience, which affords precisely that review or critique. The soul, moreover, possesses — or resonates with — objective moral knowledge or criteria. This is because it "mirrors" or is made "in the image of its" Creator, that is, it resonates with the eternal values, the eternal will, of its Creator. Human pleasures and human pain are real. Pleasure is not something which should *in principle* be repressed — our needs to eat and to procreate, properly fulfilled give us strength and lead us to love and build families. Pain is something which we should seek to ameliorate. But which forms of pleasure are admissible and which are not, and which forms of pain, should be removed, and which must be endured and come to terms with, are subject to moral decisions — by the essential, free and responsible dimension of the person: the soul or conscience.

The struggle for our times is to restore the crucial dimension of the human spirit — the conscience or soul, with its eternal moral template — which has been largely eclipsed in contemporary society and culture. It calls for a major turning in our society and culture, a peaceful revolution, which will overthrow the ethic of hedonistic materialism ("Hedonomat"). For hedonistic materialism has become inculcated into the mind of our society. The Universities teach it. Professionals, politicians, teachers, journalists, mental health workers and bureaucrats have all been educated in it. It has become their intellectual furniture. Fear can take hold of those who challenge it, and of course there is the fear and insecurity of those adherents of the Zeitgeist of hedonistic materialism — who have furnished their minds and professional practices with the thought vocabulary of hedonistic materialism — when challenged by the idea of having to refurnish.

There is the more subtle and pernicious self-accusation, of a person who wants or thinks to change, of *hypocrisy*. How, a person will ask, can I who have lived so differently, now profess a different ethic. How can a person who herself, whose niece or daughter, has had an abortion now become an opponent of abortion on demand? Is this not hypocrisy? The simple answer is that there is no hypocrisy in embracing and doing what is good and right. That is the answer of a person who is cognizant of the soul and understands its struggle with the psychophysical dimension. That struggle is dynamic: sometimes we fail morally and sometimes we succeed. We should be happy when we succeed. It is precisely the culture of the psychophysical determinism — of hedonistic materialism — which says that I am driven and immured in my psychophysical nature and that I can be no different to, or other than, my drives. The power to *turn* is the power of the human spirit.

Hedonistic materialism is deeply hostile to religion because religion both teaches that the human being has a soul or conscience in addition to a body and psyche; and also because religious tradition imparts the eternal moral compass of the soul or conscience. Yet, the acknowledgement of religious tradition as the fount of universal ethics can also make even the religious person nervous. The reasons are essentially twofold. First, because there is an ostensible diversity amongst the world religions and if so what does this say about a set of objective values and truths? Secondly, because conflict and strife has been promoted in the name of religion, does this not make religion more the problem than the solution?

The answer to the first question is that when we speak here about "religion" as the repository of traditional, objective, universal values, we are referring to the common or shared root values of the great world religions. These are a set of universal laws, with all their ramifications, known as the laws of Noah, the biblical survivor of the flood and ancestor of all humanity. They were practiced and transmitted by Abraham, the father of the so-called Abrahamic religions, Judaism, Christianity and Islam and who is also a source for the great religions of the east, Hinduism and Buddhism. They were finally and definitively reiterated at Mount Sinai more than 3000 years ago. The Noahide laws have been affirmed by great world leaders and I have indicated these endorsements and elaborated upon the world view and content of those laws at length in my book, *The Theory and Practice of Universal Ethics — the Noahide Laws*. Moreover, I have found that in interfaith activity to defend common ground against legislation hostile to this common ground, a shared resonance is experienced with these basic laws. Thus, although the individual world religions have clearly developed in different ways, the shared common denominator of the Noahide laws is that which bring them all together, and this shared religious tradition is what are speaking about here. Our object is therefore neither ecumenism or interfaith dialogue to resolve differences, but rather focus on the common ground: that is the meaning of the religious — the shared and common religious — tradition.

The second objection, that religion fuels conflict and even terror, falls away when we consider that such movements, which have promoted these phenomena, are in fact a distorted and perverted religiosity. The humility and self-transcendence of the authentic religiosity, which comes from the genuine recognition of a Creator and of one's own creatureliness, rules out the ugly hubris which covers its violence with a religious veneer — that is not real religion. Religion comes from the Latin word *religare*, which means to "bind" oneself back, to master and control, to take responsibility for, oneself — in the presence of the Creator and His laws. The hubris of violent and triumphalist "religion" reveals it as actually non-religious.

The Light of the Human Spirit

Thoughts on the Festival of Channuka

Channuka is a festival which commemorates two consecutive historical miracles in Jewish History. One was the extraordinary victory of a tiny Jewish force against the armies of the Greek-Seleucid Empire over two thousand years ago, which was bent on destroying the spiritual life and practices of the Jewish people. The other was a miracle, which has no basis in nature at all. The ritually pure oils used for the candelabrum in the inner sanctuary of the holy Temple had all been defiled in the war, and more ritually pure oil for the candelabrum could only be obtained in eight days. A single flask of oil, of a quantity sufficient only for one day's kindling of the candelabrum, was found and in fact burned for the eight days.

The festival is celebrated each year for the eight days of the Jewish calendar during which the flames of the candelabrum actually burnt from that one day's quantity of oil. To fulfil the precept of this festival at the most basic level it would be sufficient to kindle a single light in each Jewish house each night of the eight days. The custom, however, is to kindle an ascending number of lights, one the first night, two on the second night and so on until on the eighth night we have the full blaze of the Channuka candelabrum with its eight branches and flames. The time of kindling is at night or slightly before nightfall, such that the light should shine into, and illuminate, the darkness and so publicize the miracle. For this reason also, the Channuka candelabrum or "Channukia" was intended to be set up in such a way as to shine out into the street, the "public domain". What is the message of this light for the public domain of conflicting ideas (or for the domain of conflicting forces within ourselves)?

A light which is transcendent

"Light" is often a metaphor for "truth", and "darkness" for "falsehood". Most people, with a modicum of conscience, want to defend their actions and principles as true and good. The problem is, of course, that in the tides and struggles of ideas, the transformations of social values, what was yesterday's "light" is now condemned as "darkness"; and yesterday's "darkness" is now extolled as "light". We are socialized and "educated" by various media and official bodies, academies and associations, into new canons of political correctness which impart an unquestioned authority to the latest "enlightenment".

Long ago the great prophet Isaiah said: "Woe to those who call evil good, and good evil; who put darkness for light, and light for darkness; who put bitter for sweet, and sweet for bitter!" Only a prophet could so certainly and confidently tell his generation, that their version of light was in fact darkness, and darkness light. In short, the light which on Channuka is needed to be shone into public places, where the battle for values take place, in order to be a timelessly authoritative light, has to be a *transcendent* light. The place of transcendence is beyond society and history. It is with G-d, the Author of Creation and its purpose, and it is only for a prophet of the Divine tradition *and* all those who adhere to the Divine tradition or come into alignment with it, transcending self and society, to recognize an authentic light.

The light of Channuka stirs the human being to know his or her own light, the light of the human soul, which tradition has called "the candle of G-d". The human soul or spirit triumphed signally both against the physical and culture wars of a Seleucid empire and its literati who wanted to extinguish devotion to the ethical norms and beliefs of monotheism. It calls for further triumphs of the human spirit.

A light which does not change

Where history has sought from time to time to rename light as darkness and vice versa, or in the current twilight of moral relativism to mix light and darkness, we have another criterion of what constitutes "real" as distinct from transfigured light. "Light" as spirituality refracts into concrete morality. If purported "light" warrants values which do not correspond to those enduring values of the human spirit, then it is not light. And so the test of new social doctrines or New Age "spiritualities" is the actual morality which they produce.

A mark of truth is that it does not change. It is something constantly borne out, continuously verified. The positive morality associated with the Divine tradition does not change, except where *it itself* allows certain modulations for certain circumstances. The Divine morality is unchanging for two reasons. First, because, in itself, it is the will of an eternal G-d for the cosmos and the human being which He created. Secondly, because in its recipients, it is verified as such by the human soul throughout history. Authentic fundamental values constantly *return*. In the words of the great psychologist Viktor Frankl: "there are value-meanings...there are the Ten Commandments...values which have been crystallized in the course of human history and across human society." Even if today's aberrations have been taken up by national parties, and even if legislated into reality, history and society has and will reject them. For the human soul, made to model the Divine, and once allowed to emerge and become conscious of itself, will recognize these aberrations as precisely that. It is only the gross hedonistic materialism of the epoch which has effected the suppression - and even the voluntary suppression - of the instrument of spiritual discernment within humanity.

A light which transforms

There is a saying that "a little light dispels much darkness". It is experientially borne out. A small candle in a large dark room has an extraordinary power. The cloak of darkness is removed, it is shed like something insubstantial. For this to happen in spiritual terms, we, however, require an authentic light, a spiritual light. The bright dreams of a sleeper do not dispel the darkness of his or her room. The light, which, in spiritual and moral terms, transforms, even in a small measure, must be a G-dly light. The "enlightenments", which are in fact the eclipse of the Divine and the human soul, do not have that qualitative power.

The reason why the little light of the spiritual is so powerful and can push away so much darkness is because this light contains Divine powers directed against mere human constructions, edifices of new moralities. At a deeper level, the reason for this is that the animating Divine life force energizing and recreating creation is the real foundation of all being. The world conceals G-dliness, because G-d Himself has allowed the play of human choice and action to erect edifices of conduct which obscure it. By accessing transcendent Divine powers — Divine light — that concealment can be transformed and "darkness" be exposed and shed as insubstantial, as the mere blockage of light.

This explains the "disproportionate" power of the "little light" of human spirituality. For what is being brought into the "great world" of society and nature — or for that matter the "little world" of the human being — needing transformation, is a light which is qualitatively superior to the world itself. The festival of Channuka is an intimation, an ever-recurring reminder of the ultimately historically and socially un-concealable and irrepressible presence of the Divine and its mirror, the human spirit.

The commonality of the human spirit

Faith: the highest and the most humble

The most fundamental recurring fact of humanity and history is faith: the sense of a higher purpose and an encompassing meaning. What this means is that the highest faculty of the human, the most human in the human is the soul. When the human being was fashioned by G-d, it was said, "Let us make the person in our [G-d's] likeness". That refers to the human soul, the mirror of G-d, which is the highest faculty of the person, the seat of conscience, meaning and responsibility. That is what the person ultimately is. It is true that the person is also body and mind, but the rider over both of these is the human soul. They are the vehicles of the soul.

Therefore, it is not at all strange that the single most salient feature of human history should be religion, for religion is the expression of the human soul. Perhaps the greatest of all sociologists, Max Weber, saw that religion was the clue to understanding social processes and social organization for it is the master template of human purpose sought out by the soul: the control board, in accordance with which human activity is guided and directed. Even the modern phenomenon which Weber focused upon most extensively, the "disenchantment" of the world, the process of secularization and "rationalization" of the world, had been set in motion by a particular religious ethic, an ethic of good works, though this had swung back against its original religious fount and desacralized the animus which set it in motion.

The citadels of western society — the universities, the professions, the media and the bureaucratic elites — are today largely in the grip of that spirit of secularization, with a new deeply materialistic and hedonistic twist. The grass roots, however, are not so; in them the human spirit is far more resilient. The reason for that has to do with humility. Humility is the beginning of religious experience, the knowledge that there is something greater than oneself and a higher purpose to which one must tie oneself. Humility is a rigorous requirement. People of intellect and power are easy sticking points for hubris and arrogance. Simple people, on the other hand, more easily see something greater than themselves. This does not mean that humility and religious experience is *mere* simplicity; much rather simplicity is a quality which helps us to "grasp" G-d, Who is absolutely "simple" in the sense of being beyond all description. Humility is not in contradiction to intellect. On the contrary, one cannot do better than to marry humility with intellect. But this means opening up the spiritual faculty which can then properly receive from the tradition and guide, rather than being occluded by, intellect with intellect's own dangerous propensity to vanity and materialization.

The materialistic hedonism which has captured the high places of our society as a world view could be termed an idolatry of the material; indeed, it has even sunk beneath the intellectual promethean atheism of Marx to a purely physicalist materialism of Darwin and Freud.

The common core of faith

There are two models of interfaith: an older one, about which I am sceptical, and one which I want to present as the new and the more cogent. The old model was built on a premise of understanding of differences and the hope that this mutual recognition of individualities of faith would relativize a sense of superiority or particularism and so breed tolerance and harmony. The problem with this model is that its relativistic approach could ultimately dampen personal religious conviction. Orthodoxy — which believes in a G-d and in G-d's teaching — is not going to accept the relativity of standpoints which liberal faith posits, with their greater emphasis on "humanism" and "change". It is interesting to note the comment of a great modern thinker and psychologist, Viktor Frankl on the concept of tolerance. Frankl said that tolerance should be born not out of a relativism — which reasons, "Who says I'm right? Maybe s/he's right?" The truth is not relative. Rather, tolerance should stem from a spirit of love and respect for the other. The truth is the truth, and even if the other is not quite with the truth, still as a fellow human being I must feel a love and respect for this other. Moral relativism is false and it saps the spirit.

The approach to interfaith which I embrace is thus not relativistic. It looks for the common, authentic core, which we can all endorse. This is not hard to find. It is a historical and spiritual reality. These are the faith and laws by which Noah, the ancestor of all humanity after the Flood, and later Abraham, the father of a host of peoples and faiths — Judaism, Christianity, Islam and by a circuitous route also Hinduism and Buddhism (via the sons which he sent to the East) — in all, 75% of humanity. These laws can be documented and their resonance tested. My study of these laws, called the Noahide laws, goes back now many years. I have written a book on the world view and the practice of the Noahide laws called *The Theory and Practice of Universal Ethics — the Noahide Laws*. From my own tradition I knew these to be the universal law of humanity. However, recently I put it to the test before the great world religions, Judaism, Christianity and Islam. I received a grant from the Federal Attorney General in its Building Community Resilience Program to produce a "Manual of shared values of the world religions, Judaism, Christianity and Islam" (found in this volume in Chapter 6). I held seminars with distinguished religious scholars from the Christian and Islamic faiths to test the resonance of a set of root values. My special collaborators were Professor Tracey Rowland, Dean of the John Paul II Institute for Marriage and the Family and Professor Ismail Albayrak, Professor of Islam at the Australian Catholic University. The resultant manual "An education in a shared ethic", which was ratified by each of us, corresponds to the Noahide laws, the fundamental code set out in the Bible and elucidated by the tradition of commentary from Sinai. Another, more familiar term for these ethics might well be: "Abrahamic ethics". This is the true path forward in interfaith, the affirmation of our genuinely shared common belief. It also has — like all by-products of the truth — other good consequences, of which a sense of the fraternity of humanity is one.

...and of all (including "non-religious") humanity

Having quoted Viktor Frankl on the true meaning of tolerance, I would also like to quote him on human self-transcendence. Frankl has made the extremely important observation, that every person — including the supposed atheist or agnostic — once called upon to transcend his or her "psychophysical" existence in fact unlocks their innate (and often hitherto suppressed) spiritual potential. The meaning of self transcendence is linked to what we called at the outset the essential ingredient of humility. Self transcendence means taking a higher perspective than that of the plane of our psychophysical being. It means asking what it is to which we have been called, the meaning of our suffering, our circumstances, life — or as the consciously religious person says, G-d — wants of us. When a person humbly transcends his or her own psychophysical being in this way, says Frankl, he or she is in fact en route to G-d, the terminus to which the religious person is fortunate already to have been brought.

I therefore feel much confidence that these universal laws or ethics will resonate not only with those whose faith stems consciously from the Abrahamic tradition, but also with those who are willing to embark upon an honest and integral self-transcendence.

The Human Spirit in Action

Politics as a vocation

Over the years I have studied a famous essay by the great German sociologist Max Weber, entitled "Politics as a vocation". Weber spoke of the politician as one who proceeds from conviction of a world view. For Weber himself there was an inherent relativism about world views. He found no mooring in religious tradition, describing himself as religiously "unmusical" (tone-deaf). So there is something relativistic and even a little nihilistic about his view of the "polytheism" of warring or colliding world views amongst which the politician found his or her own personal conviction. Having seen in the universal ethics of the Noahide laws, a common root of the world cultures and world religions, I disagree with his relativism. Although Weber could not find any truth criterion for a particular world-view, at the very least he required of the politician a strong sense of responsibility for the consequences of acceptance of a particular world-view in politics. What I am taken by in Weber is his concept of politics as a *vocation*, as a profound and earnest calling. Indeed, I believe that the most important arena of ideas is the political arena. John Maynard Keynes said that politicians are the slaves of some *defunct* economist, i.e. that academic ideas do filter through and influence politics. Still, I would prefer that living and eternal ideas be present in politics. For politics is above all the realm of action, where ideals are within actualization. So as one who is more an academic than a politician, I have sought to arouse and inject ideas, which are living, vital and universal, rather than allow the input to remain that of a defunct academic! Here are some thoughts from the ringside of politics about what constitutes real — I would say, spiritually integral — vocation in politics.

Idealism

The first quality of a politician for whom politics is a vocation is idealism, or a commitment to goals. I believe that a genuine idealism must recognize the whole person of the individuals who make up society, namely people who are a composite of body, mind and soul. One of the appalling features of modernity has been the eclipse of the human soul. Its denial seems to me as absurd as the denial that one has a body. The exclusion — and now the occlusion — of the reality and experience of the spiritual, which is one of the most natural human experiences, is denial in every sense of the word: intellectual and emotional denial. It is irrational, though paradoxically it parades as rationality.

Action for true goals

My observation and engagements of the last few years, which produced much of the material of *Politics and Universal Ethics* — though the theoretical chapters in the middle of that book precede this by a number of years — confirms the importance and necessity for action in politics. We not only have to know what is right, but also do it. Not to be afraid of political correctness, disfavour and ridicule but to think, say and above all to do the right thing. It means saying and following (i.e. *loving*) truth. I thought that the following phrase came from Jewish tradition, but find also that Isaac Newton said (something like) it: it goes "Love Plato, love Aristotle, but love the truth more". One of the hallmarks of truth is that, for it, one is ready to put oneself on the line — in action.

Not to be bedevilled by inconsistency

Speaking about truth — indeed, thinking, saying and doing it — does not mean that I present myself as a paragon of truth and virtue and that if I am not these, I am afraid to say the truth. I am all too aware of my shortcomings. But here comes another piece of advice from our tradition, which I am sure will be welcomed by everyone: it is "accept the truth from the person who says it", not because the person has a perfectly virtuous unchequered past, but because right now what he or she is saying is true. In other words, have the humility to accept truth, and to be wary of one's prejudices which might lead one to dismiss it or fears which keep one from affirming it. Humility or acknowledgment is also a hallmark of truth.

Honesty

Honesty is another hallmark of truth. We may believe what we believe, but we have to acknowledge what we do not know. Bertrand Russell was such a person. He was a self-professed irreligious person, with many values which I reject, but he acknowledged what he did not know, and what the limits of his own understanding were. This in fact is the entrance to self-transcendence: to recognize not only the foibles of our character but also the limits of our intellect. This helps, though was not sufficient for Bertrand Russell, to open the door to the soul and its qualitatively different knowledge.

Regard for another human being

Love of one's fellow human is essential to a true political vocation — recognition of diversity, freedom and creativity — but all within the perimeter of universal ethics and with respect for Divine image of the human being. As discussed in *Politics and Universal Ethics,* within the compass of universal ethics there can be diversity, Liberal and Labor, but we must know what the boundaries are, where the compass points lie, what lines we cannot cross, and which basic shared values we are bound to affirm. I don't want a conflict of religious vs anti- or non-religious. Every human being is made in the image of G-d, every human being has a soul. Some are more activated than others, and those who are not so activated, are not to be blamed even from a religious standpoint, since we live in a culture of spiritual deactivation. With the famous psychotherapist Viktor Frankl, all

I would ask is that we all make an effort to transcend ourselves, that is to say to rise above our perceived desires and wants and our limited grasp of reality and ask ourselves, why are we here, what is asked of us and how we can make the world a better place. That is already the route to our own intrinsic spirituality, without asking anyone to make any religious affirmation. In that we will find our common spirituality and humanity. And, to repeat another word from Viktor Frankl: the true meaning of tolerance is not moral relativism — that I will tolerate another's view, since who knows where the truth is? Rather tolerance has to do with love and regard for another. It is not suspension of belief in and adherence to that which is true and universal.

Politics is a sphere in which we engage to change our lives and the lives of others. This makes it the most responsible, the most earnest of all realms of human conduct. That is why we must recover the human spirit into politics.

PART 2: MORE QUESTIONS FOR UNIVERSAL ETHICS

Chapter 3

Conflict and Higher Moral Authority

The two pieces in this chapter apply universal ethics to issues of conflict: "conflict of interests" and "conflict of loyalties". The first deals with the role of universal ethics in conflict resolution. It proceeds by way of critique of a pre-eminent model of conflict resolution known as the "Harvard Negotiation Project". It explores the idea of a common access of ultimate shared values, which in turn leads to the modification of held "interests", and so to the resolution of conflict. The second piece deals with ostensible conflicts of "loyalties". Specifically, it examines the question of whether the offence of "treason" can be said to apply where the interests of the State conflict with a higher — and ultimately "common" — moral authority, namely that of universal ethics. It is a forum on the celebrated case of Jonathan Pollard.

Conflict Resolution: An Ethical Supplementation of the Harvard Negotiation Project

The subtitle of *Getting to Yes*, the foundation text of the Harvard Negotiation Project, is "Negotiating agreement *without giving in* [emphasis added]". That is, its basic premise is that subjectively perceived and affirmed interests are the basically immutable foundation of negotiation. Negotiation has the sole task of (conjointly) maximizing and satisfying the given interests of the parties. This essay argues that the Project's methodology should and can be radically improved by focusing on the ethical dimension of the conflicted relationship calling for a negotiated solution. A shared perception of that ethical dimension can lead the parties to *modification* of their interests, after which the "rational" techniques of the Project's methodology can be brought in to fine-tune the result.

To explain this, we shall first consider the relationship between interests and the values characterizing a person's view on life. There are two models here: (1) where interests are modified by objective values — the ethical model — which is here promoted; and (2) that subjective interests constitute values — the present Harvard model.

The second task is to show (1) how it is *possible* for the parties to a conflict to come to a common ethical understanding, through which interests are modified; and (2) why such an agreement is also more *efficacious*.

The third task is to give examples of successful settlings of potentially or actually conflicted relationships, based on a revision of interests by a party or parties in the light of shared, objective ethical norms. We look at this in the contexts of family, business and international relations.

Two models of the relationship of interests and values
Values as constitutive of interests

To understand the difference between an "ethically" supplemented and an *exclusively* "rational" approach to negotiation, we need to go to a basic psychological model of the human being. This model, presented by the faith — the central historical — traditions of civilization, consists of body, mind *and soul*. Body is the seat of physical drives or needs (for food, protection from the elements, money, sexual gratification, power etc.) and emotions (love, fear etc). In the language of negotiation, all of these, whether general or highly specified, are "interests".

Interests are expressed, satisfied and also frustrated in a variety of social contexts. The family deals with many primary needs, physical and emotional. The family unit brings in an income and manages the household. It can also be conflicted. Economy and business represent a larger scale organization of the satisfaction of basic interests, and of course are also open to conflict. More comprehensively political systems are also concerned with the management of the satisfaction of human needs, where economy and business are just individual departments amongst a host of others of Government. In their relationships with other nations, Governments also famously pursue "national interest" in their political, military and economic relationships with other nations. Interests derive from the physical or material dimension — the "body" of humanity — writ small (the individual and family), medium (business) or large (societies).

The dimension of mind — reason or rationality — in the individual is the faculty with the power to review and check the spontaneous or impulsive expression and gratification of physical wants. Mind examines the consequences of acting on impulse, measuring its benefit or harm and calculating how and when impulsive need should be met: now, later or not at all. In the individual human being, reason confers responsibility and answerability upon the individual. A human being can be held responsible because he or she has this rational power of review of interests. It measures actualization of physical interests in terms of their "costs" and "benefits", including importantly their relationship to social rules. Family, business and society all draw on this rational dimension of the human personality: it has to do with the organization and regulatory aspect of the satisfaction of human interests.

The final dimension of the human being is the soul or conscience. It is the repository of the values, to which reason refers in administering the expression and fulfillment of human needs or interests. The soul or conscience decides *what* an acceptable or unacceptable benefit or an acceptable or unacceptable cost is — in moral terms. The soul is the moral compass of the individual and of all individuals. A person has a sexual interest, but that must be expressed and satisfied within a licit framework. A business needs to make money, but may not do so through fraud. A society is concerned about its military security, but may not embark on aggression, where it is not under attack or lethal threat.

The reason why the soul, the spiritual potential or receptor within *all* human beings — *when it is authentically manifested* — resonates with the *same* objective, universal values is that (in the language of religious tradition) it is "made in the image of G-d".[3] This means that the human soul was fashioned by its Creator as a microcosm of the attributes of the Divine. The soul can resonate with the Divine attributes of kindness, judgment, mercy and so on, because it too possesses these qualities in potentiality. These G-dly qualities or attributes in turn translate into practical ethics for conduct, which have been codified historically as the "Noahide laws", the collective moral and spiritual root of the world cultures and religions. The term "Noahide" refers to the figure of Noah, the survivor of the Flood and ancestor of all humanity, with whom this moral covenant between G-d and humanity was completed. This code came down through the intervening ten generations to Abraham, who transmitted it to many cultures, until it was authoritatively reiterated for all humanity at the Divine revelation at Mt Sinai through Moses.[4]

It behoves the individual to actualize this universal spiritual potential within him- or herself and to apply these Divine qualities, embodied in the Noahide laws, in practical conduct in the myriad circumstances of life. This *one*, universal ethical template, which is capable of finding resonance in the souls of all human beings, expresses the eternal, ethical will of their *one* eternal Creator.

The traditional model of the human being also teaches that the spiritual faculty is the highest, the essential and the sovereign faculty in the human being. This means, that with the actualization of the spiritual within the person, body and mind properly become *its* vehicles: it is their sovereign driver. It hones both feeling and thought. It determines (whether by direct influence upon the physical, emotional self or via the agency of reason, which it has briefed, to exercise its control over the bodily self) what a legitimate interest is, and the forms it may permissibly or optimally take. In this sense the values-set of the soul *constitute*

---

[3] Genesis 1:27.

[4] The content of this universal code at the root of the world religions and cultures has been discussed and documented in Shimon Cowen, *The Theory and Practice of Universal Ethics – the Noahide Laws*, Institute for Judaism and Civilization: NY, 2015.

— modify and craft — valid human interests in the myriad circumstances of life.

Interests as constitutive of values

The basic concept of the negotiating method outlined in *Getting to Yes* is to move from the raw conflict of individual wills over held interests to a process which rationally satisfies, to the greatest extent possible, the interests themselves. In other words, its purpose is to take the emotional static out of negotiation, moving it instead into a problem-solving mode based on rational principles: to travel from "positional bargaining to principled negotiation".[5] The idea is "to be soft on the people while remaining hard on the problem".[6]

The fundamental platform of this negotiation process is the "interests" of the parties. Down to basic stakes, these are not questioned or revised, except where they might be dysfunctional to securing more basic requirements. The goal of the negotiation process is to accomplish or "satisfy" these interests. There is no concern as to the *morality* of the interests: "*Getting to Yes* is not a sermon on the morality of right and wrong; it is a book on how to do well in negotiation. We do not suggest that you should be good for the sake of being good (nor do we discourage it)."[7] Success in negotiation is measured by the degree of satisfaction of the interests with which one came to the negotiation. Modification of those interests in the light of ethical concerns (not enforced by the laws of society) would be a case of "giving in", against which the method protects one. The negotiation principles of "communication" and "relationships" are applied, not morally but in terms of their functionality to a maximization of satisfaction interests and a minimization of conflict. "Options" and "alternatives" are also functional to the maximization of fulfillment of the interests; they do not involve a basic revision

---

[5] *Getting to Yes*, p. 187
[6] Ibid., p. xv.
[7] Ibid., p. 157. In a footnote the authors suggest some virtues that might result from the method, but this is a theme little developed; it is literally a footnote to this book.

or questioning of the interests which the parties brought to the negotiation table, but rather of means taken to that end. The subtitle of *Getting to Yes* nakedly states the negotiation project's methodological commitment to one's initially perceived interests: "Negotiating agreement *without giving in*".

Even the negotiating reference concept of "standards" does not imply objective moral criteria, but rather conventional benchmarks which *help* the negotiation to a maximal fulfillment of interests and minimization of conflict[8]. The concept of an unconscionable act itself is judged in terms of the pain (a cost) it causes one — the sleepless nights, a gut-wrenching feeling — rather than the fact that it was something *actually* wrong.[9] One is advised to use "standards of legitimacy both as a sword to persuade others, and as a shield to help you resist pressure to give in arbitrarily...Convincing the other side that you are asking for no more than is fair is one of the most powerful arguments you can make".[10] But not because the standard of fairness, which enjoys social legitimacy, from the standpoint of *universal* ethics, *is* fair.

The rationale of a "win-win" solution is often presented not on ethical grounds of reciprocity, but for pragmatic reasons: bringing the other side to agree to something which doesn't fulfill their interests can generate resentment, harm one's own reputation, and is also a fraught stratagem that could readily be seen through. "Options" are creative measures to satisfy interests, but they do not include modifying one's own basic or minimal interest stance ("BATNA" "Best alternative to a negotiated agreement": if one can't improve on this, then the negotiation has no value and one should "walk away"). Yet this "basic" interest is itself not evaluated: how many people walk away from a marriage because they have not evaluated what *really* — as an ethical ideal — matters, not just what they thought or felt at the time mattered?[11]

---

[8] "Watch out for your own interests – it's a dog-eat-dog world" might be an objective "standard" on which the parties agree; but it is not necessarily an ethical standard.
[9] *Getting to Yes.*, p. 157.
[10] *Ibid.*, p. 189.
[11] See below, section 3, on marriage.

Here, in summary, are the principal criticisms of this essentially instrumentalist methodology of negotiation concerned to satisfy interests without ethically critiquing or modifying interests. First, it is focused on the realm of human conflict, "mere" material and personal interests, rather than the human commonalities, discoverable in people's deeper, spiritual and ethical being. The focus on a "primary reality" of conflicting interests actually fosters unconsidered self-interest and a culture of conflict. This is half-wittingly acknowledged in the Introduction to *Getting to Yes*: "Indeed, the advent of the negotiation revolution has brought more conflict, not less".[12] Wrongly, from the standpoint of universal ethics, it takes as the primary human reality diverging subjective, material interests instead of the converging, objective, and unifying values of the human soul. It wrongly understands the human.

The second criticism is a moral one: the disinterestedness of the Harvard negotiation project in morality. Of course, this criticism flows from the view of the primacy in the person of the human soul or spirit, which is ethical. To ignore this is to degrade culture and to embrace relative rather than real — *ethical* — "objective standards". An amoral stance is an immoral stance.

The third criticism relates to the criterion dearest to the Harvard negotiation project: "success" in agreement. An approach tied to staked material interests — with all the co-maximization for the parties — will not bring durable agreements. For it has latched on to that which is centrifugal, not what is centripetal — the spiritual-ethical commonalities and good in relationships ("the negotiation revolution has brought more conflict, not less"). We shall return to this point.

In short, in terms of the model of body, mind and soul, the Harvard Project takes bodily or material (or emotional) interests as primary, for which reason exists as a facilitator. The soul is gone, or rather usurped by a "religion" of interests, where interests *constitute* values.

---

[12] *Getting to Yes.*, p. xiii.

Ethical commonality
Coming to ethical commonality

Viktor Frankl validated within psychology the existence of the human soul. Not only is this an "objective" faculty — notwithstanding the doomed efforts of a purely empiricist psychology to find it as a physical substance — but its *content* is also objective. The truth, which the soul properly activated and humbly exposed within the human being, recognizes, is *one*.[13] *It corresponds, he too confirmed, to the Divine image in which it is made (and translates in practice into the universal Noahide laws). But how do we come to that ethical commonality, how do we awaken the human soul?*

As part of what Frankl called "logotherapy", literally therapy of the individual oriented to Logos, or higher meaning, he devised various ways of leading the psychologically distressed individual to *self-transcendence*. "Self-transcendence" is transcendence beyond the "psychophysical" self (of body and mind), with their perceived interests and stakes, to a selfless answering to higher meaning, which can bring with it a revaluing of those perceived interests and stakes.

Physical and material wants — the interests and wants of the body — are obvious: one is sick, poor, lonely or powerless and one feels the need for their redress. Or one may have more ambitious, and less basic, needs which are unmet. Rich and poor can both be needy in terms of what they want. For them the test of transcendence is: if fulfillment of these needs is not presently available, how can I live with that — what other meaning and purpose remains in my life? Alternatively, if I can take action to fulfil these needs, with what means and in which measure and for which purpose should I do so? In terms of ethically valid goals, my opportunities and challenges, what needs should I revise, pursue or repress?

For some, intellectual needs are as powerful as (or more so than) material ones. But the life of the mind also has to face the test of

---

[13] See Viktor E. Frankl and Pinchas Lapide, *G-ttsuche und Sinnfrage*, Gütersloh: Gütersloher Verlagshaus, 2005, p. 58.

self-transcendence. Frankl tells the story of how he, a Viennese Jew under the German annexation of Austria, took with him to the concentration camps the outline of a book he wanted to write upon his liberation. He had sewn it into the lining of his coat and this future project alone gave him the will to live in the daily Hell of the camps. One day he was to be taken on a march with other inmates. But before this, his coat (with the sewn-in book outline) was confiscated and he was given instead the coat of another, presumably murdered, inmate. At that point, he later wrote, he contemplated suicide: his intellectual stake in life was gone. He then put his hand into the pocket of the replacement coat and found a page from a Hebrew prayer book, which contained the "Shema", the biblical and liturgical statement of the unity of G-d. In this moment he realized that a life lived *only* in order to write a book was not a life *truly* worth living. Life calls us to *its* tasks, beyond a particular intellectual project.

The accomplishment of self-transcendence — the exposure of the highest faculty, the soul or conscience within the person — is in asking and answering the question, *not* "what do I want of life", *but* "what does life want of me"? My material and intellectual interests are not insignificant, but they are revisable in terms of my ethical mission in life, to which the self-transcending soul alone can open.

Perhaps this can be asked of the religious person, but what of the atheist or agnostic? Frankl never required his patients to believe in G-d. He simply sought to engage them in the *process* of self-transcendence. The atheist or agnostic who sincerely asks him- or herself the question, What am I called to do?, and relativizes his or her needs to that question, is in fact *en route* to the terminus which the consciously religious person has already reached: G-d and universal ethics. For the self-transcending faculty, recognized as soul or not, *is* the soul, which is made in the image of G-d and recognizes G-d. G-d, Frankl states, will "not mind", if the atheist or agnostic, engaged in this deepest, most sincere conversation with him- or herself, presently thinks that he or she is talking only with him- or herself, and not with G-d. Self-transcendence, wherever one starts, leads to the same destination, ethical commonality.[14]

The content of ethical commonality

What follows from the notion of a universal set of ethical principles, the Noahide laws, ratified by the actualized human conscience, is that any situation of conflict involves an application of these ethical principles. Conflict in the business or economic sphere has to do with the ethics of economic exchange. A business or an economic interaction is a human relationship, to which pertain ethical criteria. A negotiation over the price of an item may not involve a particular ethical principle. Yet, when the negotiation involves an actual conflict, it is very likely that a wrong has been done by someone, or that there has been a lack of proper consideration for another. Hence, the first question in negotiating conflict should be: does an objective ethical principle apply here, and if so, what?

One does not have to break the law or commit a civil wrong to another to have a question of the application of ethical principles. Universal ethics require us not only to desist from wrong, but also, positively, to do what is right. We have not only *not to harm* the other, but also positively to *consider* the other. Marriages are preserved, not only by spouses not mistreating one another, but also by their showing love for, and giving to, one another. Business relationships are built, not only when the parties do not deceive one another, but also when they evince a degree of reciprocity and regard for the other's livelihood. Peace between nations arises through holding back belligerence, but also through expressions of good will.

If one or both of the parties do not come to the ethics of common conscience, as detailed in the Noahide laws, by themselves, then it is the task of the party that does understand, or the mediator,

---

[14] A client to a negotiation might not be particularly drawn by the intimation that he or she may have to revise perceived initial interests in terms of an objective ethical standard. In that case, a "sales" byline, such as "*discovering* and accomplishing your real interests", might be reassuring.

to state the principle and its application. One should "beam" that principle onto the spiritual "radar" of the unforthcoming party(ies). For, according to received wisdom from tradition, "even if they do not see, their souls see".[15] Presenting the ethical truth is bound to produce a spiritual resonance which eventually trickles into consciousness.

The central point here is that, within a negotiation, consideration of the application of universal ethics to the conflict can feed back to review of previously maintained "interests" in the positions of the parties. Awareness of the ethical ideal of marriage and how spouses *should* behave towards each other, can make them think again about the weight of their actual complaints and the efforts they might make. So too with the parties to a business or international conflict: their claims (or initially felt interests) will very likely be modified in the light of an awareness that their dispute is not solely a conflict of interest but equally and perhaps about a relationship which has ethical dimensions. In other words, all disputes represent a fracturing of some level of ethical community and relationship, and *that* primary consideration may well produce a secondary modification of the interests, to be brought back to the negotiation.

Success within ethical commonality

The ethical community of human beings — the way they cohere and cooperate with one another when they engage their higher, spiritual selves — is a peaceful, blessed and successful one. So it was in the biblical account of the beginnings of creation, when all the souls of humanity were contained in the soul of one person, Adam (before the sin) with whom nature bountifully and miraculously cooperated. So it will be in the messianic age, when the principal occupation of humanity will be to know G-d. Then envy and struggle will cease, and nature will deliver its bounty to

---

[15] This is the concept of *mazlaihu chozi*: "their souls see". Talmud Tractatess *Megilla* 3a and *Sanhedrin* 93b-94a. See also Rabbi M.M. Schneerson, *Likkutei Sichos*, Vol. 20, pp. 311 and 345.

humanity.[16] This is the ultimate "success" — to have what one needs, without opposition from others or from nature — and it will be a universal condition.

The long stretch, between that idyllic beginning and this idyllic end of history, is marked by a descent into an existence in which human beings struggle with one another and with nature. It was the epoch introduced by human sin, which corrupted the world as a vessel for Divine blessing. One *can* succeed in this condition too, but only "by the sweat of one's brow", with difficulty, frustration and uncertainty. This is the world of the conflict of "interests". At the same time, a person who in this world, acts and works to bring about ethical community, repairs a part of it, and there draws down Divine blessing and success: the fulfillment of genuine need and the removal of conflict.

This was stated by the Jewish Sage, Rabban Gamliel, who said "Those who are involved with the community should do so for the sake of Heaven"[17], i.e. not with an exclusive focus on personal gain, but for the ethical integrity of the community, as prescribed by G-d. The reason for this, as explained by the great commentator, the Maharal of Prague, says, is that G-d associates Himself — connects His blessing — with the realized ethical community. Rabban Gamliel also states, "Make His [G-d's] will your will, so that He will make your will as though it were His will".[18] That is to say, Do those positive acts required by G-d to build ethical community, so that He will give you what you need. And he continues, "Retract your will before His will, so that He will retract the will of others in the face of your will". This means, Refrain from those negative acts, prohibited by G-d, so that He will remove conflict from encroaching upon the good that you have. *Success*, the goal of any conflict mediation strategy, can be accomplished by working for ethical community: by doing what is ethically right and by not doing what is ethically wrong.

---

[16] See Maimonides, *Mishneh Torah, Hilchos M'lochim*, Ch.12.
[17] *Ethics of the Fathers (Pirkei Avos)* 2:2.
[18] *Ibid.*, 2:4, also according to the explanation of the Maharal of Prague in *Derech Chayim*.

Applying ethical commonality

Marriage

One of the major areas of conflict is marriage. Understanding what marriage is, as an ethical concept, can change the parties' very understanding of their own "interests" and "grievances" in a marital conflict. Marriage is perhaps the deepest union into which two humans can merge: indeed husband and wife are called two halves of the one body and soul. If so, the regard they should have for one another should be like that which the foot has for the hand and vice versa. Concerning a man's attitude towards his wife, tradition states that he should "honour her more than this own body and love her as himself". Of a wife, it states, that "she should respect his wishes exceptionally".[19] The marriage in itself — as something bigger than both of the spouses — is a Divinely ordained institution, which (a) completes and makes whole each spouse, in a unit, in which both support each other to accomplish their collective and individual tasks for the good of the world and through which (b) they accomplish their own extension in a new generation of children continuing in the betterment of the world. In the *light of, and for the sake of that ideal*, each spouse will decide what is presently an essential need, and what they can do without ("give in") and where they might act "self-sacrificially".

My brother related to me the following true or imagined — but instructive — story. A couple had a long and successful marriage. One day they were asked to tell the secret of its success. The husband began, "Well I'll tell you. The truth is that I like the white meat [the breast] of the chicken, but I always made a point to give it to my wife to make her happy, and took the dark meat [the drumsticks] of the chicken for myself, which I really enjoy less". When the wife heard this, she cried out, "What?! All these years I have been giving you the dark meat — which I really prefer, to make you happy, and taking the white meat, which I like much less!" I suppose that thereafter the husband got the white meat, and the wife the dark meat, which respectively they

---

[19] Maimonides, *Hilchos Ishus*, 15:19-20.

wanted. But that was typical of the secret of their marriage: they had modified (or changed the ranking of) their own interests, for the purpose of making the other happy.

How great was their "sacrifice"? Neither the nutrition nor the preferred diet of chicken of either spouse was compromised. But they *modified* their interests, gave up some (relatively minor) preferences and *did not even think to negotiate* to accomplish them. Had the parties to a marriage been focused on their interests — rather than on the ethical ideal of the marriage — and sought agreement "without giving in", they would not have accomplished such a good marriage.

This does not mean that there isn't a host of accommodations which could and need to be accomplished in a marriage, and that a rational approach to their solution is helpful. What it does mean is that the ethical ideal of the marriage is foreground and the differing and conflicting interests are background, and that the interests have to be seen through the lens of the ethical ideal of the marriage. This is bound in some way to refocus the interests and modify them, and that already will make them more amenable to conciliation. My preference for the white over the dark meat of the chicken drops dramatically in significance when I consider what the importance and value of the marriage is. And similarly with variety of less trivial matters.

The primacy of the ethical commonality, expressed in the ideal of marriage, works to create coherent interests and to remove conflict. The husband, who "honours his wife more than his own body" and the wife who "respects her husband's wishes (influencing him, if need be, that these be ethical wishes)", create a vessel for blessing. Where they know that "our marriage" is a good in itself, which enables them collectively and individually to do good in the world, they will approach repairing it more positively and energetically.

Business

In business dealings, conflict — as distinct from mere bargaining — is often an indicator of perceived injustice in one or more of the parties, and hence of ethical questions. An ethical approach to the situation by the parties is required, because it is right in itself; *but also* as a means, through revising initially held "interests", to help the negotiation of agreement. As in many situations of conflict, ethical requirements in business are both positive (what I *should* do) and negative (what I should *not* do). The following story was told to me by a businessman, whose life is guided largely by universal ethics. He is the proprietor of a firm which distributes light bulbs and is a reasonably large and successful business.

On one occasion his warehouse received a delivery of bulbs from a manufacturer. An employee, who was not the person who regularly received and signed for deliveries, signed the documentation for this delivery, which stated that two boxes had been delivered. It subsequently became clear that only one box had been delivered and that the person, who had irregularly stepped in to sign for the delivery of the two boxes, had not checked the delivery. When the inventory and accounts section picked up and reported the error, the proprietor asked relevant personnel to sign affidavits that in fact only one box had been received.

The proprietor then contacted the manufacturer with the affidavits and asked for a credit corresponding to the overpayment for the delivery (for two boxes instead of one). The manufacturer declined, stating that the delivery of two boxes had been signed for, and that was the end of the matter. (Presumably, the manufacturer could have checked or did check his or her own inventory and accounts and discovered how many boxes did go out, but nothing at this point was conceded). The proprietor of the distribution agency later rang the manager of the supplier and said to him, "We have checked inventory and accounts and have sworn affidavits that only one box was received, and that the person who signed for the delivery, whose task it normally was not to do so, had made a mistake. It is true that we have signed for the delivery, but you should know that the money made from payment for that second box is stolen money; and you should make it good by giving us a credit for the extra payment". The manager of the manufacturing firm did not concede the point then. Later, however, he contacted the proprietor of the light bulb distributor, and told him that the firm had decided to credit him for the payment made for the "second box".

One might argue that the supplier's decision to give a credit for the disputed second box, was a business decision to keep a client (if the client had a choice to look elsewhere), rather than an ethical one. Still, the concession was not made, *until* the ethical point was made in direct personal communication. Just as *Getting to Yes* seeks to move from positional to principled negotiation on rational (but value-neutral) principles, here the shift was to ethical principles. Over the telephone, both the negative and the positive sides of the ethical situation were stated calmly and without an audience: "You are protected legally by our signature for the delivery, and we're not going to run court costs to recover overpayment for the extra box. We can both verify by inventory checks and our affidavits that money is being wrongly taken from us. If you deny it, the money you make will be stolen money, and you will be doing the wrong thing *[negative]*. If you give us a credit for the overpayment, you will be returning stolen money and will be doing the right thing *[positive]*." He was presented with, and given an opportunity to do the right thing, which he did: to embrace their ethical relationship, an ethical ideal.

I would like here also to quote the conduct of another distinguished human being, who was also a successful businessman, a man guided strongly by universal ethics, called Moshe Zalman Feiglin:

> After his [Moshe Zalman's] passing in 1957, Frank Cameron, the township's leading lawyer told Dave [Moshe Zalman's son]: Your father was a most unusual man. One day in 1936, a farmer called Charlie Evans had put up his promising orchard for sale. Your father parked his Pontiac outside here in Wyndham St., they agreed on the purchase price, but no money had yet passed hands. Mr Evans later came back to my office, literally weeping: he had changed his mind. He continued to change his mind

back and forth three times, but your father refused to buy. He said he didn't want to build his prosperity on another man's tears.[20]

Some seasoned businesspeople might laugh at this story: business is generally not swayed by other people's tears — it is based on interests, not on the morality of motives driving deals and the impact they have on others. Yet corporate greed, which released a tsunami of tears in the Global Financial Crisis of 2008, ruined huge corporations and small individuals alike. Business relationships are human relationships and their parties are enjoined by universal ethics in specific ways to do good and not to do wrong. When the common conscience of the parties to a business conflict is awakened and the ethical stance of universal ethics is made known, a *revision* of interests becomes possible, which is the first and vital step to solving the conflict. Ethically "tenderized", the parties can *then* put forward their *revised* interests for practical, *rational* resolution by the Harvard negotiation project.

International conflicts

One of the original authors of *Getting to Yes*, Roger Fisher, wrote a book entitled *Dear Israelis, Dear Arabs* in which he sought to apply the Harvard method to resolution of the Israeli-Arab conflict. It was based largely on the Resolution 242 of the United Nations Security Council calling for (1) withdrawal of Israeli forces from territories gained during the 1967 war and (2) non-belligerency on the part of all states, with the right of each to its own secure borders. His approach, which coincides with that of many others, has not succeeded. The short explanation of the failure of this approach is that the "valid interests" assigned by this Resolution to Israel and Arabs under the authority of PLO (and now also under Hamas in Gaza) are at variance with universal ethics.[21]

---

[20] *Avraham Avinu of Australia. The Life of Reb Moshe Feiglin*, by Uri Kaploun, NY: AAA Publications, 2002, pp. 83-84.

[21] For the following, see at greater length "The Noahide Laws and the Land of Israel" in *The Theory and Practice of Universal Ethics – the Noahide Laws*, pp. 123-132.

To whom does the land of Israel belong? Both the Bible and the Koran have the same answer: it was given by G-d to the Jewish people. It has an intrinsic relationship to the Jewish people as the land in which alone all the commandments given to the Jewish people at Sinai, can be observed. This is the information from G-d, transmitted from Sinai in universal ethics. Jews and Muslims, whose spiritual receptors have been presented with and freely allowed to respond to it, agree. Who disagrees? On the one hand, the PLO and Hamas clearly disagree. They, however, are variants of the radical politicization and distortion of Islam, of which "Islamic State" is the heightened archetype. They do not open to universal ethics and in fact, in their theft, murder and corruption of justice vis-à-vis the Arab peoples subject to them, they make a travesty of the Noahide laws. Painfully, there is also on the part of some secular Israeli leaders, an equivocation about the Divine gifting of Israel to the Jewish people, and their entitlement certainly to the territories which were regained in defensive war against Arab nations. The unclouded spiritual consciousness of Jews and Arabs alike, who have the courage to say so, is to recognize in the Biblical (or Divine) framework only one State, not two: Israel.

Secular democratic thinking in Israel and the secular politicization of Islam, by leaving out the Divine framework of universal ethics, both distort the true interests of Jews and Arabs respectively. The land of Israel can never ethically be wrested from Jewish sovereignty, neither ceded by democratic votes, nor captured through terror. It must be under Jewish sovereignty because that is G-d's prescription for the land. That is the v*alid* claim or interest of the Jewish people. But the Arab peoples within the land also have a valid interest or claim: *a claim to full welfare through the Jewish people of the Arab peoples within it, who chose to live by the Noahide laws.* This is also a prescription of universal ethics, rooted in the Bible.

The problem is that UN Resolution 242 was put together without reference to G-d, human conscience and universal ethics — on the basis of which ordinary, humble, believing Jews and Arabs *could agree*. Instead it took its concepts of interests from a G-dless democratic secularism and a G-dless political radicalization of Islam. The Harvard negotiation program, which enters with its "neutral" rationality onto a platform of ethically invalid *centrifugal* interests, *itself* contributes to proliferation and protraction of the conflict. Only a revision and purification of the interests of the parties, through the *centripetal* power of ethical commonality, can bring peace.

Jonathan Pollard: to Whom is Loyalty Due?

This piece is based on a number of discussions conducted by myself, in which an Israeli lawyer, Nitsana Darshan-Leitner and an Australian academic lawyer, Professor Simon Bronnitt, were interviewed, as well as upon published writings of a former American Ambassador to Australia, H.E. Mr Jeffrey Bleich on the topic of Wikileaks. The summaries are those of the writer and were not submitted to any of the above contributors for verification. It was written when Jonathan Pollard had already spent some 25 years in prison, before his release in 2015 on parole. The discussion does not seek to take into account the full scale of Pollard's alleged crime, or whether he went about his action in the ultimately acceptable manner, but abstracts a single issue — whether a facet (at least) of Pollard's activity might be regarded as morally defensible. The question is that of loyalty to an ethical principle higher than the Government of the United States of America, with which that Government, as Pollard's employer, had appeared to conflict.

The case of Jonathan Pollard

Jonathan Pollard, an American Jew and an American citizen, working in American Naval Intelligence, was accused and convicted of turning over classified information to the Israeli Government. He indeed pleaded guilty to the charge as part of a plea bargain which would gain him a minimum sentence of several (4-7) years for making over classified information to a friendly power. The plea bargain was overturned and Pollard was sentenced to life imprisonment when, at the end of the trial, the Secretary of Defense, Caspar Weinberger submitted a confidential memorandum — which could not be publicly scrutinized or defended — purportedly outlining a massive danger to American security and its agents by Pollard. Later Weinberger would acknowledge, "[the Pollard case] was, in a sense, a very minor matter but made very important." Pollard has now served 25 years of this life sentence. Many American political leaders, and the Israeli Prime Minister Benjamin Netanyahu have sought clemency for him.

By the account in Pollard's biography, *Territory of Lies*, by Wolf Blitzer, Pollard whilst working for American Naval Intelligence became aware that America was withholding much information relating to existential threats to Israel from its Arab state enemies. These included both nuclear and biological warfare strategies and deployments. His sentiment was that the American naval intelligence was not disposed to make this information available. In his defence he expressed regret that he had not sought to change this through official representations to his superiors and had instead taken the matter into his own hands, offering to work for the "Mossad". At the same time, he stated that he had never handed over information relating to American fighting plans. In other words, his argument was that his ongoing transmission of classified information to Israel consisted only of matters which bore upon Israeli security and that in his judgment would constitute no harm to American interests and its agents.

The law of treason (discussion with Nitsana Darshan-Leitner)

The Israeli lawyer, Nitsana Darshan-Leitner, who was Pollard's attorney vis-a-vis the role of the Israeli Government in his case, did not focus on the rectitude of the treason charges made against Pollard, but on the argument that the United States had reneged on the plea bargain struck with Pollard. When asked whether individual national laws of treason can themselves be arbitrated by a universal standard or law, she stated: "It doesn't go by international law. It goes by the rule of the State, in which one lives and against which one gave information. Every country has its own law, through which it defines treason. Some countries say that where one gives information against regulation, one is committing treason. Others say that it applies only if one causes damage to the mother country. Some countries like Iran have extreme laws of treason. They can define even teaching Hebrew or being a Zionist activist as committing treason". This variety of concepts of treason highlights the question of whether there is a "right" — and an "unjust" — law of treason, which relates not only to the actions of purported traitors, but also to the actions of the state, protected by its law of treason.

That the law of treason itself needs scrutiny, and is subject to abuse, was recognized by the American Constitution. Knowing that the charge of "treason" can be used to stifle the agitation for political change and political critique, the framers of the American constitution paid it unique attention. It is the only crime specified in the constitution, which thereby limits the power of Congress to redefine it:

> "Treason against the United States shall consist only in levying War against them or in adhering to their Enemies, giving them Aid and Comfort. No person shall be convicted of Treason unless on the testimony of two witnesses to the same overt act, or on confession in open court..." (art. Iii, sec. 3)

Whilst there are many subsidiary laws in the scope of treason, and Pollard was convicted in accordance with a particular one of them, not "treason" proper, all these bear ostensibly on the concept which underlies treason, the perpetration of a demonstrable harm to one's country.

Whistleblowing and the law of treason (discussion with Professor Simon Bronitt)

Professor Simon Bronitt[22] stated in discussion that what might formally be regarded as seditious or treasonable activity vis-a-vis

---

[22] Griffith University Law School.

one's own country, in the case of liberal democracies, has to be approached with consideration of a *balance* of concerns: on the one hand, the need to maintain good order, and on the other, people's freedom to agitate for change "and to do so in ways which are fairly direct but are lawful". A form of this challenge has to do with the balance between disclosing corruption in Government and the need to protect state secrets. Autocratic states will have no whistleblowing protection. Against prosecution for divulging state secrets there may be defences of necessity. The plans of the Government may be to perpetrate war crimes or engage in torture and the individual charged with divulging state secrets concerning these could argue that they took these measures of divulging information to protect others.

The difficult case is not where you are disclosing information to *your* Parliament, ombudsman or media, that is internally, but where you are disclosing it secretly to a *foreign* nation. In the fraught environment of international relations, the risks of harm are greater. Yet here too is the issue of the weighing of evils — potential infringement of the security of the state and its institutions vis-a-vis the defence of third parties. Here, above all, the judgment must turn on words like reasonableness and proportionality. Is the action taken with its risks to one's own state proportionate to the harm which the state could itself cause. I would argue that this is the issue and the question with Pollard: his disregard for US secrecy, but in order to protect Israel, a friend of America, from harm.

Ambassador Jeffrey Bleich on disclosure of sensitive information

Ambassador Bleich is amongst the first to acknowledge that freedom of information is essential to democracy as he quotes President J F Kennedy: "we decided long ago that the dangers of excessive and unwarranted concealment of pertinent facts far outweighed the dangers which are cited to justify it". Nevertheless, his argument is that the indiscriminate — or as people have called it in the case of the "Wikileaks" disclosures, the "anarchical"

-dissemination of confidential information can be harmful to an open and democratic society itself. Privacy and confidentiality is both a right and necessity for many areas of life — medical and legal counsel — and the same applies to Government in its diplomacy.

This has to do obviously with defence concerns (deployment of troops and fighting plans, the disclosure of which to an enemy is treasonable). The Ambassador further summarizes three other areas of harm caused by the Wikileaks disclosures: (1) they impair and inhibit dialogue between States, (2) they endanger the personal security of a variety of vulnerable individuals ("religious or political activists, opposition leaders, whistleblowers, and human rights advocates") whose communication to foreign powers is essential and (3) they harm the quality of decision-making itself as it discourages "people from being forthcoming with candid observations and sensitive information, and discourage decision-makers from recording the reasoning behind important decisions for fear of premature disclosure".

On the other hand, the Ambassador writes, where the disclosure of classified information can serve legitimate ends, "a legal process exists for individuals or media organizations to seek de-classification and official release of documents where appropriate. As a lawyer, I have used that process — it is fair, it works, and it advances the public interest in accord with the rule of law." Nevertheless, a question remains for the Ambassador: the concept of "whistleblowing" is an issue of a calculus of harm. The properly motivated whistleblower seeks to prevent an entity (the State or the corporation, as examples) from doing harm; in the process, however, the whistleblower must also avoid or minimize doing harm. Very often a harm (at least a loss of reputation, if not worse, as indicated by the Ambassador) is done by the whistleblower in the course of the whistleblowing. The question is whether harm can always be avoided by following procedures: whether the corporation management will listen to the employee who knows of and wants to warn about a faulty product, or whether Government will act to redress the harm which one of its civil servants sees in its conduct. Harm *may* be travelling both ways — *to and from* the object of the disclosures — and the justifiability of the whistleblowing measures, whilst they should be calculated in advance, can often only be judged once the disclosures or the whistleblowing have occurred.

Summary and evaluation

The case of Jonathan Pollard has to do with the concept of whether an act of disloyalty to the State of which one is a citizen can be partly or wholly exonerated. The notion that nothing stands higher than the authority and sovereignty of the State in its own realm can often be a cloak which hides and protects crimes. Today, the United States with other powers has breached the sovereignty of a Government in Libya to prevent it committing crimes against its own citizens. This is an intervention which has nothing to do with the self-defence of America. The question is whether the same principle can be applied to the sovereign Governments of the United States or Australia or any other country which generally have a better record than Libya. Can a treasonable act ever be exonerated, at least partly, when it was seen to uncover a wrong, which otherwise might not have been uncovered; or when the harm it caused is *weighed* against the harm it sought to stop?

Discussion with Mrs Darshan-Leitner indicates that the problem is that states seek to adjudicate this question by themselves. They formulate and judicially administer their own laws of treason. Accordingly the legal action taken on behalf of Jonathan Pollard by Mrs Darshan-Leitner was attempted only on the grounds of a self-contradiction within the justice system of the United States itself. It is claimed that the US broke its own plea bargain with Jonathan Pollard; or that it was overturned and a life-sentence imposed on the basis of a secret document, which it has been claimed was not properly summoned or challenged. This limited internal-legal approach does not address the bigger issue. If treason simply asserts the supremacy of the state, its laws and actions, it does not allow consideration of whether the state itself might also be a wrong-doer in one of its actions, whether towards its own citizens or to a party outside the state. Can we view the purportedly treasonable action of an individual sometimes as an act of whistleblowing?

The discussion with Professor Bronnitt brings out a practical difference between "treason" applied to a conflict between a citizen of the state and the state itself, where information is divulged to one's own public. One has not here (necessarily) threatened the external security of one's country. One is simply seeking to address grievances of alleged state misconduct. A whole new realm of complexity opens when that information is divulged secretly or otherwise to citizens of another state. The external security and relations of a society is generally a far more fraught issue than its internal order. Here we need an international order of law, which applies both to societies internally and to the conduct of societies between themselves. We have to adjudicate harmful acts not only within but between nations. It is this which allows us to weigh and identify the "lesser evil" in action to be taken to set right harmful acts. I would here add that the law which adjudicates these questions has to be more than merely conventional positive international law, to which nations "decide" to subscribe. It must be an objective, international and universal law, framed by the Noahide laws — the laws of G-d.[23]

Ambassador Bleich's remarks prompt the question as to what justifies a breach of sovereignty (including the State's right to secrecy) whether in its internal or external affairs. Before an international law, states are individuals — individual masters, but individuals. We have to know what we are allowed to do to stop harm, what kind of harm, and by what measures — or at least to judge these questions fairly after the event. Pollard discovered information possessed by America, the repression of which aided existential threats, mortal threats to Israel. Israel was and is an ally of America. Was it wrong of America to withhold the information? Did Pollard harm America by disclosing that information? If

---

[23] Already the great Renaissance jurists Grotius and John Selden conceived an international law based on the Noahide laws.

he had sought to have the information made available through "normal channels", would he have been successful, or would it have led to his dismissal or transfer to another position and so have furthered the holding back of vital information bearing on Israel's security? He certainly felt that his superiors were hostile to the disclosure of the information. All these issues must be considered in relation to the application of universal principles in Noahide law which bind both individuals and nations.

The issue in the Pollard matter, in terms of Noahide law, related to "the law of a pursuer".[24] According to one reading of this law, one is obligated to act to save (not only oneself or one's own country but also) a third party from an attacker. That third party was Israel — a friend and ally of the United States, a country which in no way could be considered itself an enemy or threat to the United States. There was, accordingly, an obligation on the part of the United States to protect Israel from existential threats of which the United States knew. Pollard acted to save that third party against the ostensible refusal of the United States Naval Intelligence to do so. In the process he claimed not to have caused harm to the United States. Insert new final section:

A final, important qualification

This is the narrative account of Pollard's perceptions of US conduct — which led him to pass on confidential intelligence to Israel — while he worked in US Naval intelligence, as set out by Wolf Blitzer in his biography of Pollard, *Territory of Lies*:

> Years later, [Pollard...] would dramatically describe his deep concern over what he was convinced was the deliberate U.S. decision not to provide Israel with enough intelligence. He said the US Navy was holding back vital details from Israel: 'Despite the commonly held belief that the U.S. provides "everything" to the Israelis, the intelligence exchange from the Navy, at any rate, is anything but equitable'.
> Pollard recalled his own participation in the two formal

---

[24] See S. D. Cowen, *The Theory and Practice of Universal Ethics – The Noahide Laws*, NY: Institute for Judaism and Civilization, 2014, pp. 305-6.

intelligence exchanges with the Israelis. 'I participated in two official intelligence conferences with the Israelis and was amazed to see how high-level directives about releasing certain types of information to Jerusalem were routinely shelved by the men in the trenches, who felt that the "Jews" didn't need to know anything.'

He recalled that during one such exchange, a U.S.A. analyst, when asked for 'releasable' information on Soviet chemical warfare agents, 'turned to me laughing and said that he thought the Jews were overly sensitive about gas due to their experiences during the Second World War and suggested that they should just calm down a bit'.

According to Pollard, the underlying attitude of 'many of the American participants in these meetings was overtly racist, which produced a corresponding degree of anger and distrust on the part of the Israelis, most of whom felt that their country's security concerns were being totally overlooked'.

Pollard became increasingly angry as he witnessed these trends. 'The principal instruction I received from my supervisor was that we should only be prepared to give the Israelis enough information to get them paranoid but not enough, say, to let them figure out a countermeasure to a newly identified Soviet weapon system. When I carefully asked how they were expected to cope with all the state-of-the-art Russian equipment pouring into the region, the response was that all they had to do was lose a few planes and they'd know what radar frequencies to jam'.

This attitude was completely unacceptable to Pollard. 'As can be imagined', he said 'it was very difficult for me to work in this kind of atmosphere and not become frustrated at what I thought was an unbelievably cynical view toward Israel's survival'.

The Israelis, he said, were providing the Unites States with 'everything they had acquired, at great personal risk to many of their agents, and the Navy bureaucrats couldn't care less about reciprocating in an equally open-handed manner, as per their instructions'.[25]

The foregoing discussion of this essay explores in principle the question of "treason" where the State, of which one is a citizen,

---

[25] W Blitzer, *Territory of Lies*, NY: Harper and Row, 1989, pp. 61-62.

has demonstrably violated a principle of universal ethics, on account of which one feels called to disobey the State to rectify the violation. In such a circumstance the question becomes, in terms of an ancient formulation, "the words of the student and the words of the teacher [when these conflict] — to whom do you listen?" The answer to this rhetorical question is, the "words of the teacher". In terms of our situation, the "teacher" is G-d and His universal ethics and the "student" is the Government or leader, which should be a student and subordinate to G-d's supervening sovereignty and moral teaching. The problem is that the "student" has not heeded the "teacher" and has willed contrary to G-d's will in a matter addressed by G-d's will in universal ethics.

Under universal ethics, all things being equal, one has an obligation of obedience and loyalty, to the Government, the "owner" of the land in which one resides, which is entitled to make administrative arrangements, levy taxes and provide for the safety and security of the realm. The condition for this loyalty ("all things being equal") is that there is no conflict — or that if there is a conflict, it can be, and is, resolved — between the will of the ruler and the ethical will of G-d. If the conflict can be, and is, resolved, then the obligation to obey and be loyal to the Government, under which one lives, remains intact.

The point of "conflict of loyalties" in the case of Pollard related to the law, under universal ethics, of the "pursuer", namely, the obligation to save a pursued third party from its lethal pursuer. In Pollard's sights, Israel (an ally of America) was a "pursued" party – existentially threatened by military developments in the region, about which the United States knew — but which the United States would not disclose to Israel, thereby failing to act to save Israel from its "pursuers".

A very important final consideration arises here, however, of whether Pollard himself could have resolved the conflict of loyalty between universal principles and the ethical requirement of loyalty to the Government of the land of which he was a citizen. If he could have "gone through the channels" and successfully persuaded his superiors to pass on the intelligence to Israel, there would have been no need and no warrant for disobedience to the United States Government. Pollard himself, in Blitzer's account, intimates an answer to this question:

> 'In retrospect,' Pollard concluded, 'if I had only reported what I'd seen to the Navy's Inspector General, this anomalous situation might have been rectified through channels, without me feeling compelled to take matters into my own hands. Instead, I watched the threats to Israel's existence grow and gradually came to the conclusion that I had to do something.'
>
> Once Pollard acted on his original perception and approached the Israeli Secret Service, the "Mossad", he ran into a twofold problem. The first was that he had not properly sought to go "through channels" to alter US conduct in support of Israel's security, which had it been successful would not have required any disobedience to the United States Government. The second was that he was now enmeshed in the operation of the Mossad, which may have jeopardized his own judgment and autonomy in his transfer of information to Israel (though he insisted that none of it was harmful to US interests); as well as jeopardizing his own security (both from the American and Israeli sides) should he be apprehended as a spy for Israel. Whether and to what extent Pollard was right or wrong – in his original assessment of the likelihood or possibility of a change in the treatment of Israel by American Intelligence, and the degree to which he became involved with the Mossad – adds further nuance to the ethical evaluation of Pollard's predicament and his response, for which he suffered so severely.[26]

Postscript: a correspondence on Pollard with the Prime Minister of Australia

> The Hon Tony Abbott, Prime Minister of Australia
> 17 April, 2014
>
> Dear Prime Minister,
>
> This letter is handed to you during the Jewish festival of Passover. I include a copy of the Passover Message by yourself

---

[26] *Ibid.*, p. 62.

which was printed in the *Australian Jewish News*.

Your point about Passover as having to do with the freedom of the Jewish people is a very important one. However, the point should also be made that the freedom of the Jewish people has never been in contradiction to the national interests of lands in which the Jewish people have lived.

Balfour, the British Prime Minister who as Foreign Minister, was responsible for the Balfour Declaration in 1917, in which Britain committed to a mandate for a Jewish homeland in Israel, stated at the end of his life, that this was the most worthwhile thing he felt he had done. It never occurred to him to say that this would create a "dual loyalty" or a conflict of loyalties for Jews living in Britain or in any other country.

The reason for this is simple. The Jewish Exodus of old signified the march of the Jewish people from Egypt to Mount Sinai where they received the Ten Commandments. Jewish heritage has not been in contradiction to any civilized country. To the contrary, it has been an example. Similarly, Jewish citizenship of, and contribution to, other civilized countries has never presented a conflict with the concern of Jews for the safety of Israel.

It is in this connection that Jews feel much pain about the incarceration of an American Jew, Jonathan Pollard, on a life sentence for passing on information to Israel which he accessed whilst working for American naval intelligence. This intelligence related to nuclear and biological war threats to Israel by Iraq, Syria and other Arab countries in conjunction with the then Soviet Union. Distressed that the US was not passing this information on to a friendly country, Israel, Pollard took it upon himself to do so. He did not intend any harm to American interests. Instead of receiving a four to seven year sentence for spying for a friendly country, he was jailed for life and is now in his 29th year of this wildly disproportionate sentence. Three former heads of the CIA have called for his release as have former Secretaries for State Kissinger and Schultz. Now the US, for its own part, has acknowledged that its own intelligence gathering concerning its allies, which included tapping the mobile of the German chancellor, is simply routine. I include an editorial on the topic of Jonathan Pollard by the *Australian Jewish News*, which indicates that the plight of Jonathan Pollard is an issue which unites the entire Jewish community in Australia and around the world.

I and other members of the Jewish community would like to ask you, who, together with the Hon Julie Bishop, have shown exemplary and dispassionate principle in dealing with Israel, to intervene to secure the pardon and release of Jonathan Pollard, whose action, whatever its legality, in fact protected Israel, without harming the US. America, as you point out in your book *Battlelines* has fought altruistic war in the interest of universal values. American conduct in the case of Pollard seems strangely inconsistent with American values in the past.

Your personal intervention with President Obama would be a particularly auspicious act in preparation for the visit of the Israeli Prime Minister Benjamin Netanyahu to Australia in several months. The freeing of Jonathan Pollard is something that Netanyahu has repeatedly sought and advocated. This gesture of friendship, on your part, could also be of great benefit to Australia. In opening Australia as a "food bowl" for Asia, for it seems that Israel and Israeli technology, especially water technology and its success in making "the desert bloom", could be the most valuable partners that Australia could have in this project.

With respect and blessing,
Shimon Cowen

5 May 2014

Dear Rabbi Cowen

Thanks for your letter about the continued imprisonment of Jonathan Pollard. I will discuss this with Minister Bishop and get back to you. Certainly, the punishment seems in excess of the crime, if crime it were.
...
Yours Sincerely,
TONY ABBOTT

Chapter 4

The Basis for a Commonly Recognized Universal Ethics in the World Religious Cultures

The Noahide laws are a code for all humanity. As such they provide not only the framework for the domestic life of nations but also for the relations among nations themselves — international relations — namely, for a peaceful and civilized order both within and between nations. Yet, opposition to the application of the framework of Noahide laws in both cases comes from arguments of cultural relativity and particularism

International relations are a classic locus of conflict. Ostensibly, we find there no common authority — moral or Governmental — which can command the cooperation of the parties, in this case, sovereign states. Henry Kissinger's book, *World Order*, states that the approach to "world order" must therefore rest on a balance of "legitimacy and power", where the "legitimacy" relates simply to conventionally and temporarily accepted norms, not any intrinsic, absolute or universal moral order; and "power" means military force and deterrence. The notion of a universal law or morality, which could regulate international relations, is repudiated by Kissinger as a mere, touted "universalism", which in fact is a mask for the prejudices or private beliefs of particular cultures, the ambitions or proclamations of which have often been more disruptive, than not, to global peace.

In the domestic life of nations, the same argument is used against the existence of an objective and universal set of laws, as the broader framework of society. Cultures and beliefs, along with the varying interests which they promote or condone, are claimed to be "relative" and intrinsically diverse. It cannot — so it is argued — be otherwise.

The tradition from Sinai, on the other hand, presents and commands the Noahide laws as an *authentic* universal ethics, which can and should serve as the framework both of the order of national society and of global society. Aside from the common historical derivation of the world cultures from a Noahide root, their intrinsic universality can be tested through the "purifying" exercise of "self-transcendence". When an individual or a culture is called upon, and responds to the summons, to transcend all particular interests and stakes (and so to redefine and modify these interests and stakes) in the service of a higher good, one is in fact in a process of transcendence *towards G-d*. That act of transcendence ends as the "imitation" of G-d, as discussed in my *The Theory and Practice of Universal Ethics — the Noahide Laws*. The "imitation of G-d" means the imitation of the attributes of G-d, which in turn translate into the practical conduct of the Noahide laws. Universal acceptance of the Noahide laws is thus predicated upon self-transcendence, which is ultimately the transcendence towards G-d, the Source and Giver of these laws.

Amongst the *prima facie* diversity of the world's religious cultures, this essay examines the resources of transcendence within them, the affirmation of which serves as an important step towards their common, conscious acceptance, or discovery within themselves, of the Noahide laws.

Max Weber's typology of the world religions and its theological interpretation

The Noahide laws pertain to all humanity. They are not simply incumbent upon humanity as commandments passed on from earliest antiquity through to Abraham and then definitively reiterated to all humanity at Mount Sinai. They also resonate with the inherent make-up of the human soul — made in the "image of G-d" *(Tzelem Elokim)* — which is fitted to imitate the "attributes" of G-d. That imitation of the attributes of G-d translates into the concrete ethical practice of the Noahide laws.[27]

This "activation" of the soul of humanity, however, comes about only when people or cultures are drawn towards the first of the Noahide commandments, which is the belief in G-d. That G-d, Whose "attributes" the practice of the Noahide laws concretely imitates, is the transcendent Creator of all things. Where there is an orientation towards the transcendent Creator in an existing religious culture, or where that culture has a potential for that kind of transcendence, it becomes meaningful to test the resonance of the Noahide laws, as a universal ethics, with that religious culture.

This is not to exclude a potential affinity with the Noahide laws also in *secularized* individuals and cultures. Profound secularization has occurred under Communism in Eastern Europe, the former Soviet Union and China. Notwithstanding that, the Judeo-Christian tradition, as it falters in the West, yet sees itself in open resurgence in Eastern Europe and in covert resurgence within China today. It assuages a spiritual hunger which might well have been stimulated by the intense repression of religion in those countries for generations. In the West, where religion was not subject not to organized physical suppression but rather to an aggressive cultural hedonistic materialism and atheism, secularism has thrown down deep roots.

Nevertheless, whatever its causes and symptoms, the secularization of the ordinary, non-doctrinaire "non-believer" or agnostic, does not preclude him or her from accessing the values of a transcendent G-d. By an important insight of Viktor Frankl, even a professed atheist or agnostic — a contemporary secularist — *willing to embark upon the exercise of self-transcendence*, can also come to the source of universal ethics. This has been discussed elsewhere.[28] Still, the starting point for the evocation of a universal resonance of the Noahide laws needs to begin with the world religions themselves, for which the Noahide laws form a common historical root.

---

[27] See S. D. Cowen, *The Theory and Practice of Universal Ethics – The Noahide Laws*, Chapter 1.
[28] See S. D. Cowen, *The Rediscovery of the Human – Psychological Writings of Viktor E Frankl on the Human in the Image of the Divine*, Melbourne: Hybrid, 2020, Chapter 1

In the first section of this essay[29] we seek to examine this potential resonance in the stance of transcendence — towards the transcendent G-d — of a number of the major world faiths. We look first at the classification of the world religions, made by the great sociologist Max Weber. We then give his *sociological* typology of religious world-views a *theological* interpretation and examine their distinct, individual potentialities for an orientation towards the one transcendent Creator G-d, Whose attributes the Noahide Laws ethically translate. The patently monotheistic religions — Judaism, Christianity and Islam — have a more obvious orientation to the transcendent Creator G-d and scholarly practitioners of these faiths have affirmed their faiths' affinities with the Noahide laws.[30] Hence, it is to the less clearly established potentials for transcendence, and affinity with the Noahide laws, in the Eastern religions — Hinduism, Buddhism and Confucianism — that we here devote especial attention, in the second section of this paper.

Weber's typology of world religions

The study of the great world religions is the central focus of the work of Max Weber, arguably the greatest of all sociologists. As his sociology of religion is reconstructed and formulated by Wolfgang Schluchter[31], Weber sets out two dimensions, each with two dichotomous poles, in order to produce a four-fold classification of the world religions. One of these dimensions is represented[32] by the dichotomy of "theocentric" — centred on a transcendent G-d — and "cosmocentric" — literally "world-centred" — religions locating deity not in a transcendent realm but in nature or, more broadly, the "cosmos" itself. The theocentric religions are the Western and near-Eastern religions, Judaism,

---

[29] Much of the first half of the first section of this essay formed part of a paper entitled "Affluence in Context" presented at the Second "Living Legacy" Conference, hosted by Lubavitch House, London and held at Imperial College, University of London in 2001.

[30] See "An Education in a Shared Ethic. Common values of Judaism, Christianity and Islam", in Chapter 6, below.

[31] W. Schluchter (transl. G. Roth), *Max Weber's Vision of History - Ethics and Methods*, Berkeley and Los Angeles: University of California Press, 1979, p. 15.

[32] Schluchter here acknowledges the formulation of Jürgen Habermas.

Christianity and Islam, which focus on a transcendent G-d, that is to say, which distinguish G-d from nature. The cosmocentric or world-centred religions, on the other hand, are the eastern religions: Confucianism, Buddhism, Hinduism and Taoism, which tend to locate the Divine in nature.

The second dimension, with its polar dichotomy, has to do with world-engagement: whether the religion encourages practical engagement with, and adaptation to, the world (an "innerworldly" stance, or some sort of "flight" from it (an "otherworldly" stance). This dichotomy differentiates both the Western and near-Eastern religions as well the Eastern religions. The two dimensions with their polar dichotomies thus, for Weber, generate four categories: cosmocentric-innerworldly, cosmocentric-otherworldly, theocentric-innerworldly and theocentric-otherworldly. Each of these four categories, in Weber's view, is exemplified by major world religions, as follows:

	Theocentric	**Cosmocentric**
World-flight (otherworldly)	Judaism	Hinduism, Buddhism, Taoism
World-adjustment (innerworldly)	Christianity, Islam	Confucianism

Within the realm of the cosmocentric religions, which have an innerworldly orientation, Weber treats Confucianism. Thus, in Confucianism there is little tension between nature and deity: for Weber, it exhibits no "transcendental mooring".[33] Conduct follows from convention and the conduct of traditional virtues and this is why it did not foster capitalism. In Weber's words: "there was no leverage for influencing conduct through inner forces freed of tradition and convention. Family piety, resting in the belief in spirits, was by far the strongest influence on man's conduct"[34]. In Confucianism is thus found an active innerwordliness, conduct and ethical virtues which are adaptive to the social and natural: this world view is crystallized as one of "world adjustment".

---

[33] Quoted by Schluchter (transl. G. Roth), *The Rise of Western Rationalism - Max Weber's Developmental History*, Berkeley and Los Angeles: University of California Press, 1981, on p. 67.

[34] Quoted *ibid.*, p. 67

In Buddhism, Hinduism and Taoism, one similarly finds a cosmocentric view, where the Divine is similarly believed to reside in the natural. However, the adherents of these religions seek salvation not by action which appropriately cultivates and adjusts to the social and natural order, but rather which enables them to flee these orders. The doctrines of *kharma* and *dharma* in Hinduism and Buddhism, by which an individual eventually escapes his world-station, express this ethic of "world-flight".

The religious type joining both theocentric and innerworldly orientations is represented for Weber pre-eminently by ascetic Protestantism, and within it especially, Puritanism. Thus, the characteristic of ascetic Protestantism is the engagement in "'practical rational conduct' of a certain kind, a lifestyle of inner-worldly asceticism that combines active self-control with world mastery".[35] This ethic, which promoted "curtailed consumption, especially luxury consumption, and rewarded acquisition for religious reasons"[36], becomes for Weber the practical ethic of early capitalism. The Protestant ethic represents the dynamic of work, a restless activity to seek personal salvation through virtuous toil. To this end, it promoted the dissolution of traditional group barriers and conventions and created high flexibility in social interaction, conditions for the establishment of the market economy of capitalism. The Puritan ethic or stance towards the world is one of "world-mastery".

Similar to Puritan-Protestantism in its theocentric reference and innerworldly engagement is Islam. Weber, writes Schluchter, claims the following: in Islam, predestination, or better predetermination, is ultimately related above all to one's fate not in the world beyond but in this world: 'The prevailing conception was that predestination determined, not the fate of the individual in the world beyond, but rather his singular fate in this world, the question, for example (and above all), whether the warrior of the faith falls in battle or not.'[37]

---

[35] *Ibid.*, p. 143.
[36] *Ibid.*, p. 144.
[37] W. Schluchter, (transl. N. Solomon), *Paradoxes of Modernity - Culture and Conduct in the Theory of Max Weber*, Stanford: Stanford University Press, p. 131

The difference between the innerworldly theocentrism of Islam and Puritanism, however, is that Islam posits an acceptance of the world as it is, signaling a basic indifference to instigation of social change. Schluchter puts it this way:

> Mohammed thus related two already existing 'worlds': the world of ancient Arab tradition and the world of monotheism, one connected to nomadic and urban tribal particularism, the other, to world empires, or at least to the prospect of a world empire, ruled by a powerful universal G-d by means of His instrument on earth.[38]

This explains the more static character of Islam — vis-à-vis social dynamism and fluidity of Puritanism — which in its case served to hinder the development of the market economy and the ethic of personal striving requisite for capitalism.

Medieval Catholicism seems for Weber, on the one hand, as might well be expected, to be a source of the Protestant-Puritan ethic, but at the same time, it shares a fundamental affinity with the cosmocentrism of the Eastern religions. Thus,

> ...Weber interprets medieval Catholicism primarily in terms of its success in relativizing the tension and dialectic inherent in its world view. He is interested in the reasons that made this belief system ethically not only undemanding but an outright relief for the masses of salvation seekers. One reason is the idea of divinity, the fact 'that the Christian trinity, with its incarnate savior and its saints, is less of a transcendental conception than the G-d of Judaism, especially of late Judaism, or the Allah of Islam.[39]

---

[38] *Ibid.*, p. 143.
[39] *Max Weber's Vision of History*, p. 35. So also, Schluchter highlights its difference with ascetic Protestantism, by reference to the Calvinist thrust in Protestantism: "For Weber the Calvinist destruction of all intermediary agencies between G-d and man is historically decisive: 'The rejection of all ecclesiastic-sacramental salvation, which Lutheranism by means carried through to its conclusion, was the absolutely decisive difference from Catholicism. The great historical process of the disenchantment of the world, which began with the ancient Jewish prophets and, in conjunction with Hellenic scientific thinking, condemned all magical means of salvation as superstition and blasphemy, was here completed'." (*Ibid.*, p. 40). See below in the second section of this essay, a brief discussion of affinities between Confucianism and Catholic Natural Law theory.

What remains in the classification is Judaism. This is classified by Weber as both theocentric and otherworldly, an ethic which Weber, as explained by Schluchter, represents as an "overcoming of the world". By this is meant not the methodical mastery, but rather the expectation of a G-d-given redemption of the world. In other words, the natural, social order is not a dominant reality in itself, so much as the Divine response to human deeds. The focus moves away from natural-social order to the otherworldly, the Divine. In Weber's words:

> For the Jew...the social order of the world was conceived to have been turned into the opposite of that promised for the future, but in the future it was to be over-turned... The world was conceived as neither eternal nor unchangeable, but rather as having been created. Its present structures were a product of man's activities, above all those of the Jews and of G-d's reaction to them. Hence the world was an historical product designed to give way again to the truly G-d ordained order. The whole attitude toward life of ancient Jewry was determined by this conception of a future G-d-guided political and social revolution.

Weber may here have missed Judaism's deep concern with the refinement and sanctification of the creation through the human practice of the G-d-given ethical commandments. Yet he has rightly adumbrated the radical transcendence of Judaism and its attachment to a personal, intervening G-d.

A theological interpretation of Weber's classification

Chassidic thought[40] and Torah law *(halachah)* in Maimonides' Code[41] distinguishes three kinds of "belief" regarding G-d's relationship to the world. This is understood by reference to the notion that even though G-d wholly transcends the creation, He nevertheless chooses to channel influences through entities or powers in the creation, the stars, angels or natural forces and so forth.

---

[40] See Rabbi Menachem Mendel Schneerson, *"Ma'amar Mayim Rabim"* 5717.
[41] *Hilchos avoidas cochovim v'chukos ovdeho*, ch. 1. Maimonides describes *shituf* (without referring to it as such) as a stage between the monotheism in which a Jew is commanded and outright idolatry.

The view which relates the existence and guidance of nature directly to G-d, without any independent significance whatsoever being ascribed to the intermediary conduits employed by Him, viewing these simply as the "axe in the hands of the woodchopper", is the purest monotheism. After this, there is a perception of G-d as the "G-d of gods", where "gods" are understood as potencies which reside within creation, nature — or even nature itself. This attitude associates a measure of significance and ascribes honour to entities or potencies within creation, channelling G-d's influence. It is termed in Hebrew, *shituf*, literally "partnership". It "partners" the ultimate, transcendent G-d with an immanent power or potency. The third stance, which ascribes absolute significance to the potency within creation, or to nature alone, is idolatry. Its knows of no transcendent G-d. Inasmuch as belief in the existence and activity of a transcendent G-d is a foundation for the Noahide laws, only the first two views — pure monotheism and "partnership" — form a basis for their observance.

From the foregoing, it is evident that the theocentric religions — those with an orientation towards a transcendent Creator G-d: Judaism, Christianity and Islam — inasmuch as they are, in Weber's words theocentric (focused on the transcendent Creator G-d) all possess a *prima facie* or strong potential affinity with the Noahide world view.[42] The Eastern religions, on the other hand, *prima facie* pose an issue in this regard. If "cosmocentric" means an *exclusive* association of the Divine with nature, then we have idolatry, which of course is incompatible with the Noahide laws. In the next section, we shall look for elements of transcendence — that is to say transcendence towards the transcendent G-d — within three of the "cosmocentric" religions. Such elements would open for them to the transcendent G-d, the "imitation" of Whose attributes translate in practice into the conduct of the Noahide laws.

The key to this further exploration is to be found in further theological interpretation of Weber's conceptual dimension or

---

[42] This is obvious in the case of Judaism, since Judaism itself transmits the universal teaching of the Noahide laws from Sinai. See, however, fn 4 above.

spectrum otherworldly-innerworldly, also phrased as a distinction between world-flight and world-adjustment (or world-mastery). These terms *can also* relate to different modalities of *self-transcendence*, within the cosmocentric religions themselves.

To understand the theological significance of the otherworldly-innerworldly dichotomy with regard to the "cosmocentric" religions, we need first to revisit the treatment of self-transcendence in the work of Viktor Frankl mentioned briefly above. Frankl spoke of the human being's higher "noetic" (meaning) faculty — soul or conscience — which stands above both body and mind and has ultimate jurisdiction over them. Frankl states crucially moreover that this faculty *ultimately* discovers itself in the "imitation of G-d". That is to say, the destination of its self-transcending faculty is the discovery of itself as soul with its conscious imitation of G-d. The religious person (particularly of the Abrahamic faiths) knows and experiences this for he or she has "arrived there". Frankl, however, also, as we have foreshadowed, made the extremely important point that even the "agnostic" or the "atheist", who undertakes the exercise of self-transcendence — the relativization of all personal interests and impulses in response to the "demand" which life makes of him or her — is already *en route* to the same destination, the imitation of the transcendent G-d, without consciously knowing it.

To attain Noahide belief, a culture must, as noted several times, relate to (transcend towards) the *transcendent* G-d, in Whose imitation the Noahide laws are found to resonate. Our question will be, with regard to the Noahide "potential" of the cosmocentric religions, whether, even if they are in a sense "agnostic" about the *transcendent* G-d, they too, by virtue of distinct characteristics of their species of self-transcendence, can also transcend towards Him. We shall now seek the "hint" of transcendence towards the transcendent G-d — in the negative "world-flight" of Hinduism and Buddhism, and in the positive, self-honing "world-adjustment" of Confucianism — in these cosmocentric world religions.

The cosmocentric world religions and the potentiality of Noahide belief

Hinduism has been termed "polytheistic" and "idolatrous"; Buddhism has been described as "non-theistic"; and Confucianism has been described as not being a religion at all. Our purpose now, with the help of the analysis in the preceding section, is to look at elements in Hinduism, Buddhism and Confucianism which *do draw or could draw* these faiths towards the transcendent Divine and so to the imitation of the transcendent Divine with which the conduct of the Noahide laws is associated. In the following, I draw on the words of scholars of each of these faiths, with regard to elements of transcendence within them. This is done in the hope that these themes will be further explored — especially by practitioners and exponents of these religious cultures, themselves — in the interest of finding amongst them a common ethical ideal in the Noahide laws.

Hinduism

Whilst the common stereotype of Hinduism, particularly at the "village" or "simple, mass" level is, as mentioned, that of a polytheistic, idolatrous religion, this is not necessarily the Hinduism of its classical writings or of its Brahmin caste. The overarching deity — Brahman — which embraces the totality of worldly and natural existence is an *immanent* (a world-indwelling) deity. Yet this concept, too, has been explained to open to a dimension of transcendent deity.

The scholar of Hinduism, R. C. Zaehner, starts by stating that Brahman is not the transcendent Creator G-d of the Judeo-Christian (and, we could add, the Islamic) tradition:

> There is ... one fundamental difference between the Brahman, Self and Person of the Upanishads and the Judaeo-Christian G-d: in Hinduism there is no creation *ex nihilo*. G-d or Brahman is always the material as well as the efficient cause of creation. He emanates the universe out of his own substance and then re-enters it as its indwelling Spirit.[43]

---

[43] R. C. Zaehner, "Introduction" to *Hindu Scriptues*, London: Dent, 1966, p. x.

The focus on Brahman, as being coextensive with created existence, leads Weber to term Hinduism a cosmocentric religion. Nevertheless, from the standpoint of the Noahide laws, this stance could still have a connection to Noahide belief *if* this immanent dimension (Brahman) is *partnered* with a transcendent dimension. Zaehner indicates that the Upanishadic Hindu Scriptures do indeed acknowledge a transcendent dimension:

> The Svetasvatara Upanishad accepts unreservedly the two orders of existence, that of becoming and that of pure Being, but places the supreme G-d above both. Brahman is still the pantheistic indwelling G-d which is pure Being on the one hand and the source of all becoming on the other; but G-d, in this case Rudra-Siva, transcends and controls both orders of existence. Here self, Brahman and G-d are distinguished: by realizing 'self' as being eternal and 'isolated' as in the Sainkhya system the 'embodied soul' knows Brahman since Brahman as eternal Being is the ambience in which the 'self' moves, and by knowing Brahman in its essence he comes to *know G-d who is beyond all essences*, and by knowing Him thus he is set free from all the fetters of mortal life.[44]

Zaehner then quotes some stanzas from this Upanishad, which appears to document the idea of a transcendent G-d "beyond all essences".[45] At the same time, Zaehner writes:

> ...It will be noticed that even in this fully theistic Upanishad, 'liberation' is not interpreted as 'union with G-d'; it is having access to Brahman (VI. 10), being merged in Brahman (I. 7), 'isolation' (I. 11) as in the Samkhya system, or it is 'to know [G-d] with the heart and mind as dwelling in the heart (IV. 20)'. It is to experience G-d's immanence in the human heart, but it is not yet felt to be union with a transcendent G-d who is 'beyond all essences as they really are'...

---

[44] Zaehner, pp. xiii-xiv. Emphasis added.
[45] Yet when one turns to the actual text on p. 207, he adds a footnote to the verses "[Then will he know] the unborn, undying G-d the Pure/Beyond all essences as they really are" and states that "these epithets could be taken as agreeing with 'Brahman'".

> To sum up: the Upanishads investigate the nature of reality and their main conclusion is that in both the universe at large and in the individual human being there is a ground of pure Being which is impervious to change. To realize this Being in oneself means salvation. Once this is done, re-birth and re-death are done away with, and man realizes himself as at least participating in eternal Being. Even when he comes to a knowledge of G-d *as being transcendent as well as immanent*, he does not interpret this realization as union with G-d. The immanent G-d is everything, the transcendent largely irrelevant. This is the position as we find it at the end of the Upanishadic period, and it is from here that the Bhagavad-Gita takes on.[46]

In other words, even if — unlike the theocentric religions — there is *little* focus on the transcendent G-d Himself, the very fact that this dimension is acknowledged as the *source* of the immanent dimension endows that immanent dimension with some quality of "reflection" of transcendence. The *existence* of a transcendent G-d is known. I leave it specialists and above all to Hindu practitioners themselves, interested in the Noahide laws, to assess the degree of acknowledgment of transcendence in Hinduism — namely towards a G-d "beyond all essences", in Zaehner's words. To the extent that this is present, even if its focus is secondary, it is meaningful and important to test the resonance of the actual Noahide laws, which go with transcendence, in *this* level of consciousness in Hinduism.

The otherworldly nature of Hinduism is understood, as in Buddhism, in the goal of escaping what Weber calls "the wheel of rebirth"[47] and through *karma*, to escape the afflictions and imperfections of the world. World-flight, however, could — as we wished to suggest at the end of the first section — be not simply a flight *from* the *Karma* of this world, which it consciously is, but also as a movement *to* What is found beyond it.

---

[46] Zaehner, pp. xiv-xv.
[47] *The Religion of India*, p. 267.

Buddhism

Buddhism differs from Hinduism — at least in its classical form which is preserved today in the form of the Theravada school — in that it ostensibly eschews all discussion of deity. This, however, does not place it outside the category of a "religion" or one which might even be consistent in some ways with Noahidism, if we consider a concept of "negative" self-transcendence, applied to it.

As mentioned above, for Frankl, self-transcendence can place one on the trajectory towards G-d, even if G-d is not acknowledged. Self-nullification is the characteristic of the soul (made in G-d's image), even if the soul does not know itself as soul. Indeed, there is a remarkable parallel between Frankl's analysis of existence as "transitoriness" — into the moments of which ethical decision making must be inserted even by the sincerely self-transcending secular agnostic — and the Buddhist world view. So also, the renunciation of simple psychophysical will, or what classical Buddhism called "thirst", chimes with Frankl's "negative" act of "self-transcendence". In Weber's words:

> While the early Christian sought passion as an ascetic means or perhaps as martyrdom, the Buddhist flees passion by all means. "Passion", however, is equated to the transitoriness of all forms of existence. What is the nature of passion? It is the fight without prospects of success against the transitoriness of all forms of existence resulting from the nature of life, the "struggle for existence" in the sense of striving to maintain one's own existence which yet is consecrated to death from the outset.[48]

This *renunciation* of egotism, as typical of the world — flight *from* the world — is the source of salvation, rather than the approach *to* a G-d, which transcends the world. In Weber's words, again:

> ...it is an ethic with an absolute indifference to the question of whether there are 'gods' and how they exist...Its salvation is a

---

[48] Max Weber, *The Religion of India* (transl. H.H. Gerth and D. Martindale) NY: The Free Press, 1958, p. 209.

solely personal act of the single individual. There is no recourse to a deity or saviour.[49]

As in Hinduism, there is an ethical causality and coherence in the world — *Karma* — and it would seem that this implicitly acknowledges a Divine providence, by reference to which the human being makes sense of life. "No single world-bound act can get lost in the course of the ethically meaningful but completely cosmic causality."[50] It is simply that Buddhism lacks the *positive* concept of deity. Certainly, this negative self-transcendence (transcendence *from* self and world, if not *to* G-d) *does not deny G-d*, and the essence of the Noahide law is a *prohibition* on idolatry — a *negative* commandment — that one not worship something which is *not* G-d.

This teaching of negative self-transcendence does align Buddhism in significant ways with the actual morality of the Noahide laws that substantially overlap the Decalogue. Weber writes:

> In their original substance the advisory councils [of the founder of Buddhism] were roughly in agreement with the Decalogue, but with a broader understanding of the prohibition against killing (ahimsa), extending it to all injury of live beings, the commandment of unconditional truthfulness (in the Decalogue it applied only to court witnesses), and the express prohibition of drunkenness. For the loyal observance of these commandments of lay morality (especially of the five cardinal prohibitions: not to kill, steal, commit adultery, lie, or get drunk)...[51]

As mentioned, the foregoing relates to the Theravada school of Buddhism, the more pristine version, which is prevalent in Thailand, Sri Lanka, Myanmar (Burma), Cambodia and Laos. The Mahayana schools of Buddhism, prevalent in Tibet, China, Korea and Japan, is by contrast openly theistic. A contemporary Elder Buddhist Monk, Venerable Toby Gillies, who is aware of Noahide

---

[49] Ibid., p. 206.
[50] Ibid., p. 207. See *The Theory and Practice of Universal Ethics – the Noahide Laws*, p. 4, which references an early connection between the descendants of Abraham and the beginnings of Hinduism, especially with regard to the doctrine of reincarnation.
[51] *The Religion of India*, p. 215

teaching, has written to me:

> In my reading, the Mahayana Buddha would be relatable to the first Noahide law [belief in G-d]. Its nature is transcendent, pervasive and the true nature of all that exists. This Buddha nature is an ultimate, beyond concept or label. This ultimate truth, when realized, is Enlightenment or Buddhahood. Until realized, it is the Buddha nature of beings and their potential for enlightenment. This Buddha potential may bear the comparison to the Noahide Soul.

I cannot personally comment on the substance of this doctrine, but I do note that the writer further finds that Mahayana doctrine substantially endorses the substance of the Noahide laws.

Confucianism

In the Chinese cultural-historical background to Confucianism, there is a concept of a supreme G-d, called Tian — "Heaven". This supreme G-d endowed humanity with moral norms, in accordance with which life should be conducted.[52] At the same time, it is characteristic of Confucianism that there is little speculative focus on this supreme deity. This, the powerfully innerworldly, focus of Confucianism is expressed, not in denial of G-d (indeed it speaks of "Tian" or a spiritual dimension) but in what Mark Elvin has termed a "scepticism" about discussion on spiritual matters. This scepticism:

> is evident in his [Confucius'] refusal to talk about "supernatural events, feats of strength, disorders of nature, or the gods." Presumably he thought their reality often doubtful, and their significance, if any, even harder to determine. He insisted that an essential part of knowledge was that "if you do not know a thing, recognize that you do not know it." When his disciple Zilu asked how one should serve the *manes* [spirits of ancestors] and the gods, Kongzi [Confucius] answered: "You do not yet

---

[52] Mark Elvin, "Was There a transcendental Breakthrough in China" in S.N. Eisenstadt (Ed.), *The Origins and Diversity of the Axial Age Civilizations*, Albany: State University of New York Press, 1986, p. 328.

know how to serve men. How are you able to serve the *manes*?" Zilu then asked about the dead. This provoked the retort: "You do not yet understand the living. How can you know about the dead?" Other sayings make it clear that he did not disbelieve in the *manes* and the gods. He insisted on the practical primacy of the human world.[53]

Much rather, G-d is known from the human microcosm. Confucianism seeks positively to image a Divine morality through the instrument of reason, human rationality. Hu Shih in an exceptional essay[54] comparing Confucianism with Christian — Catholic — natural law and natural reason theory, writes:

> In an interesting passage, Mencius [...a later exponent of Confucianism] used the word *lei* in the sense of universal truth, in the sense of what agrees with "common right and wrong." He said:
>
>> "All mouths of men agree in enjoying the same relishes; all ears agree in enjoying the same (musical) sounds; all eyes agree in recognizing the same beauty. Is there nothing which all minds agree in affirming to be true? What is it then which all minds recognize to be true? It is *lei* (universal truth or law) and *i* (universal right or righteousness) ... Universal truth and right are agreeable to our mind, just as tasty meals are pleasing to our taste."[55]

In other words, it is not an act of *negative* transcendence — reaching beyond intellect — which images Divine ethical will, but rather an immanent human faculty of reason which seeks *positively* to reach towards the ethical Absolute:

> Now the sense of dismay on another's behalf is the sprout of humaneness (*ren*) planted within us, the sense of shame is the sprout of appropriateness (*yi*), the sense of deference is the sprout of propriety (*li*), and the sense of right and wrong is the

---

[53] *Ibid.*, p. 332.
[54] "The Natural Law in Chinese Tradition", p. 137, https://scholarship.law.nd.edu/cgi/viewcontent.cgi?filename=9...naturallaw...
[55] Quoted *Ibid.*, pp. 146-147.

sprout of wisdom (*zhi*). Everyone possesses these four moral senses just as they possess their four limbs. For one to possess such moral senses and yet to claim that he cannot call them forth is to rob oneself; and for a person to claim that his ruler is incapable of such moral feelings is to rob his ruler.[56]

Here we find an extraordinary congruence between the Catholic natural reason and natural law doctrine of "right reason" and Confucianism. The difference, of course, is that Christianity *also* has explicit reference to a transcendent Creator *ex nihilo* — and a debate indeed rages within Catholic thought as to whether reason, in an age of the corruption of reason, can function rightly without the transcendent guidance of revelation.[57]

Expressed somewhat differently, Confucianism knows of the existence of "Tian" — G-d or Heaven — but it seeks through reason, through a proper "directedness" (to use the phrase of major Natural Law scholar, Professor John Finnis speaking about natural reason and natural law in the Catholic tradition) to apprehend this.

Professor J. Makeham (in a communication to me) cites the later generation Confucian, Mencius:

> **7A:1** Mencius said, "He who brings his heart-mind to its complete realization knows his nature. To know one's nature is to know *Tian*. To preserve one's heart-mind and to nourish one's nature are that whereby one serves *Tian*.

The innerworldliness (world-adjustment) of Confucianism consists in the application of a refined human faculty of *reason*, an *innerworldly* faculty, directed towards Heaven. This is a species of *positive* transcendence, working via intellect and its categories, rather than negating them. The otherworldliness (world-flight) of Hinduism and Buddhism involves *spiritually driven* abnegation of the imperfect, transitory natural world, which negates both the world and its intellectual and social categories in its *negative* transcendence.

---

[56] Mencius 2A:6.
[57] See Carl E. Braaten, "Protestants and Natural Law", *First Things*, January, 1992.

Thus, Confucianism presents an interesting blend of immanence (reason) and transcendence ("imaging" G-d-likeness): transcendence through, and in, *reason*. Professor Makeham put it to me, in a personal communication, thus:

> There is [in Confucianism] no counterpart to the notion of a soul as the spiritual bearer of the human being and which is beholden to something beyond the person. In part this stems from the lack of a notion of radical transcendence in classical Chinese thought. There is no belief in a transcendent reality— instead there is a strong belief in immanent transcendence. Immanent transcendence is a realist metaphysical view (i.e., not a nominalism). It describes how, on the one hand, the referent wholly lies within the boundaries of a specifiable domain; yet, on the other hand, it simultaneously extends beyond the boundaries of that domain.

We see that what Weber regarded as cosmocentric religions can still have a connection with the transcendent G-d (held explicitly by the theocentric religions), about which they are "agnostic", even in innerworldly or world-adjusting modalities. Whilst their focus is not directly upon the transcendent G-d, the existence of a transcendent G-d is not denied: it is simply not explicitly embraced. In Hinduism, an immanent deity — Brahman — *reflects* the transcendent G-d. In classical Theraveda Buddhism, the transcendent G-d is approached negatively — by negating the un-G-dliness of an imperfect nature; whilst Mahayana Buddhism may even approach G-d explicitly. And in Confucianism, fully adjusted to the world, transcendence is modelled immanently — within the world — not as the spiritual flight from the world but through *reason directed* towards Heaven in practical conduct.

Along with the theocentric Abrahamic religions, it is thus thinkable that the cosmocentric Eastern religions might also open sufficiently to the transcendent source of the Noahide laws, to allow a true, human-spiritual commonality of the major religious cultures to emerge. When presented then with the actual definitive content of the Noahide laws, as revealed at Sinai, and as transmitted through the tradition from Sinai, the adherents of these great world faiths may well recognize and affirm the universal laws of the one G-d, as binding them all.

Chapter 5

Universal Ethics and the United Nations:
An Examination of the United Nations' "Universal Declaration of Human Rights"

What greater practical ideal could there be than that *universal values* be embraced by the organization which was meant — as its name suggests — to accomplish the unity, and draw on the common moral allegiance, of all humanity, namely, the United Nations? There is already a founding document of the United Nations, which bears in its title the word "universal". This is the Universal Declaration of Human Rights, which was adopted and promulgated by the United Nations in 1948.

In her book, *A World Made New, Eleanor Roosevelt and the Universal Declaration of Human Rights*[58] a Harvard Professor, Mary Ann Glendon, looks historically at the process which went into the formulation of this document, under the leadership of Eleanor Roosevelt. Precisely as a study of the *historical* formation, rather than providing a *philosophical* analysis, of the principles of the Declaration, it is instructive. It illuminates many key issues and problems involved in the discovery of principles, which can effectively claim universality and so act as a *uniting* and commonly motivating force for a diverse community of nations.

The Preamble to the Charter of the United Nations, which came before the Universal Declaration of Human Rights, set out four great ambitions of the United Nations: to establish peace amongst nations, to affirm human rights, to create respect for international

---
[58] NY: Random House, 2001.

law and to promote the social and economic improvement of the world's peoples. Even though the Universal Declaration of Human Rights, as its name indicates, focuses on Human Rights, the other three concerns of the United Nations are woven into it. We can evaluate this document and examine how it might be improved in terms of its universality and motivating power by examining how effectively it serves each of these four objectives. This involves understanding (1) the culture of common values which alone can be the basis for world *peace*; (2) what are truly *universal* rights and obligations, as distinct from culturally and nationally particular values; (3) the content of an international law which could command universal allegiance; and (4) how universal principles could motivate collective action towards the socio-economic betterment of peoples. The sections of this essay examine these issues in relation to the Universal Declaration of Human Rights.

A culture of common values for peace

What lessons about a common culture of values can be learnt from the historical formation of the Universal Declaration of Human Rights? The Human Rights Commission, which was assembled to produce this document, was consciously composed of members from a number of states and cultures. It was hoped that together they would create out of their various perspectives a consistent, harmonious and consensual ("universal") document. They included participants from Australia, the United States (in addition to Eleanor Roosevelt, the Chairperson), Europe (notably the Frenchman, René Cassin, who later received a Nobel Peace Prize for his work on the Declaration), a Lebanese Arab academic, Charles Malik, representing Muslim cultures, a Chinese, Peng-Chun Chang, at that stage a representative of China still under the leadership of the Kuomintang and Chiang Kai-Shek (before the Chinese Communist Revolution finally succeeded in the year following that of the promulgation of the Universal Declaration). Other representatives were Indian, Latin American and, prominently, Soviet Russian. All of these representatives from diverse, and, in certain clear instances, mutually antagonistic, nations were intended to hammer out a "universal" guiding document for the United Nations. In fact, as the work of this Commission proceeded, pretence to shared values was discarded and its task became instead to "compile" from the different representatives a collection of principles, from amongst which a mutually acceptable document could be negotiated.

It quickly became evident that this document, like the organization of the United Nations, would not form the basis for "World Government". The indomitable reality was that sovereign states, many of which were melded into blocs, would not submit their sovereignty to a world Parliament or a single conventional international law. Already the veto power vested in the five permanent members of the Security Council recognized that reality. Dreams of world-government, a world parliament with global taxation and a global military force for the United Nations have persisted to this day, but they are still dreams: they have no greater prospect of realization now than they had then. All that can command the allegiance of distinct sovereign powers, we shall argue, are *common* values and principles to which nations and individuals can *intrinsically* subscribe. Otherwise, we are left, now as then, with a clash of *particular* interests and values.

This problem beset the Human Rights Commission at its inception, as it does the United Nations today. It has to do with the approach to guiding principles. "Principles" are in fact often interests. If not naked material interests, they dress themselves up as "ideals", but these in fact represent the particular forms of individual national political and economic systems. Nowhere was this seen more clearly in the process of formation of the Universal Declaration of Human Rights than in the conflicting perspectives of the American (and European) and the Soviet (bloc) standpoints. Both the Americans and the Soviets had geopolitical interests, the establishment of friendly democracies and the extension of the international workers' revolution, respectively. And they also had a different approach to "rights", with the Americans stressing the rights of the individual *against* the State, and the Soviet bloc stressing economic and social rights to be made good *by* a powerful State, with its necessary priority *over* the individual. Consequences of the Western perspective meant limitation on the powers of the State, unacceptable to the Soviet ideal; and consequences of the Eastern bloc's perspective meant magnification of the power of the State vis-à-vis the individual, unacceptable to the Western ideal. Having made their insertions into the document, which ended up incorporating both perspectives, the Soviets in the final vote abstained from endorsing the Declaration.

The approach of the Human Rights Commission to the search for principles — "compilation" and then negotiation of principles — accorded an implicit relativity to values. There was no recognition, or maybe under the political conditions of the time little practical inclination towards acknowledgment, of a code of principles which were objective and universal for all.

There is, however, a code of ethical principles which is the common historical and spiritual legacy of all humanity. These are known as the Noahide laws, which were communicated by G-d to humanity from its inception and completed with the biblical survivor of the flood and ancestor of all humanity, Noah. These laws were passed on through the generations, until they reached Abraham, from whom they spread to the East, to Hinduism and Buddhism, but most prominently through the tradition which led to Sinai, at which the Pentateuch was given, including the reiteration of the Noahide laws; and from Sinai to the great world religions, Judaism, Christianity and Islam. There are grounds to find a resonance for the Noahide laws also in Confucianism.

Not only are the Noahide laws the root historical values of the great world religions and cultures, but they also resonate with the human soul or conscience, the human essence. This is because the human soul — made in the image of G-d — naturally resonates with the Divine attributes — G-d's mercy, kindness, justice and so forth. These Divine attributes in turn translate into the practical ethical conduct of the Noahide laws. The Noahide laws are seven in number, but include great detail. In broad outline they are (1) belief in G-d and the prohibition of idolatry (2) respect for G-d and the prohibition of blasphemy (3) sexual morality based on the identity and integrity of the family (4) the prohibition of theft and material harm (5) the prohibition of killing (6) the requirement for processes of justice and (7) the proper treatment of animals and the environment. In their detail these laws apply to every facet of the life of individuals, societies and the relationship of states amongst each other.

In other words, the Noahide laws are both the historical root of the world religions and cultures and possess a timeless spiritual resonance, a native legitimacy, within the human soul. However, to allow this common spirituality of humanity to flourish requires, both of individuals and societies, an attitude of spiritual sensitivity. The name of G-d was absent from the text of the Universal Declaration of Human Rights, and with its absence was absent the common source opening to the full substance of a *universal* ethics. A gathering of persons, who feel that they can speak of G-d, not only discovers common values, which come from G-d, but also a common "brotherhood" and "sisterhood", with a common authority that motivates their fulfilment of those shared values. This condition was not present during the formulation of the Universal Declaration of Human Rights.

If G-d could not be brought into the Universal Declaration of Human Rights in 1949, could He *now* be brought into a revised version of that document, that would endow it with genuine universality? The answer to that question appears now, more than ever before to be an unequivocal YES. With the collapse of the Soviet Union and the communist bloc in eastern Europe has come a resurgence of religion in both Russia and the eastern European countries far from the stance of their post-war representatives in the Human Rights Commission. In 2020 constitutional amendments to the Russian constitution included affirmation of belief in G-d. Similar reaffirmation of the primacy of faith in G-d is being heard in the political spheres of former Soviet bloc countries, such as Hungary and Poland. At the time of the work of the Commission on the Universal Declaration of Human Rights, China was in the throes of a civil war and an impending communist victory. This seemed to cast a shadow over the Confucian world view set forth by the then Chinese delegate to the Commission, who was a representative of the Kuomintang. But now the leader of communist China, Xi Jinping has affirmed the Confucian background of contemporary China. Though Confucianism is a practical and "innerworldly" religion, it does historically acknowledge "Heaven" and a spiritual template for human conduct, much of which can be aligned with the Noahide laws. Indian culture also has an historical Noahide background and a "summit" meeting in 2008 of its spiritual leaders along with representatives of Abrahamic faiths acknowledged belief in a "Supreme Being". And the other cultures which contributed to the drafting of the Universal Declaration through their representatives — Europe, America, Latin America and the Muslim world — now as then have a patently Noahide, biblical background, though its expression was frustrated at the time of the drafting of the Declaration. In 1991, the United States Congress endorsed the Noahide laws as the "bedrock of society from the dawn of civilization". This was followed by endorsements of the Noahide laws in 2008 by the Governor General of Australia, in 2012 by the King of Morocco and in 2014 by the President of the European Union. A leading Catholic theologian, Professor Tracey Rowland, in her review of the world faiths, has concluded, "from within all of these traditional communities, we can agree to …the Noahide laws". Now, we are on the cusp of evoking a universal culture of the Noahide laws.[59]

The emblematic "motto" of the United Nations is the inscription on its "Isaiah Wall":

> They shall beat their swords into ploughshares and their spears into pruning hooks

Less well known are the preceding verses in Isaiah, which state the preconditions of that prophecy:

---

[59] "Tradition and Rupture in Basic Shared Values", *Journal of Judaism and Civilization*, Vol. 14, 2019.

> And many peoples shall go and say: Come and let us go up to the mountain of the L-rd...And He will teach us of His ways and we will walk in His paths.

These "ways" and "paths" refer to the Noahide laws, the spiritual ethical legacy of all humanity, through which humans can merit the "world to come" and nations an enduring peace.

Universal and Non-universal Rights and Obligations

That the Universal Declaration of Human Rights was couched wholly in the language of "human rights" dates the Declaration. It is commonly acknowledged now that we should speak of obligations as well as rights. Moreover, rights are not ascribed only to humans. Animals, for example, may not be mistreated. But these issues aside, we need to ask what criteria give a posited right or obligation the status of "universality", as the "Universal Declaration" by its title appeared to claim.

We hear more and more of rights, many of which were never before touted as rights. The very fact that they are put forward as "rights" is intimidating because of the emotive and dogmatic charge in the word. But that should not prevent us from asking the question, what makes anything a "right" (or for that matter an "obligation") at all, and beyond that an absolute and universal right (or obligation)? A right or obligation presumes a value. It is the ethical pedigree of the values at the basis of claimed "rights" and obligations that will determine whether they are authentic universal rights and obligations, or not. From the standpoint of the universal tradition of the Noahide laws, this question will be answered by the consistency of purported rights and obligations with the Noahide laws.

Now there are many "rights" which are bandied about, that in fact are quite contrary to the Noahide laws. Take abortion for example. Abortion is permitted, under Noahide law, to save the life of the mother — this is an act of defence of (the mother's) life. But we hear people speaking about an *unqualified* right (of a mother) to abort a child for any or no reason. This purported "right" is dressed up — or rather obfuscated — as "reproductive rights". On the contrary, under Noahide law, this "abortion on demand" is in the category of prohibited killing. There is also touted a right to marry whomever one wants: in Sweden this is interpreted to extend to the right of siblings with one common parent to marry. The Noahide laws prohibit this as incest. There can be no "right" to commit incest, let alone enshrine it in "marriage". In other words, there is no "right" which involves an acted prohibited under universal, Noahide law.

The term "right" may also be invoked with regard to *entitlements*, which are not upheld by the Noahide laws as universal entitlements. If they were indeed universal, they would be mandatory under Noahide law. The Universal Declaration of Human Rights contains a number of such "rights". It mentions in Article 23 (1) a "right" to work. The Noahide laws mention no such right. If a person does work, various laws apply. For example, a person's wages may not be withheld; an agricultural or food processing worker may not eat from the food he or she is harvesting or processing outside the time of working. If a person is without work and has become needy, others are obligated to assist him or her with charity. But others are not obligated to provide an individual with — and an individual has no "right" to — work under universal Noahide law. The notion of a "right" to work is a value of a particular socio-economic system, typically a socialist or a communist one, which entails a strong state apparatus that comprehensively directs the economy and so can ensure full employment. The Universal Declaration's article relating to a "right to work" was ostensibly included at the insistence (particularly) of the Soviet representatives on the commission. A "right to work" — however commendable and desirable full employment might be — at all events is not a universal principle.

We have noted that the Universal Declaration of Human Rights chose the language of "rights" rather than "obligations". Yet it does place obligations upon the State, i.e. upon individuals collectively and not individually. Thus, it obligates the State to provide social security and employment to all its members (Articles 22 and 23).

The Noahide laws enjoin charity, as noted, but do not stipulate whether it is to be given through the State (social security) or by individuals. The requirement that it be supplied *through the State* is not a universal requirement of the Noahide laws. We shall return to this point.

Article 3 of the Declaration states that "Everyone has the right to life". Here, however, there is no mention of an individual's *obligation to protect life*. This means that abortion on demand is not excluded by the Declaration. Nor does it mandate an individual to save the life of another person in the face of a pursuer upon that life. Nor does it obligate a doctor to save a life. Just as purported rights — which are in fact no rights at all, but on the contrary prohibited acts by the standard of universal Noahide law — *commit* violation of universal principles; so also, the absence of obligations which Noahide law place on individuals *omits* fulfilment of universal obligations. In Noahide law, one is forbidden to take innocent life, and one is obligated to protect life.

Another shortcoming in the Declaration is its limited approach to the subjects of (i.e. those possessing) rights. The Declaration speaks about "Human" rights (and implicit obligations). The Noahide laws require that animals not be treated with unnecessary cruelty and that the environment not be heedlessly ravaged. These obligations are absent from the Universal Declaration of Human Rights. Another area overlooked by the Declaration is the acknowledgment and honour due to G-d. Its absence from the Declaration has assisted, amongst many other consequences, the rampant disregard for the free practice of religious belief and religious freedom in general, which we see in contemporary society.

In short, the quest for truly universal principles needs to proceed by deduction and inference from the universal moral and spiritual legacy of humanity, the Noahide laws. Only those principles which *can be derived from* the body of Noahide law, that has been with humanity since its origins and was reiterated to humanity at Mount Sinai are universal. What the Noahide laws prohibit can never be the subject of a purported "right"; and what the

Noahide laws mandate constitute an inescapable obligation. The Noahide laws also state both "Who" and "What" are the subject of rights and obligations. What can be derived from Noahide law is universal and what cannot be derived is not universal. Beyond this, the inclusion, in a statement of "universal" principles, of laws and principles which are not universal is not only unnecessary but can also *disturb* the unity of those (in this case, the nations of the world) meant to be guided by those principles, as we shall now discuss.

There are two kinds of law. There is universal (Noahide) law, which is mandatory and is the moral framework for all societies and individuals. Then, there is also "positive" law enacted by societies through their legislatures. In the sights of Noahide law, positive law refers to the discretionary laws — i.e. laws which do not conflict with, Noahide law. For example, a society through its legislature can decide on what side of the road people must drive; it can make laws regarding taxation. These are called positive laws, from the expression "to posit" — to assert, create, make. Positive law accounts for a vast amount of law regulating society's existence and where it does not conflict with Noahide law, Noahide law (under the Noahide law of justice) requires that it be observed within its jurisdiction.

Such positive law varies from society to society and as such accounts for the legitimate diversity of different societies. Thus, Noahide law can accomodate a variety of systems of Government and socio-economic organization within its parameters because it does not of itself stipulate the positive arrangements and laws which society can make, as long as Noahide law is not infringed. Even a centralized monarchy need not be opposed to the Noahide laws, as we see in the monarchies of King David and King Solomon. Most political systems can theoretically be consistent or inconsistent with the Noahide laws, depending on whether their specific policies and laws both fulfil the obligations, and do not infringe the prohibitions of Noahide law: a socialist society could be a keeper or violator of the Noahide laws, and similarly a democratic state, a keeper or violator of the Noahide laws.

There is, accordingly, no need to homogenize cultures and societies for them all to be united and guided under the aegis of the shared framework of universal Noahide law. But a problem does arise when particular, non-universal positive laws are included in a purportedly universal document which all societies are expected to observe. For that unnecessarily forces an alignment in areas which are naturally and permissibly diverse amongst different societies. This problem occurs in places in the Universal Declaration of Human Rights where non-universal, positive laws of *particular* political and economic systems have been enshrined in the "universal" document.

More specifically, the problem of incorporating particular positive laws in a "universal" document can be manifest in one of two ways: either it is a positive law, which expresses one particular political and cultural expression *of a* universal principle (which could equally be expressed through other positive arrangements). Alternatively, it can be a positive law, which expresses *no* universal — Noahide — principle at all. Examples of each can be found in the Universal Declaration of Human Rights. Both constitute unwarranted impositions on diverse societies and cultures.

To take an example of the first case, which has already been mentioned above. Article 23 of the Declaration states that "Everyone, as a member of society, has the right to social security". What this means is that the State is obligated to provide its individual members, who need it, with social security. Now, the Noahide laws provide that an obligation to give charity — provision for the needy — devolves upon the members of society, but it does not stipulate *how* that provision should take place: whether as an act of the State (*"social* security"), whereby the community is taxed and the State administers the charity (welfare), or whether charity be provided by individuals to one another or be organized on a more local community basis. As noted above, the emphasis on the State as the provider of welfare, whether through taxation and social security or through a commitment to provide employment for all of society's members (Article 23), ostensibly reflected the Statist perspective of the Soviet bloc in the Human Rights Commission. As such, the latter was a source of some friction with American representatives, who wanted, in accordance with the liberal capitalism of the time, a minimal role for the State: indeed, a society with a "small" state can, on a private and local level, also be a charitable society. This conflict between "big" and "small" State perspectives could have been avoided had only the universal Noahide principle, that charity for the welfare of all needy be practised in society, been stated, rather than stipulating the *positive* form that this obligation take, which is open to political differences.

We come now to the second case of positive law, which does not necessarily constitute *any* expression of universal principle. A substantial group of articles was placed in the Declaration to defend against specific summary judicial and police measures. Yet many of these articles have become highly questionable in the face of terrorism wrought by citizens against their own society. Article 9 prohibits summary arrest and detention. Does this apply to a suspected terrorist with resources of destruction as great as that of a foreign enemy? Article 10 requires under all circumstances a "public hearing": does that apply to case involving military secrets or child sexual abuse? Article 12 prohibits interference with a person's privacy and Article 13 stipulates the right of a person to return to his country. Do these apply respectively to a terrorist, whose phone is tapped, or who has been granted domicile abroad? The Noahide law of justice requires dispassionate justice. But it also has a sliding scale of exigency of circumstances which is matched by a sliding scale of stringency in the application of standards of testimony and judgment. A military court in circumstances of battle can well be different from a civilian court in times of domestic stability. There are minimum standards of justice corresponding to moments of highest social need for stability. Articles 9, 10, 12 and 13 exceed that minimum standard, and assume a high level of social stability but do not contemplate internal terrorism. They were evidently fashioned with the intention of forestalling tyrannies such as those of Nazi Germany and Stalinist Russia. Because, however, they miss the universal requirements of the Noahide law of justice, they are now dated and even, in some cases, harmful.

Accordingly, it is appropriate, in the face of the diversity of cultures and political and economic systems which the United Nations seek to bring together, that any declaration of shared principles should involve *only* universal (Noahide) principles and not positive laws. For raising non-universal, positive laws to the status of universal principles curbs the natural diversity of, and creates frictions between, the legitimate positive arrangements, of different societies. This point is illustrated by one writer:

> The conceptual integrity of human rights was a victim of the Cold War, and human rights divided into two treaties: the International Covenant on Civil and Political Rights (ICCPR) and the International Covenant of Economic, Social and Cultural Rights (ICESCR). The Western countries, led by the USA, argued for the supremacy of civil and political rights, which often amounted to denying that economic and social rights were, or could become, human rights. The Soviet-led communist and/or socialist bloc argued that economic and social rights should take precedence over civil and political rights, which often resulted in the denial of civil rights and political liberties. Secondly, this protracted process lasted until 1966, when the two Covenants were adopted, and it took ten additional years for them to come into force.[60]

A rectified "Universal Declaration": the Noahide laws in international law and the betterment of humanity

How would a revised version of the Universal Declaration of Human Rights, or a wholly new document, incorporate the Noahide laws, and thereby provide universally resonant principles for international law and spur the socio-economic betterment of peoples — the last two of the UN's objectives?

Let us begin with the first Noahide law, which is the prohibition

---

[60] Katerina Tomasevski, "Human Rights – Fundamental Freedoms for All" in E. Childers, *Challengers to the United Nations – Building a Safer World*, London: S Martins Press, 1194, p. 84.

of idolatry, but more generally signifies the belief in G-d. Why was the name of G-d absent from the Universal Declaration of Human and Rights and so also from the subsequent covenants of the United Nations? We have mentioned the Soviet presence in the Commission and that the official atheism of its communism must have contributed to a standoff on any mention of G-d. Yet, it was also an "Enlightenment" liberalism in the European and American side which wanted an exclusive focus on "*human dignity*", without consideration of whether human dignity actually derived from the Divine likeness in the human soul. Eleanor Roosevelt herself was a religious woman, but felt that G-d should be kept out of the Declaration, notwithstanding a strong religiosity in American culture, which would come to striking expression in President John F. Kennedy's statement that "the rights of man come not from the generosity of the State but from the hand of G-d". The Latin American contingent in the Commission to draft the Declaration did not feel squeamish about mentioning G-d, though they carried no sway in the matter. Perhaps the American and European liberals of that time in the Commission still sufficiently possessed the moral compass of the religious tradition, that they assumed the moral compass associated with religious tradition would stay, without mention of G-d. If that is a true interpretation of their intentions, these were certainly belied by the dismantling of the received universal moral compass by a runaway liberalism and social dismantlement of the last 50 years in the West, which has made "man", not G-d, the measure of all values. Nevertheless, the overall fact remains that some 84% of humanity is religiously affiliated and most of it is comfortable with the word "G-d". Why then must the default position of the UN's documents be to omit the name of G-d and to use the language of a secular humanism? Perhaps the belief in G-d (of the 84%) should be the UN's standard position, with tolerance of the 16% the world's non-believers, rather than that its default position and values be those of a secular humanism (of the 16%), with tolerance of the 84% — the world's believers.

Just as literacy and numeracy are global ideals, so too should be spiritual development and spiritual literacy of humanity and especially of youth. The global plagues of suicide, depression and drug-abuse, especially amongst youth, attest to the social repression of the spiritual and the sense of higher meaning and purpose. The United Nations should include in its educational objectives the promotion of spiritual literacy in the education of youth. The conduct of a lawful society and of a lawful world draws its motivation from the *conscience* of individuals. Conscience is nurtured and internalized, not by the fear of being caught by an inspector or authority, but by the sense that one stands in the presence of G-d, Who sees, hears and expects of one, in one's solitude.

We come now to the Noahide prohibition of blasphemy. This has to do with the respect for, and honouring of G-d. We hear of the dignity of the human being in the Declaration, but nothing of the honour due to G-d. Fundamentally, it is the honour of G-d which establishes the dignity of the human being, who is made spiritually in G-d's likeness. Respect for G-d translates into respect for human religious freedom. The social engineering, which has overturned traditional values, has in recent decades been accompanied by a fierce attempt to crush the freedom of religious institutions, professionals, academics and individuals who adhere to those values. Freedom of religion is mentioned in UN doctrines, but it requires greater specification and explicit defence.

We come next to the Noahide law which prohibits killing. The Universal Declaration of Human Rights tells us that everyone has a right to life. But it is not clear whether this is merely a right, which can equally be waived through suicide or voluntary euthanasia — or whether life is something sacred. Accordingly, as mentioned above, it does not exclude "abortion on demand" or regimes of euthanasia and so-called assisted suicide. The absence of the name of G-d in the Declaration weakens the sanctity of life. For the essence of the prohibition of killing is that the soul bears the Divine likeness and as such life is Divine property, not at a person's disposal.

The area of sexual morality is the subject of the next Noahide law. Section 15(3) of the Declaration speaks of the family as the basic unit of society, which is entitled to the protection of the state. It does not, however, tell us what the family is. The Noahide laws state that the family consists of parents, a mother and father, and offspring, boys and girls. Biological relationships and individual biological identity are crucial to human identity and the "commissioning of children" for alternative relationships constitute a deep deprivation to children of full parental biological ties and identity.

We come to the Noahide law of theft. What is missing here in the provisions of the Declaration is the heart of the human relationship which negates theft and exploitation: reciprocity — the idea that it is a fellow human being whom one faces in an economic exchange or commercial relationship. We have huge corporations which do not acknowledge their clients as fellow human beings, who should not be treated differently from themselves. And we have rich countries which do not view the poor countries, with which they trade, as possessing an equal dignity. The dignity of the other, and the fullness of the obligation of reciprocity in dealings, is inwardly acknowledged and guaranteed when the other is understood to possess the likeness of G-d, the foundation of human dignity.

Justice is an area substantially treated in the Declaration, but one of its most glaring lacks is the absence of a requirement that judges themselves have a sense of, and be beholden to, ultimate universal values, the Noahide laws. Without this background requirement, judges can wreak havoc with their decisions, freed as they are from electoral or parliamentary accountability. A revised Universal Declaration of Human Rights must require judges to be knowledgeable of the universal principles of the Noahide laws as the ever-present background framework of their decisions.

Finally, the Noahide law prohibiting consumption of the limb of a living animal frames a comprehensive ethical relationship to nature. This Noahide law states that animals may be used and consumed for human needs, but without unnecessary cruelty. So also, natural resources are available for human utilization, but without needless destruction. It calls for circumspect treatment of nature, though without the hubris which would install the human, instead of G-d, as the manager of the cosmos.

The Noahide laws also require the practice of charity. One of the great ambitions of the United Nations was the socio-economic advancement of the poorer nations of the world. Yet, in this area, as evidenced by the so-called "North" (rich industrialized) / "South" (largely poor) divide, there has been a significant failure. The removal of scarcity is itself one of the conditions of peace, both within and between societies. Maimonides in his portrayal of the era of redemption, writes that

> In that time there will be no hunger and no war, no jealousy and no rivalry, for material well-being will be widely diffused.[61]

Since the absence of hunger and want is a characteristic of a peaceful domestic and international society, it behoves us now to work towards that state. Generosity is required of societies and individuals, both towards their own or fellow citizens and to other peoples.

In the present, even where aid has been made available by the rich nations to the poor countries it has often been with "strings attached" — with political and economic agendas. One of the most important aspects of charity under the Noahide law, which certifies it as proper and ethical charity, is the *intention* with which it is given. It should not be given with an ulterior intention — to aggrandize the giver and indebt the receiver — but for the genuine welfare of the recipient. Assistance given with self-interested motives may both vitiate charity and turn it into its opposite. Socio-economic and financial assistance given consciously in fulfilment of a Divine imperative of charity is quantitatively and qualitatively different. It is given to help, not manipulate, the recipient. Aid then becomes more an expression of altruism than interests.

The United Nations has been concerned in its documents both

---

[61] The end of the Code of Maimonides *(Mishneh Torah)*.

with the principles that should guide the internal life of nations as well as their interactions with one another. The same is true of the Noahide laws. They are the basis of the domestic life of nations, but they operate also at the level of the interactions among states: just as the individuals of societies may not steal, or kill and are subject to processes of justice, so too nations may not steal or kill, and they are bound to judge and sanction societies, which violate the Noahide laws.

We noted at the outset that "World Government" cannot be vested in an organization such as the UN because of the inherent plurality and individual sovereignties of the actors on the international scene. "International government" can only be a Government of laws. These are the laws of G-d, Who alone has sovereignty over nations and has the native claim to the allegiance of all persons and peoples. G-d is known in religious tradition as the "King of Kings of Kings". That meant, He is King over the guardian angels (Kings) of the leaders or governments (Kings) of sovereign nations. G-d's authority and expressed will is in His laws, the Noahide laws. It is to G-d that all humans and societies have a common allegiance, ratified by the common resonance of their souls with G-d, as nurtured by religious and spiritual tradition. No organization — including the UN — can set itself up, in place of this set of universal laws, as a "super" State, with its own military force and "universal taxation". The United Nations as an organization does not intrinsically possess this authority. We have witnessed the military impotence of the UN as an expression of this fact. Its small armed force cannot be present in a region without the permission of the local states. The United Nations *can*, however, be an international advocate of — and instructor to the nations in — the Noahide laws which bring, and can be universally experienced to bring, peace, benefit and unity.

A purely secular international law depends on subscription. It is customary. It depends on the voluntary acceptance and the conventions of nations. That acceptance is not assured and has not been seen historically to be so. Noahide law, as the law of G-d, on the other hand, is law to which persons and nations, as mentioned, have an intrinsic common allegiance. The original architects of modern international law, Grotius and Selden reached, however imperfectly, for Noahide law.

The prophetic statement of Isaiah on the UN's "Isaiah wall", which speaks of the abolition of arms, refers to an epoch in which Divine law prevails both within societies as well as between them. For the twofold purpose of arms — as the deterrent to lawlessness within societies and the means of settling conflicts between societies — will then no longer be required. May the United Nations be instrumental in achieving Isaiah's prophecy of the abolition of arms through its promulgation of Isaiah's Divine ethical prescription for this peace — the Noahide laws.

PART 3:
POLITICAL APPLICATIONS OF UNIVERSAL ETHICS

Chapter 6
Education and Spiritual Literacy

Spiritual literacy is a vital educational objective of a society seeking to create a resonance with shared, universal values, accessed by the human spirit. The first essay in this chapter is in fact an educational "manual" of universal ethics, which was sponsored by a grant from the Department of the Australian Federal Attorney General to encourage harmony amongst the major faiths and "community resilience" at large. It is entitled "An Education in a Shared Ethic: a Manual of Shared Values from Judaism, Christianity and Islam."

The second essay explores the relationship between good citizenship and a spiritual education. It looks both theoretically and empirically at the internalization of values in the everyday conduct of children who have received a religious education and those who have not. It is entitled "Why should a Kid pay for a Ticket on a Train? An Argument for a Spiritual Education" and was written together with an eminent educationalist, Professor Ramon Lewis.

There follow contributions on two revisions of the Australian "National Curriculum": one, a submission to the National Curriculum Review in 2014, which explored the possibilities — to which the Review still seemed open — of spiritual content in school education, the second, a critique of the published 2021 National Curriculum Review, which effectively drained all spiritual content from national public education.

The final essay, "Aging and Spirituality", deals with the unique needs and abilities of the aged for spiritual engagement. The importance of a spiritual education in early life in preparation for "old age" thus becomes evident, and especially so in an "aging society."

An Education in a Shared Ethic

Common values of Judaism, Christianity and Islam

Compiled by Rabbi Dr Shimon Cowen

on behalf of a reference group of Jewish, Christian and Muslim scholars

The Department of the Attorney General of Australia has supported, primarily in the interests of social *harmony* and *community resilience*, this project to outline and emphasize the shared values or ethic of Judaism, Christianity and Islam. This manual begins by explaining the value of a believed shared ethic for citizenship in terms of motivating good individual conduct and creating unity around common aspirations and values. It refers secondly to the sources of this ethic, both in the human spirit and in social, historical tradition. Finally, it documents the substance of this ethic, as affirmed by Judaism, Christianity and Islam.

Citizenship and a shared ethic

Belief and the motivation of social conduct

What is the role and significance for citizenship of belief in a particular ethic? This can be answered where citizenship begins: in the education of children. The education of children involves imparting skills, but equally or perhaps even importantly it has the goal of producing an individually conscientious good person and good citizen. In terms of the latter goal, the practical question could be asked, How do we educate a child not to steal? The use of a service without payment is theft. How then do we educate a child to pay a train or bus fare with an "honour system", where it is up to the passenger to purchase his or own ticket — when no conductor or inspector is on board? This is the challenge of providing an education which *internalizes* values in children and positively *motivates* good citizenship. The question has been addressed by Emeritus Professor Brian Hill, who was consultant to a Federal Australian Government on values education in schools. His argument is that beliefs and meaning frameworks, rather than the application of some kind of free and critical reason, are the primary source and motivators of desired conduct. At a seminar, he stated:

> A school might choose to teach "honesty" for a week and then "resilience" for a week. It may be helping the student to understand what the term means and maybe even to say "That's a good thing, I like that". [Yet, t]he question — "So what?" — is still hanging in your actual living, in the way you behave. It doesn't seem to translate to the playground. Values are not just understandings — they are priorities — which are determined *not only* by our reason… It seems to me that a lot of talk about values education falls short of recognizing that it must be nested within the project of helping students to understand how people live by frameworks of meaning or life worlds or religious viewpoints. In fact one of the things that seems to be necessary to say is that many who say that they have no religion actually have a religion called "no religion", that they are in denial of the investigation of spirituality that other people hold so valuable. So for this reason I wholeheartedly support…the necessity of seeing that values do not just hang loose in space but come to us from wider views of what life is about as human beings.[62]

The level of internalization and self-motivation to ethical conduct in students can also be measured by its *converse* — the extent to which students see their behavior as dependent solely on rewards and punishments. Professor Ramon Lewis, a consultant to the Victorian State Government on school classroom management and discipline, reports,

> In a survey I conducted in 2010/11 of 4225 students in Victorian schools in years 4 to 10, the majority of students said that if there were no punishments, no rewards, no reports and no teacher (dis)approval, their behaviour would become worse or much worse (compared to a little worse, the same or better). Fear of punishment, more than internalized values, tends to mould conduct. School teachers once asserted authority: "We're the teachers, you're the students. Do as you are told". They also had punishments which hurt; but these are no longer available.

---

[62] *Interface*, Vol. 2, 2008, pp. 13-14.

> Both of these kinds of power — authority and punishment — have waned and teachers need to look for something else. One of the things we aim for is that people will behave well because they understand it is right, not because they are being forced to do it. Now what makes good behaviour right could be that people have rights in a community — and therefore it is right and proper to treat them in certain ways (for example treat them with respect). This would be a belief. Another equally motivating source for such a belief is to say, G-d has stated how people should be treated and valued, and that's what makes it right.[63]

It is true that religion itself also has concepts of reward and punishment, but these are explicitly associated with norms and values, and are part of the one belief-complex: the norms and the rewards and punishments. If our student on the train has *no* such a world-view or belief, with its embedded norms, he or she has *only* the possibility of punishment to motivate purchase of a ticket. The same goes for classroom behavior. Ostensibly the teaching *ethical norms in the widest framework of beliefs which children have already inherited*, is thus of fundamental importance for this aspect of education. This — sometimes called "bonding social capital" — makes for connected, ethical communities.

As distinct from their motivational value, a further essential characteristic of belief- or meaning-frameworks is that they supply a coherence and consistency which a supposedly independent and critical "reasoning between alternatives" by students may not be able to provide. Professor Hill has put it this way:

> Sometimes values conflict. In fact, a lot of the decisions we have to make regarding values are in dealing with one good thing versus another good thing — but which is the most important in this particular case? And the answer to these questions is to get away from this idea of a smorgasbord of values and to recognize that we make judgments over our priorities not just on the basis of individual values like "honesty" and so on but because of where we are coming from as a whole person.

---

[63] See below in this chapter, "Why should a kid pay for a ticket on a train? An argument for a spiritual education."

So, people have talked of the framework of meaning that individuals have as a self, as a whole person. And basically, however long we live, our life world can be boiled down to those three constituents — (1) with whom do we relate as persons and (2) how do we relate to the natural world, and (3) who do we think we are in our most inner selves.[64]

These three dimensions — personal, interpersonal and our relation to nature — are filled out in detail by the comprehensive, shared ethic of the Abrahamic religions, as we shall see.[65] Teaching a shared, inherited ethic analytically and in its entirety supplies an educational ideal of "coherence and consistency" and fosters the ability of the *individual* to engage and integrate ethics with life and intellectual experience. Teaching this ethic from the "inside" — for believers (who elect this study) by believers — rather than from the "outside" as a comparative, relativizing study of religion, acknowledges the reality, integrity and strength of *belief* in this shared religious ethic.

Religion and the unity of cultures

In the realm of citizenship, the consciousness of a shared ethic is important also for social harmony. As the common core of Judaism, Christianity and Islam, this shared ethic provides "bridging social capital"[66] — that is, connectedness between those communities and cultures, which together domestically and internationally form the dominant cultural mix in the world today.[67] Not only do they discover that they believe in the *same* values; but that they are *together believers* in those values. The spirit

---

[64] *Interface,* Vol 2 (2008), p. 13.
[65] See the last section of this essay, "The substance of a shared ethic", in which the key shared values of the Abrahamic religions are set out in each of these categories.
[66] On the concepts of "bridging social capital" and "bonding social capital" (mentioned above), see Professor B. McGaw, "Education and Social Connectedness", *Debate* (2008), Issue 2, 16–19.
[67] Liberal democracy, in order to "work", needs an underlying motivational ethic. Professor Hill notes: "The Judaic and Christian traditions have together brought cultural development to the point where people felt safe in such a society such as to propound the theory of liberal democracy. And that coheres with what Rabbi Cowen was saying about the idea of common values that pop up when you look comparatively at traditions." *Loc. cit.*, p. 14

which they value in themselves, they find in their fellows in other faiths. What is of most value to the one, is seen to exist also in the other. It is this which forms the deepest bonds of unity. Here the motivational power of belief is actually harnessed to a foundation of this shared ethic itself: the unity and fellowship of the human spirit.

There is an alternative approach to achieving harmony amongst religious groups. Rather than seeking a shared ethic, it wants to teach comparatively about differences and diversity of religions, with the hope of encouraging tolerance. The goal of tolerance is praiseworthy but the prospects of this method may be weaker in the quest for harmony. This is because, in stressing difference and diversity, it tends to relativize religious belief. Where belief is suspended in relativity, the power (and integrity) of religious belief is lost. One of the great secular commentators of our day has himself acknowledged that purely secular concepts of community have failed to motivate individuals and to bond communities.[68] The motivation which comes from the religious belief in a *shared* ethic lends cohesion and solidarity to the society built on that ethic.

A mistaken argument or assumption of one approach to social harmony has been that religion is itself necessarily a source of social conflict. For this reason it seeks to focus on diversity and to relativize differences and thereby deflect competing claims for truth in different religious groups. The argument of the "clash of civilizations" and the "clash of religions", to the extent that it does contain truth, relates largely to cases where religion has been politicized. The posturing of chauvinistic, political and other particularistic interests as religion is the opposite of the self-transcending stance of authentic religion. It is generally the work of individuals, who want to make themselves and their dreams — not G-d — great. Typically, it is ordinary people — "grassroots" — who, without political mobilization or demagogic manipulation, exhibit the true humility of self-transcending

---

[68] Jürgen Habermas in J. Habermas and Cardinal J. Ratzinger (Pope Benedict XVI), *Dialectics of Secularization*, San Francisco: Ignatius, 2005, p. 46.

spirituality; who want a peaceful, cooperative life. (Intellectuals, albeit challenged by the hubris which tends to be associated with intellectual prowess, are capable of this too!) Mr Aydin Nurhan has expressed this idea with regard to the Muslim masses in his *Reflections of a Turkish Diplomat*:

> ...any policy which does not reflect the genuine sentiments of ordinary people is doomed to fail... We wish our leaders, politicians, intellectuals, and media give an ear to the commonsense of our peoples and turn their mutual sentiments into action...I, as a Muslim, believe in the fraternity and cooperation between our innocent, ordinary *ummah* [nation]...[69]

The authentic heart of religious experience is found in humble self-transcendence, and the sense of personal finitude beside an infinite Creator. In this the "ordinary, innocent" people of world faiths of Judaism, Christianity and Islam come together in their orientation to a single transcendent source with its moral compass.

The same Muslim writer expresses in his *Reflections* the hope that the concept of a "Judeo-Islamic-Christian culture" would replace the narrower concept of a Judeo-Christian ethic. With this, he is intimating the concept of the shared fundamental values of the world religions, in which these world religions manifest not conflict but in fact a deep unity. The common values making up this shared ethic are found in the Abrahamic stem of the world religions, Judaism, Christianity and Islam. They in turn take root in the concept (and the reality) of the human spirit, and in continuous social and historical tradition.

The sources of the shared ethic

The human spirit as source of a shared ethic

The world religions and cultures — and certainly the Abrahamic religions, Judaism, Christianity and Islam — have always known that the human being is a composite of body, mind *and* soul. The third element, the soul, is today a much ignored, repressed or

---

[69] Self published, p. 180.

ridiculed aspect of the human being. The soul has traditionally been understood as the "mirror of G-d" within the human being. The significance of this is that the human soul naturally resonates with and "models" G-dly qualities. "Just as G-d is called gracious, so should you be gracious, just as G-d is merciful, so should you be merciful" and so with all the Divine attributes. This occurs when the human soul emerges to become conscious of itself and is informed and energized by its attachment to religious experience and tradition. The soul's imitation of these Divine qualities translates concretely into objective and eternal — Divine — laws of good and right conduct. These form the shared ethic at the root of the world religions.

Within the human complex of body, mind and soul, the soul has traditionally been regarded as the *highest* faculty. It "has"[70] at its disposal the faculties or "vehicles" of body and mind. In the body resides the whole instinctual and emotional personality of the human being. The mind, on the other hand, reasons, analyzes and strategizes. It has the ability to check and control the body and its impulses. But mind does not and cannot supply the first principles of its reasoning. It can only work with, and build upon, first principles, that is, values and basic axioms, which come to it from somewhere else. Because these are prior to reason and are simply *accepted* by reason, they are called beliefs. These beliefs may originate in the soul's knowledge and religious experience, or they may come from attitudes and dispositions which do not have a spiritual source. In the traditional view, the soul exercises its sovereignty by guiding mind and body. The mind is subordinate to the soul in the sense that it works with the soul's first principles; and then the body is subordinate to the mind which guides it with the principles it has received, organized and developed from the soul.

There is another potentiality which the human has by virtue of possession of a soul, "the mirror of G-d". It has to do with a freedom to create and transform: to actualize within oneself

---

[70] See the references to the work of Viktor Frankl for this concept in S. D. Cowen, *The Theory and Practice of Universal Ethics – the Noahide Laws*, Chapter 1.

and one's surroundings goodness by the Divine standard. Only a human being can grasp, and choose between, good and evil.[71] In religious perspective, this freedom flows from the tension of body and soul — with the mind in between the two and potentially able to act on behalf of either body or soul. If I had no soul, I would have no freedom. I would simply follow the dictates of bodily impulses as an animal follows its instincts. Mind would function simply to organize the fulfillment of my desires. If, like an angel (a spiritual being), I had no body, I would also have no freedom. For as something which mirrors G-d, the soul wants only to imitate G-d, and to follow the eternal and objective values of the life prescribed by G-d. Mind would translate that into the unswerving service of G-d. The human — as body, mind and soul — has the power and the choice to actualize the good or to actualize something other than the good.

These two concepts of the human spirit or soul, namely as "knowing" the good and being "free" to actualize the good, translate into a religious educational ideal. This is an education which *elevates* mind and body to become true vehicles of the spirit. For the mind, that means (in addition to a general skills base) a religious education which makes the soul's knowledge *intellectually literate*. That is, it makes spiritual belief and experience conscious and rigorous and able to engage intellectually with all the questions which come to it from the society, culture and science. For the body — emotion and feeling — it means a development of character, training impulse and emotion in accordance with spiritually informed ethical virtues. Spiritual literacy and character development are the actualization of the common human spirit, which the world religions know the human being to possess. It is the foundation of their realized shared ethical humanity.

There are those who do not steadily — or at all — experience what religious people spiritually know and feel. We could call them "secularists". Within the secularists are those who do not determinedly reject religious belief. These are "non-doctrinaire

---

[71] Here the Biblical verse states that the human being has "become like one of us [i.e. like G-d] knowing good and evil" (Genesis 3:22).

secularists", and as we shall later discuss, religious beliefs and ethics may not necessarily be a "closed book" for them. Then there are "doctrinaire secularists", who not only do not experience religious belief, but also reject the claim to truth of religious belief. It is important to note, however, that the "first principles", which underlie their alternative view of reality, and upon which their reason builds, are also beliefs. They believe, as do religious people, but not in the human soul, a Divine Creator and a Divine ethics. Rather their purportedly "critical reasoning" is simply based on an axiomatic acceptance of a metaphysics of materialism, in one variant or another. On intellectual and educational grounds, the "religion of no religion", as some have called it, has no greater claim or right to displace the common religious ethic passed on by tradition by the great majority of humanity. Some seventy percent of Australians profess an affiliation with one of the great world religions. It is not unreasonable that an Australian education should permit and facilitate (at least for those who want it) an education in their shared religious ethic, especially where it also serves the ends of citizenship: social harmony and good human conduct.

History and society as transmitters of a shared ethic

That which expresses itself naturally in the human spirit has also historically found expression in our society. It has been pointed out that our society is founded on a "Judeo-Christian" ethic. The interaction of Islamic culture with the Judeo-Christian culture, both in Australia and globally, has now made it desirable to seek a deeper common denominator, which we have here called the Abrahamic values. The Prime Minister of Australia, Ms Julia Gillard, describing herself not as a religious but rather as a secular person, is reported as having referred to the biblical strand of this legacy as an underpinning of this society:

> I think that there are some important things from our past that need to continue to be part of our present and part of our future...I'm on the record as saying things like I think it's important for people to understand their Bible stories,

> [...because] what comes from the Bible has formed such an important part of our culture.[72]

The Leader of the Federal Parliamentary Opposition, Mr Tony Abbott, has also spoken about the ethical principles, which cut across all cultures, and seem clearly to have roots in the religious traditions which formed those cultures. In a condolence motion on the passing of a former Governor General of Australia, Sir Zelman Cowen, he said,

> Perhaps one way in which we could further honour his memory is by seeking the ethical principles which might be regarded as common to all cultures and to all people – principles such as keeping commitments, respecting human life and caring for the vulnerable.[73]

The universal ethics, shared by these great world religions do not have to be invented or discovered. They are present and transmitted within an historical ethical heritage. But they are also ratifiable by the human spirit or soul at all times which naturally resonates with them.

A set of laws, representing a pristine covenant between humanity and its Creator was completed with Noah, the biblical survivor of the Flood. They were practiced by Abraham, ten generations after Noah. Abraham, as known, is the progenitor of the great world religions, Judaism, Christianity and Islam, the adherents of which account for the majority of humanity. These Abrahamic laws, known also as the Noahide laws (after Noah), also appear in the early modern secular tradition of the Renaissance, when the great jurists and founders of modern law, both international and domestic (or municipal, as it is called) — the Dutchman Hugo Grotius and the Englishman John Selden — referred to them as foundations of law. In recent times the United States Congress in 1991 in its preamble to an Education Day Bill referred to them as the foundation of American society and the "bedrock of

---

[72] *The Daily Telegraph*, March 21, 2011
[73] *Hansard*, Reps, Tuesday 7 February 2012, p. 2.

society from the dawn of civilization".[74] In 2001, then Australian Governor General Michael Jeffrey stated that they "apply to all contemporary issues and therefore play an important role in our day-to-day lives".[75]

The major world religions, which have grown upon the Abrahamic stem of these basic principles, have added and elaborated further theological concepts and practical precepts. These differences — the way cultures have developed around beyond this stem — do not detract from the educational template of this shared ethic and do not disturb it. Thus, for example, included in the precept of belief in G-d within this ethic, is a concept of redemption. Redemption is often associated with the notion of a Messiah. As to the identity of the Messiah, Judaism, Christianity and Islam have differences. Yet as a Christian theologian, Victor Styrsky, profoundly interested in the unity of the faiths wisely responded to this difference, "it is G-d's business". Each of the world faiths, with their own answers to this question, can "live with" this answer and keep it as "their" and "G-d's business". It has been noted that the religious language of United States Presidents has been largely that of a neutral (i.e. a non-denominational) ethical monotheism[76].

The presence of a programme or a study of the shared ethic of the Abrahamic religions does not challenge the concept of "pluralism" or open discussion and enquiry in a state sponsored and supervised education. For just as the "religious" individual has to form a response to a secular syllabus, so equally might a "non-religious" individual be invited to respond to a religious study. For the non-doctrinaire secularist, the question is then open: can one conceive and accept the same objective, eternal historical and cross-cultural values? The question has been addressed by the philosopher and psychotherapist Viktor Frankl. Frankl argues that once one begins to transcend beyond particular, personal

---

[74] US Congress, H.J Res. 104.
[75] *Interface*, Vol. 2, 2008, p. 4.
[76] See here Dissent of Justice Antonin Scalia on the verdict of the Supreme Court of the USA, in McCreary County, Kentucky, *et al. v.* American Civil Liberties Union of Kentucky *et al.* (2005).

emotional stakes and material interests, one can come to the sense of an objective higher good and set of values. Such a person, in Frankl's methodology, will be ready to respond to the question, is there something — other than what *I* want, or to which *I* feel driven — which is asked of me by life (or G-d)? When then presented with the Noahide laws, such a secularist might then say "yes, that is it" (for the Divine image is discoverable in all persons). Or he or she might not. But, whether or not they are joined from the ranks of secularists, the many whose faiths have borne them in the tradition of this shared ethic in this society should surely be granted the right to an education in it.

The substance of the shared ethic

The shared values of Judaism, Christianity and Islam as Abrahamic religions are the moral rules by which Abraham lived before these religions developed. These religions absorbed, elaborated and added to these stem Abrahamic values, but have continued to acknowledge them as central. At the Divine revelation at Mount Sinai, of which the Ten Commandments are the centrepiece, these pre-existing universal laws were reiterated by Moses. Judaism, Christianity and Islam acknowledge Moses as a genuine transmitter of these values to their own prophetic traditions. These ethical laws (as indicated above) bear upon (1) personal identity (2) interpersonal relations and (3) the relationship to nature.

Ethics and personal identity
MONOTHEISM

G-d and the human soul The Abrahamic faith was monotheistic and this is the common legacy of Judaism, Christianity and Islam. This means that not only is there one G-d, who is the Author and Sustainer of creation, but that this G-d can also in some way be known by human beings. Whilst prophets and revelation may have been the way G-d was made known to humanity, it is the human soul — characterized sometimes as the "mirror of G-d"— which individually resonates with and personally ratifies the knowledge and values communicated through revelation and prophetic tradition.

Monotheism The Abrahamic faiths all share the ideal of monotheism. The simple meaning of monotheism is understood in terms of the relationship of G-d to the creation. Everything in it is brought into existence by G-d, and even the greatest powers within creation, be these physical or spiritual, are all subordinate to G-d. This ultimate source of all being is one, a unity.

G-d's dominion over the creation There are three classical dimensions of theology, or knowledge of G-d's relationship to the world, in which the Abrahamic faiths concur. The first is that G-d is its Creator and Sustainer, and that the creation is wholly dependent on G-d. The second is that G-d has revealed a moral code or compass to humanity, with norms which are eternal. This Divine teaching has been indicated in Scripture and elaborated in religious tradition. Finally there is a redemptive process, guided by G-d, aimed at a reconstituted creation freed from evil and imperfection. This is accomplished through an interaction of Divine providence or intervention and ethical human conduct (informed by Divine teaching), through which creation is brought into alignment with the Divine.

REVERENCE FOR THE DIVINE

The respect for the Divine Not only belief in, and knowledge of, G-d is required to produce a civilization based on G-dly values, but also a respect or reverence for G-d. It is this which actually motivates the moral conduct communicated through revelation. The service of G-d by Abraham in fact was based not only on reverence or awe, but also upon a positive reverence, the love of G-d. The reverence for G-d expresses itself initially in avoiding forms of disrespect for G-d, for Divine teaching and for those who teach and guide in relation to it.

Reverence as a foundation for the integrity of human relationships The respect due to human beings is significantly associated with the respect due to G-d. Thus, the respect due to parents is associated with, though subordinate to that for, G-d. The respect due to fellow human beings stems from the fact that each person has a soul, with its special affinity with the Divine. Finally, the respect for G-d is the foundation of the keeping of an oath, which invokes G-d's Name. By extension, keeping one's word and fulfilling promises means not profaning the G-d-given power of speech.

The service of G-d Respect (and love) for G-d translates the knowledge of G-d as Creator and Sustainer of the world, into prayer in which one seeks the help of G-d, and active acknowledgment of what G-d has given one, such as one's food and sustenance. It translates the knowledge of G-d, as a Revealer of Divine norms, into the active study of the moral law communicated by G-d. Finally, it activates the knowledge of Divine redemption into concrete moral conduct; and the desire to return to G-d, which means to repent and alter those aspects of our conduct, which need to be rectified in the light of the moral code.

HUMAN SEXUALITY

Sexuality and human identity Even though human sexuality involves an individual with others, it is still within the compass of personal identity. This is because the normative heterosexual union of marriage (of permitted partners) is deeply tied to the identity of the individual. It has a procreative potential: the individual came from such a union, and from it he or she has an extension in the future through children. The individual participates and is defined through the union of a man and a woman. Because sexuality relates to personal human identity, it cannot be modified by "consent", as in certain interpersonal relations where consent would remove "harm".

The normative sexual union The sexual union which the Abrahamic faiths view as normative is the heterosexual union of man and woman. Properly this should be in the context of marriage, which represents a public commitment of the two to an enduring relationship. Adultery, incest and bestiality are forbidden unions. So also is homosexual practice. Whilst acknowledging with compassion a variety of challenges which individuals may face in limiting sexuality to a committed heterosexual union, the Abrahamic code sanctions this union alone as the only permissible, and Divinely normative union.

Modesty and guardedness against promiscuity Human sexuality has the ability to be destructive when directed or channeled improperly (whether as a factor leading to marriage breakdown, "unwanted pregnancy" outside marriage, dangers to health), aside from moral considerations. Accordingly, a sexualized culture, with high commercial exploitation and promiscuity, is not desirable. Modesty is a virtue in all persons.

Ethics and interpersonal relations
JUSTICE

A system of justice A society must necessarily have a system of justice, which brings society into alignment with its laws and moral principles. The task of justice is to hear evidence as to whether travesty of the law (incorporating also universal Abrahamic ethics) has occurred; judge the evidence; and to hand out appropriate sanctions and remedies for the injustice. The most fundamental characteristic of justice must be its objectivity and its impartiality.

Testimony A witness, as one of the agents of the process of justice, needs to understand the importance of coming forward to testify; to know the prohibition of testifying falsely, to have basic qualities of character, integrity and maturity such as to make testimony is reliable; and to be untainted by personal interest. Testimony must of course be subjected to examination.

Judges Judges must themselves be learned and observant of the law, both conventional and of the universal ethics constituting the Abrahamic faith. They must resist any bribery. They must strive to treat litigants equally and remove disadvantages from parties in presenting their cases, and should apply adequate standards of proof.

Punishment Punishment can only be applied to persons, who possess responsibility for their actions. A child or individual of diminished mental capacity is not subject to normal punishment. Ignorance of law is a mitigating factor only in special circumstances. Ignorance of fact is, in most cases. Compulsion or duress can also be a mitigating factor except in compulsion by another to kill. A differentiated liability attaches to the accessory to a crime vis-a-vis the principal. The kinds of punishment used by a society reflect the severity of the crime and their utility and appropriateness to restoring social order.

KILLING

The severity of killing The prohibition on murder is one of the most fundamental ethical rules of social order taught by the Abrahamic religions and its strictures are the highest. The prohibition against destroying life applies not only to the life of the viable human being, but also the incurably ill person and the dying person. The foetus is also a life which cannot be taken at will. Similarly, the premeditated direct act of killing and indirect causation of death are both regarded as forms of murder. There is liability also for unintended killing — manslaughter.

Suicide, self-injury and self-sacrifice A person's life is not considered as his or own "property" to dispose of at will. The same applies to self-harm. A person's body is given in trust by G-d, and it may not be subjected to suffering or pain except where this has legitimate therapeutic value for the person. The permissibility of self-sacrifice is limited primarily to a circumstance where rather than transgress a moral law, an individual surrenders his or her own life, such as where one is forced to kill or be killed.

Permissible killing exists in the case of individual self-defence, or collective self-defence and this is the justification for war. Not only in self-defence, but also in the defence of a third party it is permissible to kill the pursuer-assailant, if that is the only way to stop the danger to the life of the third party.

THEFT AND MATERIAL HARM

Direct or criminal theft. This is the taking of another person's property or body without that other's consent. This can be theft of the body, abduction; or of another's property or money. Theft is also incurred by withholding wages, or fees due for a service. It can also be through exceeding entitlements and benefits permitted by the workplace. Even where a person knowingly parts with his or her property but does so under compulsion or, as in the case of fraud, is deceived into parting with it, this is theft. Theft is subject not only to punishment but also restitution.

Harm to persons or property. This is commonly called civil wrong or tort, and it is often monetary remedy or damages, rather than punishment (though punishment may also be applied), which rectify this harm. This applies to harm done either to another's body or property. The harm caused may be direct or indirect, but in both cases carries a liability. It can also extend to a failure of duty of care for the other.

Regard for others and their property. Not only should one desist from theft of, or harm to, the property or person of another. There is also a moral norm of regard and care for one's fellow human being. Exploitative overcharging is something which on this account should be avoided. In a positive vein, regard for another entails restoration of lost property to its owner. The attitudes of greed and coveting, even without an act of theft, are reprehensible. Examples of positive, normative regard for another is charity and fellow love.

THE ETHICAL RELATIONSHIP TO NATURE

The human appropriation of nature. The human being's use of nature is something clearly granted by Abrahamic belief. The human being was granted a dominion over nature for constructive purposes. Thus the "consumption" of nature is permitted where there is a legitimate human benefit. The human being can cause pain to animals, where this is necessary for a useful purpose for human beings, such as in their slaughter for human consumption, other utilization and medical research.

The minimization of pain and destruction of natural resources. Notwithstanding that pain may be caused to animals, for the above reasons, it must still be minimized; to cause gratuitous suffering is forbidden. The goals for which pain may be caused to animals must be substantial and proportionate to the pain inflicted. Thus, clubbing animals to death, so as not to cut their furs (through normal slaughter) is not warranted by the value of wearing a fur. The pollution or contamination of natural habitats for mere convenience in disposal of waste is not warranted.

The prohibition of gratuitous pain to animals and purposeless destruction of natural resources. The consumption of part of a living animal is an ancient prohibition and furnishes a source for the prohibition of cruelty to animals. Similarly a prohibition on the destruction of useful resources, which serves no useful or constructive purpose, is found at the root of Abrahamic belief.

Why should a Kid Pay for a Ride on a Train? An Argument for a Spiritual Education[77]

With Emeritus Professor Rom Lewis

The question and a short answer

Despite the increasing sophistication of monitoring systems, it is possible to get a ride on a metropolitan train without paying for it. The problem with doing this is that it is stealing. Not only may we not pocket and take away another person's property, we may also not use a service offered for payment, and not pay for it. The reason why a person can get away with it, is that it is at least partly an "honour system" backed up by spot checks by inspectors, who can impose a heavy fine on a fare evader. That is the risk and the deterrent of not paying for one's ticket (or topping up one's

---

[77] This is the expanded version of an essay which appeared in the *Yeshivah Shule [Synagogue] Magazine*, May 2015.

MyKi card, or whatever it is).

The function of an education, we are sure and hope everyone would agree, is not just to teach literacy and numeracy and lay the basis for a young person to acquire the skills to have a job. It is also to produce a citizen who does not steal, who respects life, justice and upholds a variety of other basic universal values. We have the deterrent and punishment of a *possible* fine for a child (discussed here, and not an adult, because we are talking about schooling) who was thinking of not paying for a ride on the train. But do we settle for such processes as a way of training kids to pay for their rides on public transport?

We had the pleasure of finding out about, getting to know, and involving in a seminar, a distinguished emeritus Professor of Education, Brian Hill, who had been consulted by an earlier Federal Government on the issue of values in schools. At the seminar, he stated that a teacher can talk to a child in the classroom at any length about a particular value or principle of conduct, but out in the playground (without close supervision), the child will not abide by it unless he or she actually *believes* it.

Professor Hill made it clear that he meant "believing in it" in the sense of reference to an ultimate view of the world, such as religion, but also a secular world-view, presents. The behaviour which the child would hopefully replicate in the playground, away from the eyes of the teacher, would be consistent with an ultimate framework of meaning in which the child believed. For those raised in the faith traditions, this belief relates to a human faculty, engaged in religious experience and commitment, called the soul or conscience. It is not the same as heart (feeling) or mind (reasoning). It is an experience of and resonance with Divine, and the values, ethics and conduct associated with the Divine, which the *soul* has, or to which the soul responds, and which it acknowledges. Since the Divine is not something which can be accessed by the physical senses or conclusively proven by logic, it is something else in the person, which ratifies the Divine: something which is like the Divine, namely, the human soul (described by the Bible as made "in the image of G-d").

The religious person, who believes in G-d, and knows that G-d has prohibited us from stealing — from taking a ride on a train without paying for it — interconnects the belief in G-d and G-d's laws, including the one not to steal. The connection might be that having accepted G-d as the ultimate authority in one's life, one cannot disobey His ethical commands. But deeper than this is the idea that fulfilment of His laws and attachment to Him are bound up with one another. Through living the moral life required by G-d, one is bound up with G-d and feels His presence more closely. His laws are actual conduits of attachment to Him. So whether or not the inspector is on the train with me, G-d is, and I do not want to weaken my connection with him by breaking (not only the State's) but also His law, not to steal. A child, who has internalized this view, is likely to be a good citizen with regard to paying for train rides. That is a basic argument for a religious education just as at the giving of the Ten Commandments and the related revelation at Mt Sinai, humanity not only heard what we have to do and not to do, but fully experienced Who was saying it.

Why is belief different?

We have used the word "belief" here in a religious sense, as a function of the human soul in its unique perception of, and relationship to, G-d and G-d's ethical will. The word "belief", however, is also used in a secular sense to signify a person's irreducible and undiscussable first principles and assumptions. When one of us went as a postgraduate student to Germany to study the work of a group of philosophers, known as the "Frankfurt School", he made an appointment to visit one of the group, a philosopher called Jürgen Habermas, who ran an institute in a small town in Bavaria. Already familiar with his ideas, he walked into the courtyard of the Institute, where Professor Habermas was sitting and talking with colleagues at a table, and recognized that he was enunciating a fundamental assumption of his thought, thumping the table as he said it. This was a principle, a foundation of Habermas' thought, which itself is not established by any antecedent reasoning, but is for him a self-evident first principle. And so it occurred to me to call the basic predispositions of secular thinkers, from which their reasoning proceeds, the "table thumper": this is the way it is, and that's it. Now although that could also be called "belief", we do not want to give it that name, because it is essentially a disposition or an assumption, which this thinker has and others do not. It is variable and ultimately arbitrary, even if it is supported by evidence: because many different paradigms can explain the same phenomenon, and there is no criterion in reason and evidence alone for the *absolute* truth of the paradigm.

The belief of the soul, on the other hand, is different. The soul, made in the image of G-d, is universal and its capacity to "imitate" the Divine, which means the ability to model in ethical conduct the Divine attributes, which translate into universal laws and ethics, is common to all humanity. It is not relative or arbitrary. And across cultures, people can and do resonate by virtue of this common spiritual faculty with the universal ethics known as the Noahide laws.

We have distinguished differing *intellectual* frameworks with their anchoring first principles from the common values of the human soul. How much does the factor of arbitrariness and personal will enter into the more basic *emotions*, desires and reactions of people at the sub-intellectual level of feeling. Personal will (to have something) is much more palpable than the will (to see the world in a certain way) underlying an intellectual system. These are simply raw material and emotional interests: "I want money, I want food, I want...."

Back on the train with our school child, let us consider how belief, intellectual frameworks and simple material interests play out when it comes to paying the fare, with no inspector in sight. When it comes to simple material interests, we have the biggest problem. If a person wants the simple gain to be had through not paying — through stealing — there is little impediment, only the calculated risk of a spot check by the Inspector and a fine. Is the fear and likelihood of the punishment sufficient to outweigh the desire to keep a few dollars for oneself? A moot point. It could be that many children (and adults) do not think beyond this calculation. There is very little internalized morality here.

With regard to intellectual frameworks, let's suppose, that the child was brought up in an educated *secular* home and has gone to a fairly sophisticated *secular* school. The child has a rudimentary intellectual understanding of why stealing is bad for society. It violates the Kantian categorical imperative (imagine if everyone did it) and the Millsian principle of liberty (your freedom stops where it infringes that of someone else). But these intellectual frameworks (learnt or imbibed) are also dependent on a personal will and perhaps one can be persuaded (in conjunction with the desire to spend the few dollars on a coke instead) by another "rationale" that the trains make enough money and it is unfair to expect a kid to pay. Reason is easily bribed.

What is left is the soul or conscience. The whole concept of the soul or conscience is that it stands over and against what I (as body or mind) want. It is the higher, the real "I", which is aligned with G-d, and which has the ability to discipline both the (simply wanting) body and (rationale-generating) mind. It is not "will" — personal and arbitrary — but an "internal" authority, the soul, linked and identified with the greatest "authority", G-d. This is why conscience is vilified as "guilt" and "socially internalized repression" by the wilful body and mind: it can and does stand in their way sometimes. But it is the best bet on the train for stopping stealing. It has no will of its own, and therefore is the strongest will; it has Divine assistance. This is the argument for a spiritual education: it nurtures and internalizes conscience — the knowledge of G-d and the package of universal ethical principles which goes with that. Amongst which is the prohibition on stealing. Full stop.

For the sceptically and/or empirically minded

For those who don't understand this talk about a "soul" and "G-d", most probably because they have not experienced them, or are sceptical for other reasons, there is suggestive empirical evidence that a religious education produces good citizenship of the train-fare paying kind. We recently designed and implemented surveys of students in Victorian religious and state schools. The religious schools included Jewish, Christian and Islamic schools. One survey set out questions relating to universal values. These were placed in the two dimensions: one, of conduct between persons (what we could call "citizenship values", such as not stealing, avoiding cruelty to animals, marital fidelity, honesty, charity, respect for property and life, a concern for justice); the second in the relationship of the individual to G-d and belief in a personal and providential G-d[78]. A second survey related to classroom behaviour (important to the health of our schools) and the factors motivating it. The principal findings of the surveys were:

(a) A significant positive correlation between measures of expressed belief in G-d and stronger citizenship values.

We were unfortunately not permitted to survey State School students on their belief in G-d. However within the religious schools, we observed that as the belief in G-d rises, so do positive citizenship values, such as paying for a ticket on a train, where no inspector is present. [This should not be a surprise since citizenship values are actually classical religious values in origin: "Do not steal", "Do not kill" are amongst the biblical Commandments].

(b) A significant positive correlation between attending a school which incorporates a religious education (Jewish, Christian and Islamic schools) and citizenship values. Students who attended religious schools had stronger citizenship values than did those who attended a State School.

(c) Internal motivation more strongly relate to appropriate classroom behaviour than external motivation.

---

[78] For the questionnaire, see below Appendix "A".

In terms of motivating responsible classroom behaviour students were presented with a range of motivators which were empirically grouped into two categories. The first, "internal" motivating considerations (because of self-concept "I am a good person", because it is "right", it is "the rules" or because "G-d wants me to") and "external" motivating considerations ("reward", "punishment", "approval" and "disapproval"). Across all schools, the stronger motivating factor towards good classroom behaviour was found to be the "internal" one.

(d) The strength of "internal" or internalized motivation is greater for students attending a religious school than it is for students attending a State School.

(e) Stronger citizenship values and even more so, belief in G-d, are associated with more internalized motivation.

It is *empirically* indicated that a religious education and a nurtured religious consciousness in children is associated with stronger citizenship and more appropriate classroom behaviour.

In concluding these empirical observations we need to emphasize that our study was only a pilot study and comprised an investigation of students with only four schools. Nevertheless, the findings are highly suggestive.

The option of a religious education for students in *all* schools

Because a religious education is provided in religious and some independent schools, what we have said is really an argument for (at least the option of) a spiritual education *in State schools* and for the State to recognize religious studies *in all schools* as a worthy subject up to matriculation level, to be credited like any other matriculation subject.

The Australian census indicates that about 70% of Australians express a religious affiliation. However, 65% of Australian school children attend Government Schools. Assuming (exaggeratedly) that all the children of religiously unaffiliated families (30%) attended Government Schools (and that birth-rates amongst religiously and non-religiously affiliated families were the same), there would still be more children from religiously identifying families than from religiously non-identifying families in Government schools. This is ostensibly particularly so in the case of ethnic minorities which arrive from strong religious backgrounds, but cannot afford to send their children to private schools.

Nowhere is it written, to our knowledge, in the legislation of the Australian States or concept underpinning Government schools, that they must *exclude* religion from their purview, and disallow the teaching of religion, whether as part of general curriculum or for those who want a religious education. Their task is to provide a *free* education for all children, who require it. To claim that no teaching of religion should be permitted in Government schools is a result of aggressive secularism, which has no place in our culture, and is contrary to both the Victorian Charter of Rights and Responsibilities and section 116 of the Federal Constitution, which guarantee religious freedom.

In gaining ethics approval for the study reported herein, the Victorian Department of Education and Early Childhood Development permitted only one question about G-d to remain in the survey carried out in the State Schools. They requested removal of four other questions seeking beliefs related to the existence of a personal and providential G-d who influenced individual life outcomes and experiences. The remaining question assessed the extent to which students reported that their appropriate classroom behaviour is associated with doing "what G-d wants me to do". The students were asked whether this motivation was "exactly" like, "very much" like, "like", "little" like, or "not at all" like them. Sixty three percent of the State School students responded that it was, at least "like" them to agree with such a statement (i.e., 63% stated that it was either exactly like, very much like, or like them) to experience this motivation. There is, apparently, belief in G-d in the State school included in our sample, and possibly in many others. However, there is no adequate education to nurture spirituality, which is a requirement of the Melbourne Declaration and National Curriculum Review Report in its recommendation that

> ACARA *[Australian Curriculum, Assessment and Reporting Authority]* revise the Australian Curriculum to place more emphasis on morals, values and spirituality as outlined in the Melbourne Declaration, and to better recognise the contribution of Western civilisation, our Judeo-Christian heritage...

There are three alternatives with regard to the teaching of values relating to practical ethical conduct in schools: To do nothing and to rely on reward and punishment alone, which internalizes little moral sense in students; to offer a religious education to all who want it (which could focus on the universal template of the Noahide laws at the root of the world religions), and a third alternative, to be discussed now.

This, third alternative to avoid teaching values, and to teaching religion, is to attempt a secular approach to values. This alternative may take two forms: one, a secular treatment of religion itself and the other, a purely secularly based approach to values. The first form has its paradigm in Sweden where students are not taught religion but rather the study of religion. That is to say, religion is not a living reality, but rather it is a "problem" or phenomenon best treated by a relativising and comparative study of religions. This fits with the largely atheistic society of Sweden, which has cut loose from many traditional values. In Sweden both homosexual and incestuous (between half-siblings) marriage is permitted, and there is a program to bring up children "gender-neutrally" until they are ready to "choose" their gender. In Australia, there are also offerings which take up historical, sociological and philosophical studies of religion, but none of which necessarily leave religion intact, or its adherents happy with religion. This is not a religious education but an education "about" religion. Rather than tapping into the soul life of its students, it tends to negate and sap the objective reality of the soul and its life.

A variant of the secularist approach has been to try to develop an ethics curriculum as an alternative to religious instruction in State Schools, as found in the "Ethics" programme piloted in NSW primary schools. This is a programme which professes by discussion alone to draw children to their "own" moral positions. The problem however is that the children do not have the fundamental principles by which to arbitrate between different ethics. Since the animus of this programme is antireligious, it is clear then that its instructors will import first principles, which are at variance with those given by religious tradition. Otherwise, there is no way that children can create their own world-views. When all is said and done, however, the principles imported by children, or insinuated by their secularist teachers, will be ones which are dependent for their observance on the arbitrary will of the students, not something anchored in the soul or conscience, as fine-tuned by the spiritual tradition.

Let us then return to the middle alternative: to offer a religious education to all who want it, in State Schools. It would seem that there are two ways to do this. One is through the vehicle of Special Religious Instruction (SRI), which has been subject to all kinds of vicissitudes, relating to its status as a subject, the paucity of time available to it, its relative lack of rigour and professionalism (through no fault of its own as a minor ad hoc addition to the curriculum), and the new arrangements of "opt in", all of which seem to have presented major administrative barriers both for parents and schools to its implementation. The *coup de grace* has anyway just been delivered to SRI in Victoria with the Government decision to push SRI outside class time.

An alternative to this, which was acknowledged in the Review of the National Curriculum 2014, would be to present basic shared religious values — both in terms of broad theological categories (creation, revelation and providence) as well as shared practical ethical values of the world religions.⁷⁹ These do not have to be invented or researched. They exist in a body of ethical teaching and theology known as the Noahide laws, the ethical covenant completed with Noah, and upheld and transmitted by Abraham, the father of the great world religions, and reiterated again at Mt Sinai. These common core values and theological positions have been endorsed, among others, by the American Congress, an Australian Governor General, a President of the European Union and the King of Morocco, an Islamic state. To teach these values and theological categories would resonate with the major world religions and would also form the common template for a rigorous curriculum in religious studies. As such it would not be subject to any of the hazards and difficulties of SRI: it would have its proper weight in the syllabus, for those who chose it; it would be taught by trained teachers, obviously with personal conviction and would have a substantial and rigorous syllabus. But in all this it would still be *lived and learned* religion; not a secular and relativising lens on religion, but a study rigorous *and germane* to the human spirit — proper and real spirituality. The proposed substitute in Victoria for the displace SRI is a "world histories, cultures, faiths and ethics curriculum". If this turns into a relativising, secular study of comparative religion, rather than the lived and learned experience of the common denominator values of the world faiths as real and authentic believed values, it will not have replaced SRI. It will instead have nailed shut the coffin on spirituality, which both the Melbourne Declaration and the National Curriculum Review said must *live* in State Schools.

---

[79] As the author of the Review of the National Curriculum (for schools), Dr Kevin Donnelly writes:
One approach to dealing with religions and belief systems is to design specific subjects taught over a number of years. As noted in the Review of the Australian Curriculum Final Report, such is the recommendation by Rabbi Shimon Cowen, who argues for a stand-alone subject provisionally titled Theology.
"Such a subject, instead of focusing on what distinguishes various religions, would focus on "common theological categories and ethical principles". Cowen makes the point that the Abrahamic religions, including Judaism, Christianity, Islam and Buddhism, have common origins and embody similar ethical and moral values.
Dr Kevin Donnelly, "Religion has a place in the School Curriculum", printed in a number of places including the *Daily Mercury*, 23 March, 2015.

For the secularist, who does not naturally turn to religion — and here is not meant the doctrinaire secularist, but rather those who do not know or have not experienced the lived life of religious experience — there is a strong practical argument for a proper, voluntary religious education in State schools. This goes beyond the argument from the standpoint of freedom to learn about and (so better) practice one's religion. It is that (as suggested by the data discussed in this study) there is a profound social utility or value — sometimes called "social capital" — in nurturing and deepening the religious faith of students (at least for those who want it) in the State school system. A religious education is positively correlated with *better citizenship*. Or to come back to our kid on the train deliberating whether or not to buy a ticket, an education which lets G-d on the train might work better than, or at least form a vital supplement to, having only an inspector on the train.

Appendix: Citizenship values school questionnaire

1. If you were on public transport, and there was not much chance of being caught by an inspector, would you save your money and have a free ride?
2. Imagine you saw somebody damage another kid's property (e.g. Mobile phone) at school but they didn't own up. You didn't know either kid very well. Would you tell a teacher who did it?
3. A friend had a billy cart and tied up his dog to pull it. It was heavy for the dog to pull so it didn't move. Your friend asks you to hit the dog to make it pull the cart. Would you hit the dog?
4. Imagine that as a grownup, charities are ringing you quite often for donations. If you gave something to all of them you might be giving away about 5% of your earnings each year. Would you choose to keep the money and generally not donate?
5. Your friend is bouncing a ball on ants outside in the yard, to kill them. He asks you to join in the game. Would you refuse?
6. Many celebrities (singers, film stars, etc.,) are having relationships with other people's partners. If a good friend of yours became a celebrity, would you encourage your friend to do this too?

7. Imagine you are a parent of a child who was caught stealing your money. A month later there's some more money missing, but he says he didn't do it. Would you punish him before you heard his side of the story?
8. Imagine in about 10 years one of your school mates went to a party to farewell a friend going overseas. He or she had too much to drink and driving home accidentally killed someone. Would you help them to avoid punishment?
9. Imagine you found a wallet with 100 dollars in it, and there is identification (a driver's license). Would you hand in the money and the wallet to the police?
10. Imagine you have a friend who is sick in hospital. The only time you have free to visit is on Sunday afternoon, but you would have to take a tram and a train to get there and back. Would you just forget about it and save the hassle?
11. Imagine your aunty died. You used to go and play with your cousins there when you were younger. Would you go to the funeral?
12. Imagine that you saved hard to get the latest iPhone. Just at that time a friend gets very sick and needs an expensive operation. You are asked if you can loan money to help pay for the operation. Would you lend the money you saved knowing it may not be paid back for a couple of years?
13. Imagine a close friend of yours was married but had not been happy in the marriage for a few years. By chance, your friend fell in love with someone else. Would you encourage them to wait until the marriage was formally over before they began going out with their new love?

The Spiritual Component in School Curriculum

Submission to the National Curriculum Review (2014)

The "Melbourne Declaration" on the "spiritual" development of young Australians

The Preamble of the programmatic "Melbourne Declaration"[80] (p. 4) includes the following statement: "Schools play a vital role in promoting the intellectual, physical, social, emotional, moral, *spiritual* and aesthetic development and wellbeing of young Australians, and in ensuring the nation's ongoing economic prosperity and social cohesion [emphasis added]."

Under "Goal 2" of the section "The Educational Goals for Young

---

[80] *The Melbourne Declaration on Educational Goals for Young Australians*, affirmed by all Australian Education Ministers, December 2008.

Australians", the Melbourne Declaration (p. 9) states: "[Confident and creative individuals] have a sense of self-worth, self-awareness and personal identity that enables them to manage their emotional, mental, *spiritual* and physical wellbeing [emphasis added]."

In its section "A commitment to action", the Melbourne Declaration (p. 14) states "The curriculum will enable students to develop knowledge in the disciplines of English, mathematics, science, languages, humanities and the arts; to understand the *spiritual*, moral and aesthetic dimensions of life; and open up new ways of thinking [emphasis added]."

In summary, the Melbourne Declaration puts spiritual development on a par with mental, emotional and aesthetic, moral and physical development. It recognizes that just as children should become literate and numerate, just as they should be entitled to stable emotional development and have physical education and sports, an opportunity to develop artistic or musical expression, so too they are entitled to spiritual development. Ostensibly, as numeracy requires actual mathematics and physical education involves actual sports — spirituality entails an actual training in the knowledge and ethical practice of faith.

The integrity of spiritual development

The meaning of spiritual development for the overwhelming majority of humanity, and for the seventy percent of Australians who named a personal religious affiliation in recent Australian censuses, is quite simply: traditional religious belief and observance. New Age spiritualities and the like — which eschew reference to traditional religious languages — may also be present. But they do not constitute the default sense and content of religious experience for the majority of humanity or the majority of Australians. To the contrary, they frustrate the religious and spiritual needs of most people.

We find that the offerings in various State syllabuses, in the area of religion, invariably present religion through the lens of another discipline. Any true school discipline is one which is available all the way through to the completion of schooling, like maths, English, sports and art. So let us look at the offerings in State syllabuses which bear on the topic of religion, the obvious receptacle for developing the spirituality of students. One of these, in an investigation I made some years ago was a Tasmanian subject in which religion would be treated through the perspective of philosophy. Others are the subjects "Religion and Society" and "Text and Tradition". These last two subjects respectively treat religion (or "spirituality") through the lenses of sociology and history. And it is not only that religion is being treated through a "foreign" subject filter. That filter is also one which often carries a secular critique of religion. When I confronted such a curriculum official on this issue, I was told that students could mount their own defence of religion. It is highly unlikely that students should be able to challenge that secular perspective or critique, when school curriculum has developed their powers of secular critique, but has done nothing to develop their spirituality, i.e. their reflective knowledge and practice of their faith.

The previous working group on religion under the Australian Curriculum, Assessment and Reporting Authority (ACARA) used the work of a researcher, who advocated a Swedish school subject of comparative religion rather than the study of religion from the "inside" as believed and comprehended faith. What this serves essentially is to relativize religion from the outside and thereby to sap belief, rather than to nurture belief and human spirituality as something taught from the inside for those who believe by those who believe. The former study has not to do with the *spirituality* of students, but offers another kind of *humanities* subject. Theology engages the actual spirituality of students.

Traditional and for the majority of humanity, contemporary, spirituality as *religion* needs to be a subject which is precisely that, taught on its own terms: for believers by believers. This does not mean that it should be done in a way which is non-rigorous and non-intellectual. To the contrary, universities — to which school curricula lead — have faculties of Theology, just as they have faculties in all other school subjects. And just as University faculties of theology provide a rigorous, intellectual presentation and analysis of faith, so should school curricula in this area.

The disenfranchisement of the spiritual in contemporary curriculum thinking

Football is played with one's feet and a musical instrument is played with one's hands, together with an education addressed to the mind which instructs the foot to play better football, and the hand to play better music. Similarly, spirituality is pursued through the human "spirit" (or as it has traditionally been called, the "soul"), which an education, addressed to the mind, can also develop. Faith in its integrity recognizes the unique sense or "instrument" of faith, which for most of humanity is the human soul. An aggressive secularism which wants in education either to deny and discount both the soul and the traditional faiths with which it has been associated, is in fact disenfranchising the spiritual dimension of the human being, which the Melbourne Declaration affirmed.

Such a position is stated by a Curriculum Manager in the Humanities of the Victorian Curriculum and Assessment Authority, in a paper[81] which addresses the Melbourne Declaration's requirement for the development of students' "spirituality". This is the starting point of her statement:

> How can the development and management of spiritual wellbeing be expressed in curriculum beyond faith-based settings, so that it is indeed supported for all Australians? This paper outlines and then uses a way of articulating the spiritual that is independent of adherence to religious tradition or belief in the divine, to inform themes of secular spirituality that could be manifested in secular curriculum, and the skills and capacities that can be brought to these themes. In doing so, it aims to capture what is distinctive about the spiritual in the context of curriculum.

---

81 Victoria. Work Education Curriculum Committee. (Vic. :). Curriculum newsletter.

The answer she presents is a concept of teaching the sense of "awe and wonder", without any traditional religious content. The desideratum of the above quoted paragraph encodes the prejudice against an integral spiritual education, in the form of the rigorous education of faith on its own terms.

It does this first, by insisting that it be supported by "all Australians". But is classical music and art practised by all Australians? We do not see this in the numbers of candidates in music and in art in the upper years of schooling. Is football played by all Australians? We do not see this in the teams fielded by schools. Are physics or foreign languages studied by all Australians? We do not see that all students pursue exclusively sciences or humanities towards the end of schooling. In short, the spiritual in the sense of traditional religion is not affirmed by *all* Australians although the *overwhelming majority* of Australians *do*. Music may not be for all students, but it is offered in education. Similarly traditional spirituality in the form of religion might not resonate for *all* students, but it should be available for those with whom it does. In short even if, after an initial exposure to traditional religion, there are students who do not wish to pursue it, it should remain an elective for those who do want it — and for whom it would constitute an essential spiritual growth.

Secondly, the suggestion that the default position be one which makes no reference to a Creator, is in fact a secularist position which negates traditional religion. It is a totally eviscerated spirituality which is irrelevant and contradictory to the historical and contemporary spiritual experience of the majority of Australians and humanity. The invention of a neutral spirituality, which the education officer wants, as a relationless sense of "awe and wonder" is historically spurious; and it is a minoritarian secularist imposition on the beliefs of the majority. Her default position is a concept of "secularist" spirituality, a contradiction in terms for most Australians. It does nothing to develop the spirituality of young Australians in the sense in which the majority of humanity and Australians understand this concept. It is educationally discriminatory and of no educational value in the realm of spirituality as this has been culturally and historically understood.

Even those groups which are avowedly anti-religious and did not want religious instruction for their children in State Schools in NSW and sought to set up an alternative secularist syllabus in "ethics", did not promote the *exclusion* of traditional religious education for those who want it. However, the agenda apparent in this education officer's paper, in fact excludes a traditional religious spirituality even as an option and elective strand for those who want it.

If the National curriculum wants to acknowledge those Australians who seek a "spirituality" which is "independent of adherence to religious tradition or belief in the divine", then let it be offered as an alternative to the traditional and majority conception of spirituality, not as the default position which drives the traditional view of spirituality out of the curriculum.

In summary, the proposal to satisfy the development of "spirituality" with a "secularized" spirituality, which makes no mention of traditional religion or the Divine, eviscerates the objective and historical meaning of spirituality for the majority of Australians and humanity. If a secular minority wants no truck with traditional spirituality as religion, then it should be offered a secular alternative to traditional spirituality; it should not be allowed to drive out and wholly replace traditional spirituality.

The separation of religion and state

The prescription of the Australian Constitution in section 116 prohibits the establishment of any *one* religious sect as an affiliation mandatory for the holding of office in Australia. It does not prohibit the expression of or education in religious beliefs. On the contrary, it actively requires freedom of religion and conscience. There is no suggestion that the provision for spirituality in the National Curriculum should teach one faith only. It should be possible for students within the provision of a Theology subject to study those general theological and ethical categories shared by a *variety* of faiths in Australia.

Australia is a party to international treaties which provide for the rights of parents to educate their children in their own faiths. What is evident today in the world of ubiquitous media is that a kindergarten or Sunday-school or home education in religion is wholly inadequate to a young person's spiritual development. The right to educate is only fulfilled when it is an education which follows the entire process of intellectual maturation of the student throughout schooling such that he or she is capable intellectually of answering challenges to belief which enter, so to speak, through every "pore" of their being by contemporary media. Parents, who cannot supply this education, often see the spiritual destruction of, or at least damage to, their children, who have been given no maturity, sophistication or conceptual "infrastructure" in their belief, which alone would equip them to survive spiritually: in short there is little or no spiritual *education*.

In summary, the imposition of a uniform secularization of the content of "spirituality", or in other words the removal of all traditional religion taught, believed and lived from the "inside", has nothing to do with the Constitutional Provision for the separation of religion and State. To the contrary it infringes the Constitutional requirement of freedom of religion, which is not truly possible without religious education. It also infringes international charters which provide parents with the right to have their children educated in their religion. Without a religious education which advances throughout the school years, for those who want it, there is no real spiritual education, given the pervasive and overwhelming impact of modern media, with its indifference or hostility to religion.

The transmission of values and the preservation of a common ethic

Our society is built on what has commonly been called a Judeo-Christian ethic. Whilst, as we shall argue below, this can be widened to an "Abrahamic ethic", which also makes Muslims,

Hindus and Buddhists comfortable, it is important to understand why society should want to preserve an identifiable ethic, which has a faith root. The primary reason for this is that a world-view is the primary motivator of desired civic conduct and morals. People internalize and act upon values, not because they enter upon an on-the-spot rational reflection on each ethical situation, but because they believe in certain basic ethical imperatives at a deeper, inner level. Ultimately, our society is based on the *faith* or *belief* traditions of the great western religions and the values which they have taught.

Unless there is an education in these values, which is renewed and taught to children with increasing sophistication paralleling their intellectual and emotional maturation, this ethical tradition and foundation of our society is endangered. Gone are the days, when values instilled in the home alone and in early childhood were sufficient to carry a person for the rest of his or her life. Pervasive media and social connectivity outside the home, and the breakdown of much family life, have weakened the family as a transmitter of values. Faith now needs to be educated, and educated in schools, for those who choose it. Without basic spiritual literacy, the beliefs which have been historically articulated by religion and the moral values which religion has passed on, become fraught in their sustainability.

In summary, the Judeo-Christian ethic (which can be broadened to an Abrahamic ethic) as the foundation of our society has meant two things. One, an *ethic* — that is to say a set of values, upon which our society was based. Secondly, it had a faith foundation — it was *Judeo-Christian* — and it was this belief and faith tradition which anchored, internalized and motivated the practice of these values. The Judeo-Christian (or broader Abrahamic) ethic cannot be preserved unless it is *taught*.

How would a subject, "Theology", be structured?

Without a proper subject within the National Curriculum, which is studied as a regular subject and examined externally at year 12 level, spirituality cannot be adequately catered for in the National Curriculum. All the educational areas with which spirituality are put on a par by the Melbourne Declaration — the "mental development" afforded by the traditional subjects such as Maths and English; the aesthetic education, afforded by art and music and even physical education — are given the status of matriculation subjects in different Australian jurisdictions. As mentioned, this can be an elective subject. And for those wanting a secular alternative on ethics, that can also be devised, but it should not displace Theology as an integral subject on its own.

Clearly different faith traditions — such as can be accommodated by the educational system — should be able to work within the one subject template. One way this can be achieved is by examining the common categories at the root "Abrahamic" level from which the world religions spring. This is an exercise which I — as a Rabbi — have already successfully undertaken with Christian and Muslim colleagues. We were able to agree upon a number of common theological categories and ethical principles within which each of Judaism, Christianity and Islam work. It is my belief that this Abrahamic template could be extended also to Hinduism, and possibly also Buddhism, inasmuch as these also have a connection with the historical Abraham and the tradition transmitted by him. My research into this shared template was supported by a Government Grant and has been published as "An Education in a Shared Ethic".

The common template can be further elaborated to provide a rigorous framework for the elective subject "Theology" and teachers (who themselves are adherents and believers of the various world religions) can be trained to teach this subject. Just as my own work with Muslim and Christian colleagues has disclosed basic theological categories of belief and ethic principles upheld in common by Judaism, Christianity and Islam, so this template should be extended and developed by a special team of the National Curriculum. Societies *seek* a unifying common denominator faith-based ethic. Americans have described this in their context as an "ethical monotheism", Australians a "Judeo-Christian ethic". Part of the task of the National Curriculum in this area would be to identify this ethic with its basic shared faith tenets (which will be seen to be compatible with other indivudual religions as well).

Finally, there is a very big dividend of social cohesion in teaching theology (from the "inside") but out of the one template. The fact that through this template, adherents of the great world religions see that they have common denominator theological categories and a common set of basic shared values, actually builds mutual respect and a sense of community and solidarity amongst the great faiths. Not only this, it also effects a spirit of moderation amongst the faiths. Any sentiments of chauvinism within an individual faith are automatically attenuated and negated when the starting point is that there is a common template and a common root. Thus, work which I did in preparing the manual "An Education in a Shared Ethic" was indeed funded by a Department of Government which was interested less in education than in social cohesion and moderating religious extremism.

In summary, the subject "Theology" can admit both rigour and variety of participation. Its *common* template additionally promotes respect and harmony between the faiths.

The National Curriculum of 2021 as an Instrument of Secularization

Perhaps the most striking feature of the new National Curriculum put forward by ACARA in 2021 is its 180-degree reversal of a key position of the "Melbourne Declaration" on the goals of school education signed by every State Education Minister in 2008. In three places the "Melbourne Declaration" placed the "spiritual development and wellbeing of children" on a par with their "intellectual, physical, social, emotional, moral and aesthetic" development and wellbeing. This is gone from the new curriculum.

The educational understanding that the child is also a spiritual being has direct bearing on the ability of the child to grow and develop as an ethical being. As Professor Brian Hill, a former Professor at Murdoch University and a consultant to Government on education, wrote, what ultimately anchors and motivates moral conduct, personal and interpersonal, as well towards the things in the child's environment[82], are his or her beliefs. Professor Ramon Lewis, a former Head of the School of Education at Latrobe University, observed in a survey that children from religious schools were more likely to act out basic "citizenship values" consistently with conscience as distinct from the threat of punishment than students in State schools who did not have the same religious component in their education[83]. In short, internalized ethical conduct is rooted ultimately in conscience, which is the domain of belief.

The 2021 National Curriculum has ostensibly eliminated the spiritual dimension from childhood education. It is there when considering the culture of indigenous Australians and in the general brief of "intercultural understanding". But the vast majority of students in Australian schools are not presumed to have any objective spiritual legacy. There is, it would appear from the 2021 ACARA curriculum, no objective values-set that they — unlike the indigenous Australians — have inherited as part of a common religious heritage.

Perhaps unwittingly, the National Curriculum is thus chasing the *Zeitgeist* of a moral relativism and hedonistic materialism, which holds that life has no objective sanctity, that the human being in sexual terms has no objective identities and that human institutions such as marriage have no objective normativity. There is nothing in ethics which a child could be taught. Rather, as set out in the "Elements and sub-elements of the Ethical Understanding learning continuum", children will "explore ethical concepts", "examine … the range of norms" which relate to ethical behaviour and make their own "ethical decisions".

---

[82] See the earlier essay in this chapter "An Education in a Shared Ethic".
[83] See the essay in this chapter, "Why should a Kid buy a Ticket on a Train?"

But how, and with whose help, will children arbitrate between ethical concepts, affirm specific norms and make their ethical decisions? Will they generate these out of their own "feelings" and "perceptions", or with the input of social and general media, or in accordance with the dispositions of their graduate teachers? Where will these ethics come from and what will they be?

The word and concept "spiritual", which has been basically removed from the new Curriculum, has historically referred to an objective entity called the "spirit". It relates to the conscience or the soul of the individual. That individual, human spirit also implied a great correlate, the Creator, to Whom all the major faiths have in some way related. It also meant that there was a template of common values that resonated in the human soul or conscience, because the soul was made in the likeness of that Creator who gave those values. Unfortunately, the new National Curriculum seems implicitly to deny these interrelated principles. It has so become an instrument of further secularization.

This negation of the spiritual in the student deprives the student of the power of self-transcendence which is what spirituality is all about. It also robs the student of the deepest resource of motivation for ethical conduct, namely the beliefs — accessed by, and "stored within" the spirit — which anchor ethical norms. Finally, inasmuch as the spirit is a crucial instrument of meaning, the suppression of the spirit opens the door wider to confusion and meaninglessness. We see this in the statistical trends, which correlate with ongoing secularization, of depression, suicide, substance abuse and the failure to establish lasting homes and relationships. Unfortunately, the National Curriculum, with its excision of the spiritual, is here not building stronger and more resilient individuals. Rather, in chasing the trend of social secularization and eliminating the key spiritual aspect of human personhood, it serves to weaken human resilience.

Aging and Spirituality

In seeking to grasp aging in philosophical terms of religious — in my case Jewish — tradition, we are presented with a paradox. On the one hand, it is clear (as indicated in many sources) that the person who remains occupied with a life of religious study and observance, with engagement of all, and particularly one's intellectual, faculties is meant to be in a process of continual spiritual ascent and personal refinement. This is so even to the extent that the day of one's departure from this world, death itself — the end of life — is grasped as a spiritual summation and revelation of an entire life's service of G-d. All this is certainly true in the dimensions of wisdom and character refinement (putting aside the intrusion of the illness of dementia or other organic sicknesses which can overwhelm and obscure the spiritual ascent of the person through age).

On the other hand, in physical terms, life would seem over the greater trajectory of its passage to be a process of decline. One's physical strength and one's ability to pursue goals in terms of physical stamina wane. Illness finds a far more vulnerable object in old age and of course death itself generally overtakes an old person through the very wear and tear of the body. Assuming that this is more than a mere paradox, the question to be addressed then is, what is the *functional inter-relationship* of spiritual ascent and physical decline. What, in other words, is the relationship between acquired wisdom and character-refinement, on the one hand, and the waning of strength and stamina on the other. What is the meaning of the adage that "the weakness of the physical is the strength of the soul and the weakness of the soul is the strength of the physical"? What is the explanation of their "inverse" relationship?

A feature of aging is that, after an early peaking of physical strength in one's twenties or perhaps even thirties, one begins physically to decline. We are accustomed — and rightly — to understand the physical and the spiritual forces with a person as engaged in what is called a "zero-sum game". The ascent of the physical is the descent of the spiritual; the ascent of the spiritual is the descent of the physical. This is associated with the aging process, since one is born with an undeveloped spirituality and a mature (that is to say, a powerful) physicality, that is to say, with definite and conscious desires. Since youth is associated with physical passion, and age with physical retirement or resignation to some extent, it would appear that automatically as one gets older, one should have less trouble from the physical dimensions of one's being.

So here then is the question. Can we see life as two intersecting curves: a curve which early on begins high and declines through life — the physical curve; and a curve which begins low and ascends throughout life — the spiritual? The significance of their intersection — might this be at the half-way point of life (of the biblically blessed life of 120 years) that is, the age of 60? Is that a point reached midway where one has gained significantly in wisdom and has not yet significantly declined in strength? In short, is this the point, where one has enough energy to utilize it properly with the significant advance in understanding: the equilibrium stage of strength and understanding?

The Tradition also states that as the wise get older, their understanding becomes more settled; whilst, as the boorish get older, their understanding becomes more disturbed. Now a problem with this statement of the Tradition is that some of those who are "wise" in fact become demented. The resolution of this contradiction must be that this dementia in fact results from an organic illness which has affected the physical mind of a person who has been "wise". Yet, what we can still observe in some of those who have cultivated wisdom — but have become demented — is the persistence of character refinement *notwithstanding* the dementia.

The nature of the service, called for spiritually, at each stage of one's life is actually appropriate to the physical condition which one possesses at that time. A young person with naturally strong memory should be crammed with knowledge in childhood and early adulthood. At the height of his or her strength, he or she can go into the world to establish a livelihood and a family. As this begins to plateau in one's forties and fifties, one is able to pull back from the active physical engagement and gain the distance which is requisite for analysis and counsel. But both of these are yet active agencies, requiring a degree of physical strength and stamina. One seizes opportunities, one embraces them and seeks an active role.

In the second half of one's life, perhaps beginning around sixty, however, one's acceptance of G-d's providence becomes deeper. It is not one who chooses the role, but rather accepts what is required of one. There is a passivity which indicates a receptivity to task. Part of the strength which comes to one under these circumstances is from one's students, one's children and those who support or honour one. The strength is given to one at this stage by others. The same applies to the sick, elderly person. Their spiritual development proceeds, but its actualization comes about through the others who learn from, honour and physically support or follow the elderly, weakened person. This in fact brings out the infamy of the culture which rejects respect and honourable care for the aged. Just as youth is idolized because of its natural vigour, old age is despised or disregarded because of its physical weakness. But it is the spiritual greatness of the old, and perhaps even sick person, which is brought out through the attention to him or her by others. In short, the physical condition is not one of decline; it is one which is suited to a more purely spiritual service. As it ascends — as years go on, it needs more to be heard by others.

With this we can understand perhaps the special accomplishment associated with the age of 60. There is still energy, but one spies physical weakness and dependence. The novelty of this age is that perhaps one's service is no longer geared to asserting goals as *personal* goals. One's attitude is that it is important that the goal be accomplished, less than that I am to be the one who will necessarily do it. The personal — psychophysical — stakes wane vis-à-vis the spiritual goal itself. I — the psychophysical self — matter less (— and in fact that makes it easier to attain it, gives one a purer energy and motivation to accomplish it).

The beauty of the quality of equanimity (which one can carry forward) is that the goal is clear in focus, and whilst one would be satisfied to be the one to achieve it, there is also a satisfaction in the achievement of another of that same goal. After all good was brought into the world. And in the realm of truth there is no jealousy, because jealousy exists only over material things, in which ego has a stake. This is the quality of equanimity. I do not have to be *the* achiever, I am happy when another achieves goodness. I am not frustrated, because I understand that goal is bigger than me, and my stake in it is less important than that it be achieved, than that the suffering of others be alleviated. Consequently, it does not matter what role is chosen for me by the Creator: I shall embrace it with equanimity.

The question of how it could be that the elderly and even those who have used their minds and are scholars, and are yet struck by organic illness which affect the mind — despite the assurance of the words of our Sages — is not really a problem. These are organic diseases, diseases or debilitation of the *physical* brain. The quality of "understanding" intended by our Sages, may also have had a spiritual dimension: the Hebrew word for understanding — *da'as* — means "attachment" to the spiritual concept, and the elderly and even those who have organic illnesses of the brain, may not lose that quality. In fact, I have seen myself, a distinguished and refined member of my community who spent his life in learning struck by severe dementia. And yet the profound refinement which this person had acquired through a life of learning and religious practice never left him, even in dementia. One could see that his spiritual life was fully intact. Viktor Frankl has something very similar to this about the great philosopher Immanuel Kant whose mind became sclerotic in old age. This is what Frankl writes:

> Does not the piano tuner have an opportunity to marvel at the virtuoso who can play better on an untuned piano, than a bad player does on a good piano. [The great philosopher] Kant [in old age] had the use of no more than a brain in a condition of *status cribrosus* [a condition marked by dilations of

the perivascular spaces in the brain]. In the last days of his life, he exhibited a severe amnestic aphasic condition [- an inability to name objects or recognize objects by their names -] but what words were drawn from this "instrument"! His doctors wanted him for a meeting to discuss his medical case and [when it eventuated,] waited long — in vain — for him to sit down. Eventually, they understood that their patient had refused to take his seat so long as the doctors themselves had not sat. Once they did, Kant wrestled from his atherosclerotic brain the profoundly moving words: "I have not yet lost my sense of humanity". Behold: a virtuoso plays on a bad instrument.[84]

What this suggests is the human soul has a life of its own within the human being, which in a certain sense is independent of its housing in mind and body. The soul — or the spirit — though pristine and pure, still undergoes a progressive development throughout life, and unless the person is coarse and has sought no self-refinement, that spiritual faculty continues to develop. What this may mean is that we can contact and engage this faculty even in the individual whose mind is demented and whose body is significantly weakened. How could that be? I can only say from personal experience of giving talks on religious subjects in Jewish old age homes, that elderly people can sit around quite rapt, even though it is not evident that intellectually they always understand much. Unless one were cynical and responded, that they have nothing else or better to do or do not have the strength to protest or take themselves away, one is tempted to say that this is an application of what we say: "the soul hears". I personally believe that this is the case and think that people are ennobled by subjects which indeed the soul does hear, spiritual topics. The intellectual filter or conduit is less important, because the content — the light which is being transmitted in those words — is the main thing. So perhaps in old age, when generally people have become more spiritual, because the ego and the lusts have become weaker, there is a special reason to appeal to the spiritual within them. For it is stronger in some sense than ever before, and it "hears". I

---

[84] *The Rediscovery of the Human – Psychological Writings of Viktor E. Frankl on the Human in the Image of the Divine*, p. 152

notice that various programmes in certain systems of Age Care such as "Baptcare" have set up programmes of life writing by the elderly. This is something which is spiritual. It is about meaning and reflection and the very expression of it is ennobling. What I would say is that old age care needs to encompass a very important dimension which speaks to, and as far as possible, engages the spirituality of the elderly.

For this reason, I am dismayed when I see old people in homes for the aged being entertained like children, with balloons being bounced in front of their faces and bingo games being featured as highlights of the week. And above all when they are "put out to graze" for hours in front of a television set. Without entrapment or compulsion, it might be good simply to expose the elderly to spiritual subjects, rather than waiting for them to request or agree to it. For what is refusing to hear is not the spiritual faculty. Let the spiritual faculty have a chance to hear. Especially when the elderly are gathered together for some kind of social occasion or even celebration or entertainment — when they are otherwise happy to be there — it could be most appropriate to allow a spiritual theme to be heard. Maybe even before or after the bingo game.

The trajectory of life brings out, particularly in old age, the support, strength and enrichment conferred by spirituality. It is in old age that we see whether this path has in fact been taken and the extent to which, in earlier stages of life, one has been educated in it.

Chapter 7
The Assault on Conscience and Religious Freedom

A derivative of the attack on religion itself is the attempt to foreclose the ability of those who believe to practise and manifest their belief. The first essay in this volume, "The Repression of Religious Freedom", is a comprehensive treatment of this topic. It was placed in the introductory part ("The New Challenge to Universal Ethics") rather than in the present part "Political Applications of Universal Ethics" because its theme is emblematic of the current challenge to universal ethics: the *actual hegemony* of hedonistic materialism, expressed most pointedly in legislation to repress the expression of religious tradition, which has been the principal bearer of universal ethics.

This chapter begins with two pieces on the coercion of conscience involved in legislation legalizing abortion on demand. The first relates to coercion of health practitioners in Abortion Reform legislation in two Australian State Parliaments — the Victorian (in 2008) and the Tasmanian (in 2013). The second analyses a political moral failure to correct the excesses of the Victorian law by a Parliamentary leader who knew it was wrong.

The third and fourth pieces in this chapter have to do with breaches of religious freedom in judicial decisions and legislation blocking access to psychotherapy for unwanted same-sex attraction and gender dysphoria. The third piece relates to the trial of a clinical psychological organization "JONAH", offering such psychotherapeutic assistance in the United States. The fourth is part of a representation made together with a leading paediatrician, Professor John Whitehall, to the Federal Parliament of Australia for legislative protection of autonomy in access to therapy.

Abortion and the Coercion of Conscience

From the Victorian Abortion Law Reform Act 2008 to the Tasmanian "Reproductive Health (Access to Terminations) Bill 2013"

"It is repugnant that a doctor who has a conscientious objection to abortion — and many doctors and health practitioners do — will be forced by this legislation to refer a woman to a practitioner who they know will perform an abortion. I think that is wrong."

(*Victorian Hansard*, 9 September 2008, p. 3354)

Dr Denis Napthine, in the debates on the Victorian Abortion Law Reform Bill of 2008.

"…a very sad and retrograde [piece of legislation]"

Comment of the Attorney General of Victoria, the Hon Robert Clark, prior to the 2010 elections in which the coalition came to power and he became Attorney General, on the Victorian Abortion Law Reform Bill of 2008.

(cited in *Politics and Universal Ethics*, Ballan, Australia: Connor Court, 2011, p. 115)

The religious conscience position of many doctors

The Institute for Judaism and Civilization was fortunate to be supported by the Federal Attorney General with a grant under its "Building Community Resilience" Program to produce a Manual of Shared Values of Judaism, Christianity and Islam. This work was produced with the collaboration of major religious and academic scholars of these three faiths. Amongst the shared values of these three major faiths is the opposition to abortion on demand (where there is no danger to the mother or other compelling reason). An example — perhaps the most egregious and capricious example — of abortion on demand is an abortion performed because the parents of the foetus would rather have a boy than a girl, or vice-versa. Yet this is precisely what Victorian and proposed Tasmanian legislation permits.

The standpoint of the great world faiths is that pre-natal life cannot be disposed of at will and this relates in part to the great preciousness of the human soul, which is also present in the foetus. This does not mean that there are no circumstances, which warrant abortion (such as danger to the mother's life), but the notion of this Bill — that pre-natal life is in principle disposable at will — flies in the face of an ethical and civilizational heritage of over 5000 years. It is this ethical heritage which informs the consciences of very many human beings, including doctors.

The Victorian abortion law and the coercion of conscience

The Abortion Law Reform Act, passed by the Victorian Government in 2008 provided for abortion to 24 weeks with no questions asked, and up to birth with two recommendations. What made the Victorian Act one of the most radical abortion bills in the world was its provision in section 8 (1). There it compelled a doctor with a conscientious objection (to aborting a foetus where there was no danger to the mother's life) either to perform the abortion or to refer the woman to another doctor who would.

When I informed one of Australia's greatest (now retired) judges, of this legislation, he was appalled. He explained his response in something like these terms. The underworld uses the expression "to take out a contract on someone". This means hiring a thug to kill a person. If someone comes to me and asks me to take out that "contract" I will of course refuse. Similarly, if I am then told, "All right you don't have to, but give me the address of someone who will", I will also refuse: I will not be, and must not be forced to be, a principal or an accessory to such an act. To tell a doctor who, on conscientious grounds does not want to perform an abortion, that he or she must then refer to a doctor who will, or face penalties under legislation, is in the same category. It is a direct attack on freedom of religion and conscience of those Jewish, Christian or Islamic (and for that matter many other) doctors, who on the grounds of their faith and values — which are also the underpinning values of civilization — will have nothing to do with many requested abortions.

Even those who favour abortion on demand, have rejected this clause. Such is the view of one of America's leading constitutional lawyers, Professor Arnold Loewy. He wrote to me of the Victorian law that it forces

> a doctor into the cruel trilemma of (1) give up medicine, (2) commit a crime, or (3) lead an unborn child to slaughter... [B]ecause the law seriously burdens the conscience of some doctors and is not necessary to secure abortion rights of the patients, I think it is a bad law that should be repealed.

The extension of coercion

The proposed Tasmanian Bill explicitly unpacks and extends the coercive potential of its model, the Victorian legislation, expanding compulsion directed against conscience and religious freedom from (a) the doctor (and auxiliary medical staff) to (b) the counsellor and (c) forms of protest.

The Bill's compulsion of the doctor and medical staff

Ostensibly anticipating and accommodating the protest which met the Victorian legislation, the Tasmanian Bill provides in section 6 (1) "...no individual is under a duty, whether by contract or by any statutory or other legal requirement to participate in [an abortion...] if the individual has a conscientious objection to terminations" (this refers to cases where the mother's life is not in danger). However, in section 7 (2) this seeming acknowledgment of conscientious objection is immediately cancelled by the requirement that "if a woman seeks a termination or pregnancy options advice from a medical practitioner and the practitioner has a conscientious objection to terminations, the practitioner must refer the woman to another medical practitioner who the first-mentioned practitioner knows does not have a conscientious objection to terminations." The law is identical to the Victorian law forcing a doctor to carry out, or be an accessory to, what his or her faith teaches is an unwarranted killing, by sending the person to a doctor who will perform the abortion.

The first draft of the Tasmanian Bill specified a penalty of 500 penalty points or $65,000 for a doctor who refused to refer. In the face of the two thousand submissions made on the bill, of which the overwhelming majority were against the Bill, the revised Bill omitted the penalty, with the Bill still requiring the doctor to comply. What does this mean? In a press release the Tasmanian Minister for Health stated that the refusal of a doctor to refer would instead be treated as a case of "non-professional conduct", to be dealt with by medical boards. What does this mean? Recently, in Victoria, a doctor said on a blog or Facebook page that, *were he faced with such a situation* he would not refer. He was brought before a medical tribunal and told that this was "unprofessional conduct" and that were he to persist despite caution and warning, serious consequences were in store, a clear intimation he would be de-registered as a doctor. Currently another case is being tested in Victoria, with a doctor, Dr John Hobart, who has refused to refer a couple, which came to him for an abortion because they wanted a boy instead. Clearly the Tasmanian directive is the same as the Victorian one. There is no $65,000 fine now. Instead, there is implicit deregistration as a doctor — damage worth more than $65,000. For doctors (and the same applies to nurses and auxiliary medical staff), this is a violation of freedom of conscience guaranteed by the International Covenant on Civil and Political Rights (article 18, providing freedom of religion and freedom of conscience) to which Australia is a party. The Australian Medical Association has also indicated its opposition to this legislation.

The compulsion of the counsellor

The Tasmanian Bill extends compulsion against conscience to another group of persons, which the Victorian legislation does not even mention: pregnancy counsellors. This it does in section 7(3): "If a woman seeks pregnancy options advice from a counsellor and the counsellor has a conscientious objection to terminations, the counsellor must refer the woman to another counsellor who the first-mentioned counsellor knows does not have a conscientious objection to terminations." The revised version of the Bill reduced the penalty on a counsellor for refusing to comply from $65,000 to $32,500.

This provision for coercion of the counsellor is in a way more disturbing than the coercion of the doctor. The patient came to the doctor with a request for an abortion. The patient came to the counsellor for *advice as to whether* she should have an abortion. She has not yet made up her mind whether to have an abortion or not, but the Bill wants to get her eventually to a counsellor who will recommend the abortion. If the Bill wanted her to have a genuine range of arguments for and against abortion, then if she first visited a counsellor *without* objections to abortion, the Bill would have insisted (under pain of a fine up to $32,500) that the pro-abortion counsellor send her also to a counsellor, who *does* have reservations against abortion. But the Bill does not do this. It is concerned only that woman with questions whether to abort, should end up with a pro-abortion counsellor. It has vitiated not only the concept of conscience of the counsellor, but of the very concept of *counsel itself*, sought by the woman with questions as to an abortion. This provision is also in violation of the rights of a pregnancy counsellor to freedom of conscience under the International Covenant on Civil and Political Rights, to which Australia, as mentioned, is a party.

The compulsion against protest

The Bill finally in section 9 seeks to punish a variety of actions or protests (which might also include a prayer vigil) within a radius of 150 metres of an abortion clinic. For infringement of this proscription the maximum $65,000 fine *or 12 months imprisonment or both* applies. This includes apart from protest and other actions unspecified "any other prescribed behaviour".

Protests may indeed be upsetting. Yet, when a trade union peacefully pickets workers who want to work, notwithstanding the union's strike or industrial action, the picket is legal under Australian law. There is, to my knowledge, no "150 metre access zone" which qualifies this. Under Australian law, "freedom of assembly" is a fundamental freedom, which is extended to peaceful protest. I am not aware of "150 metre access zone" which qualifies this. Yet a peaceful protest within 150 metres of an abortion clinic would be punishable for its participants individually by a fine of up to $65,000 *or 12 months imprisonment or both*. Freedom of assembly for the purposes of peaceful protest is a fundamental human right guaranteed also by article 21 of the International Covenant on Civil and Political Rights, again to which Australia is a party.

The "practical" argument against conscience

When pressed for a reason for the coercive measures against freedom of conscience in the Victorian Act (and the Tasmanian Bill copying and extending them), their proponents offer the following standard answer. Picture the case of a teenage girl, in say a rural or ethnic area, who has relatively little exposure to the world and little sense of access to facilities and wants an abortion. She goes to a doctor who refuses in principle to refer to her to an abortion clinic. The result, they argue, is that this is the end of the line for her and practically she has no recourse to an abortion facility. This scenario is presented in order to justify a universal denial of freedom of conscience, under all abortion circumstances to doctors and nurses in Victoria. But let us examine the case itself. Does this teenager have an iPhone? Is she able to "google" an "abortion clinic"? Does she know or can she find no sympathetic adult, or have no more savvy friends, who can guide her to an abortion clinic — just as she could be guided (or find her own way) to the State's welfare agency, Centrelink? A negative answer seems highly unlikely.

Yet this extraordinary scenario and justification hides the real facts and the real reasons for the attempt to coerce doctors and nurses to comply with abortion on demand in all circumstances. *Time Magazine* (14 January 2013) tells a story of how in America it is becoming increasingly difficult to obtain an abortion, not simply for the modelled 15 year-old teenager, but for mature, worldly women. This is manifestly because doctors increasingly do *not want* to perform abortions. Why? Very probably because they are struck by the wrongness of a great many of them. The movement behind this coercive legislation, however, wants to force total and immediate availability of abortion on demand for all women through any doctor. What is this philosophy of coercion?

The philosophy of coercion of conscience

What concept of an entitlement to abortion on demand can trump an established human right of freedom of conscience and religion, guaranteed by article 18 of the International Covenant of Civil and Political Liberties? Or (as in the Tasmanian Bill, additionally) freedom of assembly and a right peacefully to protest granted by its article 21? What has emerged in discussion overseas is the assertion of a new supposed positive "right to abort". Also clothed as "reproductive rights", it claims that a woman's right to abort under any circumstances for any or no reason is an expression of her very being and autonomy. An abortion of a foetus is thus conceptually no different from the removal of a benign tumour or even a corn from her foot. To deny her this complete sovereignty over everything occurring within her body is thus claimed as a right more fundamental than other rights, including the freedom of conscience of doctors who want no part in abortions for such reasons. According to this claimed right, an abortion sought for reasons of sex selection (because a boy is preferred to a girl or vice versa), becomes a woman's fundamental right. Needless to say this deeply materialistic philosophy collides totally with the religious traditions on which our civilization is built, for which the claimed equivalence of a nascent human being and a benign tumour is abhorrent.

In providing for abortion on demand, the Victorian law and the Tasmanian Bill not only go against the ethic of Judaism, Christianity and Islam, and more generally of 5000 years of civilization; they also contradict contemporary international instruments which were mindful of that legacy. The International Declaration of the Rights of the Child, promulgated in 1959 by the General Assembly of the United Nations in Principle 4 stated, "The child shall be entitled to grow and develop in health; to this end, special care and protection shall be provided both to him and to his mother, including adequate *pre-natal* and post-natal care" (emphasis added).

To uproot a fundamental ethical principle of civilization - which regards abortion as a form of killing, where there are not special grounds such as danger to the mother's life — needs a revolution to support it. It resonates in the consciences of "too many" people. The proponents of radical abortion laws know that when a doctor is asked to abort a child on demand, for example, because the parent(s) would rather have a child of a different sex, this will frequently repel the moral sense of the doctor. Often a doctor does not want to have anything to do with this travesty of traditional human values, even by referring onto another doctor.

Deeper than international treaties, are the universal recurring values, which have been ratified generation after generation for thousands of years. It is the human soul, the mirror of its Creator, which resonates with these values prescribed by the Creator and which have been transmitted by the great world religions. This is why societies return to these anchor values of civilizations, notwithstanding short historical aberrations. One of these values is the value of life, including pre-natal life, which may not be disposed of at will. To shut out the human being's deep resonance with this fundamental value, a very powerful mechanism of repression is required, and that is what was set out in the Victorian Abortion Law and has been extended and expanded in this Bill.

The perversity of this bill, with its extraordinary apparatus of coercion is indicated by the fact that it occupies the "highest" rung in the "progression" of levels to which a society can go tending towards legislative entrenchment of abortion *on demand.* These levels are:

(i) To prohibit, criminalize, and prosecute for, it. In truth, according to the Abrahamic religions, this is the right stance in that foetal life may not be taken on demand, i.e. without specific justification. Yet it may be impractical to prosecute and punish especially where society has provided no education about sexuality within committed relationships, and where there is a culture of promiscuity, sanctioned even within secondary education

(ii) To prohibit, criminalize but not to prosecute. This (not prosecuting) recognizes that there has been nothing to educate away from the culture of "unwanted pregnancy", but it at least does not give the approval of law to abortion on demand. This means that the law is *not* educating that abortion on demand is *moral because it is legal*.

(iii) To legalize and decriminalize abortion on demand, but not to fund through Medicare its more capricious forms, such as abortion for sex selection. This legalization teaches that abortion on demand is moral, though it does not yet reward it as a fundable entitlement in *all* cases.

(iv) To legalize and decriminalize abortion on demand and to fund even its most capricious forms, such as abortion for sex selection. This funding enshrines abortion on demand as more than moral: as a right and entitlement in any and every case. (The Bill put forth by Senator Madigan in the Federal Senate challenged this.)

(v) To do all the above in (iv), and *in addition to punish* those who, out of conscience, do not wish to facilitate abortion undertaken on such unwarranted grounds. This has now happened with proceedings being undertaken against Dr Mark Hobart, who refused to refer a couple for an abortion because they did not want the sex of the baby.

It seems incredible that we have come so far away from the moral position in the ethical tradition of our society to its absolute antithesis, punishing those who wish to adhere to the position, which religious tradition has taught as moral.

Government must create moral, social and cultural conditions which strive to effect that children are conceived by, and born to, mature and committed couples. By servicing — with abortion on demand — a trend which runs against this ideal, Government in fact fortifies and fosters the culture which produces "unwanted pregnancy". By punishing those who object to abortion on demand, Government is participating in a repression of traditional values and the active degradation of the value of life.

Charters and overseas judgments supporting conscience

Australia is a signatory to the International Covenant on Civil and Political Rights (ICCPR). Article 18 (1) of the ICCPR states: "Everyone shall have the right to freedom of thought, conscience and religion. This right shall include freedom to have or to adopt a religion or belief of his choice, and freedom, either individually or in community with others and in public or private to manifest his religion or belief in worship, observance, practice and teaching". Article 18(2) states: "No one shall be subject to coercion which would impair his freedom to have or to adopt a religion or belief of his choice".

Ostensibly, this is relevant, in our discussion of section 8 of the Victorian Abortion Law Reform Act of 2008, to a doctor's refusal in a non-life threatening case to carry out or refer for an abortion which his religious beliefs regard as immoral. The Victorian Charter of Rights and Responsibilities includes in its article 14(2) the provision that "A person must not be coerced or restrained in a way that limits his or her freedom to have or adopt a religion or belief in worship, observance, practice or teaching". The rub in the Victorian Charter is its section 48, which makes as an exception to all human rights set out in the charter those associated with abortion: "Nothing in this Charter affects any law applicable to abortion or child destruction".

The difference between the impact on the Victorian Abortion Law Reform Act by the Victorian Charter and the ICCPR is that the Victorian Charter in section 31 provides for its being overridden in whole or part by other acts of Parliament. It is a guide but itself a piece of legislation which can be supplanted by the Victorian Parliament, including its strange removal of abortion from all consideration and application of rights and responsibilities.

The ICCPR, on the other hand, is an international enactment to which the Commonwealth of Australia has given recognition and it appears as Schedule 2 of the Australian Human Rights Commission Act (Cth) 1986.

The European Convention on Human Rights in article 9(2) provides similarly for freedom of conscience and religious practice. Whilst Australia is not a party to that convention, its similarity to the ICCPR's provision, makes it instructive for us. In various bills put before the English Parliament to permit "Physician assisted dying" for the terminally ill, recognition was made — in accordance with that article of the European Convention on Human Rights — that conscientious objection must extend to any aspect of participation in the process in which a doctor is involved: whether it be commission of the termination of life or referral to another to do this. The conclusion of the English Parliament's Joint Committee on Human Rights was

> ...that imposing such a duty [of referral] on a physician who invokes the right to conscientiously object is an interference with that physician's right to freedom of conscience under the first sentence of of Article 9(1) [of the European Convention on Human Rights], because it requires the physician to participate in a process to which he or she has a conscientious objection. That right is absolute: interferences with it are not capable of justification under Article 9(2).[85]

There seems to be a reasonable analogy between referral for euthanasia and referral for abortion. Both have to do with the termination of life, and because of this the roles of principal and accessory are both stringent (as we find in general the law penalizes in the realm of killing, both intentional murder and unintentional manslaughter as well as both direct and indirect causation of death). In other words, any kind of participation — performance of the termination or participation in the process leading to termination — in abortion are all regarded as areas of possible infringement of conscience.

---

[85] Quoted in Mark Campbell, "Conscientious objection, health care and Article 9 of the European Convention on Human Rights", *Medical Law International* 11 (4), p. 300, fn. 66.

In April 2013, the Court of Session in Glasgow Scotland upheld the appeal of two midwives working in a hospital who argued that "that their right to conscientious objection should extend to refusing to delegate, supervise or support staff looking after women undergoing terminations". The court ruling in the words of one of the judges was that "In our view the right of conscientious objection extends not only to the actual medical or surgical termination but to the whole process of treatment given for that purpose."[86] The judgment was made in accordance with Article 9 in the European Convention on Human Rights, analogous to the ICCPR Article 18, to which Australia is party. Here again we find that all aspects of a medical process, which conflict with conscience, are reasonably considered as infringements on freedom of conscience and religion. So, too, should be referral for abortion.

Conclusion

Abortion *on demand* up to 16 weeks, which the present Tasmanian Bill supports, runs against the beliefs of the religious traditions, to which many doctors, medical ancilliary staff and counsellors adhere. Its contravention of these standards, finds its epitome in the concept of an abortion carried out simply because the parents prefer a boy to a girl or vice versa, and this has revolted public sentiment. It deeply disturbs the conscience of those who experience the religious roots of civilization. Yet the Victorian law and the Tasmanian Bill permit and enforce abortion on demand with a repression of freedoms of conscience and assembly unheard-of in today's world (in advanced democratic societies).

The Victorian Parliament which broke a path for this development in Australia should rescind the clause denying doctors freedom of conscience by forcing them to refer for abortion in non-life-threatening circumstances. The Parliament of Tasmania, which

---

[86] *Doogan & Anor v NHS Greater Glasgow & Clyde Health Board* [2013] ScotCS CSIH 36 **at [37] per the Court (**Lord Mackay of Drumadoon, Lady Dorrian and Lord McEwan).

took the Victorian Act as its model, should strike down the provisions for the coercion of conscience which its Bill contains.

Put in a positive light, it would be a great merit for the Tasmanian Parliament to remove the anti-conscience and anti-assembly clauses of the Bill, just as it would be for the Victorian Government to rescind the anti-conscience clause in its Act. The rescinding of this clause should not be a matter for a conscience vote: *there cannot be a conscience vote as to whether there should be conscience.* The Tasmanian Parliament should never allow this coercion to take hold by enacting such a piece of legislation. Thereby these Parliaments would kindle a first, small light to dispel the gathering darkness in this domain of Western society.

The Consequences and Cost of Moral Capitulation: the Failure to Amend the Victorian Abortion Reform Law

The irrationality of the fear

The inside information is that Dr Napthine acquired the leadership of the Liberal Party and became Premier of Victoria after the resignation of the previous leader, Mr Baillieu, on the undertaking that he would not introduce reform of clause 8(1)[87] of the Victorian Abortion Reform Law during the remainder of the term. This, however, was understood not to preclude him from being open to a private member's bill to change the law (which he himself, consistent with his views, would have supported). He stated that the Government would consider a private member's bill on its merits. Now, as we approach an election year 2014, comes the sudden and disturbing statement in his video of 3 December 2013 that the Government would not entertain any legislation which would limit a woman's "choice". What was the issue he had in mind? Precisely the one that was seething beneath the surface: a doctor's freedom not to participate by referral in an abortion to which he or she had a moral objection. This supposed "obstacle" to "choice" was the one to which the Premier was clearly referring

---

[87] Forcing doctors with a conscientious objection to an abortion to refer to another doctor known to have no objection, as set out in the previous essay.

when he said that the Government would entertain no revision of legislation on the abortion limiting "a woman's choice".

With this he not only overturned the reportedly unopposed resolution of the Victorian Liberal Party Conference to amend the law and provide freedom of conscience. The Premier also went against his own conscience. His predecessors, Mr John Brumby and Mr Ted Baillieu themselves had no personal sense of the wrong involved in forcing doctors to be complicit in abortions to which they rightly had moral objections. In a "free" cross-party vote, they both voted for the legislation, as it presently stands. Dr Denis Napthine, however, who opposed the bill generally, did understand the particular evil involved in this clause, and in the Parliamentary record, *Hansard*, one can read the words with which he described it: "wrong" and "repugnant". Notwithstanding his grasp of this evil, he has now chosen to act against his own conscience and the conscience of his party and to close freedom of conscience in this matter in Victoria. He has now with his new blanket statement ostensibly ruled out amendment of this clause should he be granted another term of office.

The fear which appears to have driven him to go against own conscience and that of his party is irrational. The extremity of the fear of losing office at the next election has brought him to a position *more radical* than that of the mainstream Press, which — unlike him — actually supported the regime of abortion on demand introduced by the 2008 Victorian Abortion Law. *The Age* during the debates on the Abortion Bill in its Editorial on 24 September 2008 opposed the cancellation of conscience in this legislation. In its words:

> And there's the rub. It is not necessary to coerce conscience in this way in order to decriminalize abortion. Indeed, such coercion may make the goal harder to achieve, because of the deep divisions in the community over abortion. Some argue that to remove the clause from the bill would deny the right of patients to full information, but information about pregnancy termination services is already widely available, and its availability will not diminish when abortion is decriminalized.

What would diminish, though, is the respect in which the rights of conscience have hitherto been held — a respect that is an integral part of a flourishing liberal democracy.

Five years later, in the heat of continuous and climaxing argument about the (anti-) conscience clause of the Abortion law, *The Age*, in its 9 November 2013 Editorial, *continued* to oppose clause 8(1):

> [At the time of the decriminalization of Abortion] the AMA [Australian Medical Association] shared the Catholic Church's concern that the legislation went too far by requiring a medical practitioner who has a conscientious objection to abortion to provide a referral to another health professional who does not have such an objection. As *The Age* argued, the law to that point had not forced doctors to provide a service they believe to be unethical or immoral and it was not necessary to require conscientious objectors to assist in obtaining an abortion in order to decriminalize the practice. A pro-life doctor is now the subject of a Medical Board of Victoria investigation for refusing to provide a referral. This should never have been required of him. The right to act on conscience is central to a free society and the law would be improved by repealing section 8.

Support now lent to the most irrational arguments

Dr Napthine's capitulation to fear of the spectre of extreme abortion advocacy promotes the most irrational elements in the debate over conscience. *The Age* which, as quoted above, itself editorialized against abortion ran several articles by those who wish to preserve the present regime. One of these reiterated the strange rhetoric of "reproductive rights", which means a purported right of a woman to have a foetus destroyed under any circumstances and for any or no reason *and* to force any medical practitioner or medical staff to be instrumental, whether as principal or accessory, to this act.

The same article wanted to make the anti-conscience clause an issue of "class war" between men and women over abortion. The assumption is: "men are against abortion, women are for it". This statement is absolutely false as a matter of fact: one will note leading critics of abortion laws who are women, and protagonists of the current abortion laws, who are men. By capitulating to the clamour from this extreme abortion advocacy groups (which the mainstream press discounts) the Premier only gave credibility to a false and inflammatory rhetoric in the abortion debate. His statement bolsters a hysteria and gives credence to the most irrational elements in the abortion debate.

Sanctioning the compulsion of abhorrent conduct

A Government which maintains an injustice is as culpable as the Government which allowed it to be instituted. Clause 8(1) of the Abortion Law, to repeat, compels a doctor with a conscientious objection to a particular abortion, where the mother's life is not at risk, to be complicit in that abortion by referring the client to a doctor who is known to be willing to perform the abortion. A case has come up which shows exactly what this clause means. Under this legislation, Dr Mark Hobart faces possible deregistration as a doctor because he refused to refer a couple for an abortion, which they sought because they did not want a girl.

There is a simple ethical principle that one should not force a person to participate in an abhorrent deed (even if the law does not punish such a deed). Dr Hobart was revolted at the idea of being complicit in the abortion of an unborn girl simply because she was a girl. His sentiment was a right sentiment, consistent with the basic values of our civilization. Under the Victorian Abortion Law, an abortion carried out for this reason is not criminal. But it is bad. No doctor should be punished for refusing to follow uncivilized conduct like this: to be instrumental to an abortion of a girl because she is a girl.

Indeed, the *Medical Observer*, a journal of Australian doctors, on 11 November 2013 reported that "82.6% of 500 respondents to an *MO* online poll agreed with Dr Hobart's decision to act on his conscience. Just 12.6% disagreed and 4.8% were unsure".

Depriving others of a good when you don't need to

The second ethical principle is that one should not withhold a good from another person, where one lacks nothing by letting that other person have it. Were one deliberately to park over two parking spaces where one does not need the second spot, in order to prevent another from taking it, one would be transgressing that principle. Putting this positively, if I do not need that second spot, I should let you have it and not to let you have it is perverse or worse. This principle is also violated by the conscience clause 8(1) of the Victorian Abortion Reform Law, as follows.

Under the decriminalization of abortion established by the Abortion law, anyone with a mobile phone or computer can "Google" a doctor or clinic which will perform the abortion. Why then must a particular doctor, with a moral objection to that abortion, be compelled to be instrumental to it with a referral? The individual seeking an abortion does not lose out on the abortion, and yet under this law the other is forbidden the immense good of living by *his or her* conscience.

These ethical principles are about preventing wrongful compulsion and deprivation: compulsion to act against good moral instincts and the deprivation of the freedoms of others by those who anyway have what they want. When society weighs in with sanctions — as it does with section 8(1) of the Victorian Abortion Law Reform Act — against these ethical principles, it turns not only against the values of civilization but also against democracy. As noted, *The Age* said this at the time this bill was being debated, when it editorialized that this clause would "diminish...the respect in which the rights of conscience have hitherto been held — a respect that is an integral part of a flourishing liberal democracy". One does not have to be religious to sense a deep injustice and inversion of compassion, as well as a danger to democracy, in the law which has put Dr Hobart in his predicament. For the sake of our society and democracy the (anti-)conscience clause of this law must be repealed.

The political costs for the coming election

Archbishop Hart has already raised his voice against this tyranny against conscience and its corruption of human moral fibre. In a previous communication to the Parliament I relayed messages from both the Rabbinic Council of Victoria and the Board of Imams Victoria stating how the anti-conscience clause 8(1) forces believing Jews and Muslims to act against their consciences and faith on pain of punishment.

Dr Napthine will not win another term for his Government[88] by trampling the beliefs of the Abrahamic religions, Judaism, Christianity and Islam, which have formed society, and particularly by forcing their adherents to act against them; or for that matter the democratic significance of freedom of conscience. 82% of doctors believe that he is wrong. With his video of 3 December he has now stated what a victory for the Coalition in the coming elections would signify: another four-year term of repression of human conscience.

The very fibre of our society is at stake in this issue. Australia is one of the most civilized nations on earth. It upholds a strong ideal of justice and compassion in its social welfare. In its good management of these it is an example to the world. There is something also about the character of Australians which is exemplary: our mateship ethos indicates a real sense of social solidarity and caring. In many areas we are a flagship of civilized and democratic values. But by this very standard of our society, it is important that we make sure that we pass an essential test for civilization and democracy in the rectification of the conscience clause 8(1) in the Victorian Abortion Law Reform Act. It should be done before the summer recess of the Parliament.

The Premier said he wants to put aside this issue and get on with delivering material "infrastructure". The essential infrastructure of a society is the value-set by which it stands and lives. Totalitarian and cruel regimes have delivered material infrastructure very well. What are roads and trains for? What kind of a life will people

---

[88] In fact, Dr Napthine's Government lost the election.

live who travel in trains and ride on roads in a penal colony of human conscience? Is this infrastructure for the smooth activity of morally anaesthetized drones who live within imprisonment of the human spirit?

Every member of Parliament must ask him- or herself, when they supposedly "risk" their seat pre-selection and political careers for matters of principle, and in particular for the repeal of this iniquitous anti-conscience clause: "Why am I in Parliament? Why should my party rule?" Public representation and Government are not and cannot be goals in themselves, especially if their legacy is complicity with a law for which the Premier himself has spoken the epitaph: "wrong" and "repugnant".

Psychotherapy and Religious Freedom: The Trial of JONAH[89]

The original case

Around the world a movement has arisen to seek by political and legal means to prohibit therapy for those seeking help from unwanted same-sex attraction (and now also gender dysphoria), or who seek it for their children. It is portrayed as not only impossible but harmful. This is a mantra repeated vociferously by politicians and media, who have no critical understanding of psychology or the actual data. More disturbingly, it is repeated by professional psychological and psychiatric associations, which *do* have access to the data. The "Report of the American Psychological Association Task Force on Appropriate Therapeutic Responses to Sexual Orientation" (2009) was prepared by a committee of seven psychologists. I am informed[90] that politics went into the composition of this committee: of the seven members, six were homosexuals and therapists and one was a heterosexual but gay-affirming therapist — hardly a scientifically balanced panel. Notwithstanding this, the conclusion of the Report, concerning

---

[89] The first part of this essay "The JONAH Trial" is reproduced from S.D. Cowen, *Homosexuality, Marriage and Society*, Redland Bay: Connor Court 2016, pp. 68 -70. "The sequel to the Jonah Trial" is the text of a talk held in the United States in 2019.

[90] By Dr David Pickup, one psychologist who sought to be included in the committee.

purported harm arising from reparative therapy, was as follows:

> There are no rigorously scientific studies of recent SOCE that would enable us to make a definitive statement about whether recent SOCE is safe or harmful and for whom.[91]

Nevertheless, the twin political (non-scientific) statements of professional psychological associations — (a) that homosexuality is a "normal" variant of sexuality and (b) that it is unethical to treat it — have formed the basis for legal and political persecution of homosexuals and parents wanting, and therapists willing to facilitate, change. Two examples are the JONAH trial verdict in the USA in 2015 and the Health Complaints Act passed by the Parliament of Victoria, Australia, in 2016.[92] The latter is the seed of the new proposed legislation by the Government of Victoria to criminalize the provision of therapy, by those seeking it, whether for gender dysphoria or unwanted same-sex attraction.

The JONAH trial

A Jewish organization, set up to assist Jews seeking help with unwanted same-sex attraction (JONAH — "Jews Offering New Alternatives for Healing"), was fined and ordered to close down by a New Jersey Court in 2015 on the grounds of "consumer fraud". The case was brought against JONAH by a "gay activist" organization, The Southern Poverty Law Centre, which found disgruntled individuals willing to be its plaintiffs. The charge was consumer fraud, namely that JONAH could not deliver what it offered, namely help to those seeking change with their unwanted same-sex attraction. The turning point of the case was the Judge's acceptance of the plaintiff's argument that JONAH's expert witnesses, licensed therapists, who were ready to testify about their success in helping individuals alter their homosexuality,

---

[91] Page 83 of the Report.
[92] And now the most egregious example of this policy is the Victorian Change or Suppression (Conversion) Practices Prohibition Act 2021, described above in Chapter 1 in the essay "The Repression of Religious Freedom in Australia". It is arguably the most punitive expression of this policy in the world.

should be barred from testifying. The Judge excluded the expert testimony *a priori* and out of hand on the basis of the cited pronouncements of the American Psychiatric and Psychological Associations that homosexuality was a "normal" variety of human sexuality and that therapy should not be undertaken to modify it. A case which was being heard on "consumer fraud", that the therapy did not work, would not hear testimony that it had worked. Early in the trial, Nicholas A. Cummings, a former President of the American Psychological Association (who himself had supported the declassification of homosexuality as an illness) made this statement:

> The Southern Poverty Law Center has done amazing service for our nation in fighting prejudice. But it has gone astray in its recent New Jersey lawsuit charging JONAH, formerly Jews Offering New Alternatives for Healing, a group that offers to help gay people change their orientation, with committing consumer fraud. The sweeping allegation that such treatment must be a fraud because homosexual orientation can't be changed is damaging. The lawsuit is the opening salvo of a wave of activism intended to discredit therapy offered in 70 clinics across 20 states, according to the SPLC.
>
> When I was chief psychologist for Kaiser Permanente from 1959 to 1979, San Francisco's gay and lesbian population burgeoned. I personally saw more than 2,000 patients with same-sex attraction, and my staff saw thousands more. We worked hard to develop approaches to meeting the needs of these patients....Of the patients I oversaw who sought to change their orientation, hundreds were successful.
>
> I believe that our rate of success with reorientation was relatively high because we were selective in recommending therapeutic change efforts only to those who identified themselves as highly motivated and were clinically assessed as having a high probability of success.
>
> Since then, the role of psychotherapy in sexual orientation change efforts has been politicized. Gay and lesbian rights activists appear to be convincing the public that homosexuality is one identical inherited characteristic. To my dismay, some in the organized mental health community seem to agree, including the American Psychological Association, though I don't believe that view is supported by scientific evidence.

>...[C]ontending that all same-sex attraction is immutable is a distortion of reality. Attempting to characterize all sexual reorientation therapy as "unethical" violates patient choice and gives an outside party a veto over patients' goals for their own treatment. A political agenda shouldn't prevent gays and lesbians who desire to change from making their own decisions.
>
> Whatever the situation at an individual clinic, accusing professionals from across the country who provide treatment for fully informed persons seeking to change their sexual orientation of perpetrating a fraud serves only to stigmatize the professional and shame the patient.[93]

In purely professional terms, this was a closure of patient autonomy — a wrongdoing. On a broader scale, it was not only a wrongdoing, but a punishment for what many people, according to their faiths, was doing right.

The sequel to the JONAH trial

The situation in which Arthur Goldberg and his colleagues find themselves today — as a consequence of two successive court rulings — in my view constitutes one of the greatest and most insidious infringements of religious freedom of which I have ever heard or could imagine. Because of his situation, for reasons I would like to set forth, I believe it is not only our duty to act but it is also a tremendous merit for us to act affirmatively in regard to it. Major dangers to humanity and society are uniquely encapsulated in his case. I therefore implore you to recognize that we can make a difference. If his case can be publicly rectified, we may achieve something of far-reaching importance.

My argument links both universal ethics and religious freedom with Goldberg's case. The significance of universal ethics from a religious standpoint is that the human soul is fitted to "imitate G-d". What this means is that the human soul is capable of resonating with Divine attributes: with G-d's manifestations of

---

[93] Nicholas A. Cummings, "Southern Poverty Law Center wrongly fighting against patients' right to choose". *USA Today*, July 30, 2013.

love, judgment, mercy and so forth. Practically speaking, the imitation of these attributes or qualities translates into laws which G-d revealed to humanity. These commandments are set out in what are known as the Noahide laws, the common denominator and shared core of the great world faiths. These laws are known to the soul; they are the content of human conscience, opened to G-d. One of these laws relates to Divinely lawful forms of sexual conduct. Specifically, the Divine law, given at Sinai, enjoins only the heterosexual union of man and woman, and prohibits homosexual unions.

The problem is that, in addition to a soul made in the image of G-d, one which resonates with the Divine law, the human being also has physical and psychic selves, which often project desires and perceptions contrary to the norms of moral conduct known by the soul. Accordingly, *the most fundamental freedom of the human being is the ability to engage the soul or conscience in struggle with these physical desires and perceptions and to check, or if possible, to transform them in accordance with the Divine dictates of the soul.* This energy actualizes the freedom to live the life of conscience or religious belief. This freedom is an integral aspect of freedom of religion, which is protected by the First Amendment of the US constitution.

The original case made against Arthur Goldberg and his associates concerned the organization he established to assist Jewish (and any other persons) in their struggle with unwanted same-sex attraction. JONAH was set up to enable those who wanted to live their life in accordance with their religious beliefs. Such beliefs often clashed with or were impeded by contrary impulses and perceptions. As related above, an activist law group called the "Southern Poverty Law Centre" (SPLC) sued JONAH, Goldberg and others under a law relating to consumer fraud of the State of New Jersey. The SPLC argued that the therapies offered under JONAH's auspices or referred by them to independent counsellors were like a faulty second-hand car: that they did not and could not work; in short that JONAH and Goldberg were involved in a form of fraudulent commerce. The SPLC won their case and shut JONAH down. It was the first case to ever apply this law to a duly constituted not for profit organization, a holding that particularly runs contrary to the concept of consumer fraud since Goldberg and his co-director worked for 15 years without ever receiving any personal compensation.

By comparing therapy for unwanted same-sex attraction to fraudulent commerce, like selling bad second-hand cars, the SPLC were able to repress what was, in fact, the pursuit of religious freedom — the freedom to struggle with oneself (with the help of a therapist and/or clergy) in order to keep G-d's laws. But in order to this, the SPLC themselves had to carry out a fraud. The alleged fraud perceived by the judge and jury was that the alteration, management or transformation of unwanted same-sex attraction was impossible. In other words, this was like a second-hand car that had the mileage on its odometer changed.

The plaintiffs persuaded the judge with a statement from the American Psychiatric Association, which had itself been manipulated as a result of an internal political struggle, that homosexuality was a normal form of human sexuality. On this basis, as mentioned, the judge barred JONAH's expert witnesses, which included licensed therapists, from presenting their personal experiences of successes in therapy for unwanted same-sex attraction. In fact, the judge in the initial 2015 case was so against the idea that change of sexual orientation was possible that he chose to compare the experts he barred from testifying to those who believed the earth was flat. The therapy was never examined, to see whether it worked or not, but still the so-called "fraud" was proclaimed. So, in my view, not only was a religious right violated through the banning of therapy, but this "finding" was also supported by a suppression of facts and a refusal to consider the evidence. It is up to the legal experts to investigate whether this violated proper judicial due process.

After the first court ruling shut down JONAH and ordered that it desist from all therapy or promotion of commerce in this therapy, the SPLC got permission to access 70,000 of Arthur Goldberg's emails to examine whether his newly formed Jewish Institute for

Global Awareness (JIFGA), a totally different organization with an entirely different mission statement was defying the court order by continuing to carry out the work of JONAH. Indeed, they found that Arthur Goldberg, as co-director, had referred a patient to a therapist in another state, and that this therapist had paid a commission to the organization for the referral. Under the "cure provisions" of the 2015 decision, Goldberg cured this by refunding the monies received for that referral.

But the new judgement — on the claimed breach of the first court ruling — went far beyond this to indict Arthur Goldberg's continued support for therapy for unwanted same-sex attraction even though he neither provided nor organized the therapy itself. The plaintiff found in Goldberg's emails that he had spoken in favour of the therapy, and that he had attended a weekend gathering of like-minded persons. In other words, even though Goldberg was not dealing in the therapy, which the court had deemed a forbidden activity, he was found to have spoken in favour of it and to have associated with others who believed in it. All of this was cited for the major penalty which the Court imposed in its new 2019 ruling. In this, it seems to me that the new court ruling went beyond its initial abridgment of religious freedom to provide and undergo the therapy by creating two additional abridgments of freedom: the right of Goldberg *to speak* about his beliefs (the therapy itself) a right also protected by the First Amendment, and Arthur's right *to associate* with others with similar beliefs. The latter right of association is not explicitly included within the First Amendment but has been upheld by the Supreme Court as a constitutional right.[94] Whilst the court's second ruling, on Goldberg's supposed breach of the first ruling, grappled with the issue that Goldberg's promotion of the therapy through his speech and association had primarily occurred outside New Jersey with its consumer fraud law, it concluded that

---

[94] As stated by Justice John Marshall Harlan II in majority decision of the Supreme Court in *NAACP v. Alabama* (1958), "It is beyond debate that freedom to engage in association for the advancement of beliefs and ideas is an inseparable aspect of the 'liberty' assured by the Due Process Clause of the Fourteenth Amendment, which embraces freedom of speech."

"Nevertheless, Goldberg's location is irrelevant because he is restrained from partaking in any activity that promotes conversion therapy, no matter where it is located". In plain words, there was no venue anywhere and no moment in time that Arthur Goldberg could be free to speak about, or associate with others to discuss, the religious right to live in accordance with conscience though therapy for unwanted same-sex attraction.

The new ruling which was excessive, disproportionate, and punitive compelled him to pay more than $3 million dollars of the plaintiff's legal expenses and closed down his new organization (JIFGA) which dealt with universal ethics and morality. In addition, the new ruling forbade him and his associate from holding office in a New Jersey not-for-profit organization ever again. If I may say so, as an observer from overseas, these two rulings — which pursued and relentlessly punished the provision and "promotion" of therapy for unwanted same-sex attraction as constituting an act of consumer fraud — actually deprive citizens of the United States of their constitutional rights to pursue their religious beliefs, to speak of them and to associate with others who share these beliefs.

The refusal to consider hard evidence of the successes of therapy for unwanted same-sex attraction allowed the perpetuation of the lie that all such therapy is a "fraud". The scientific fraud was on the other side.

The putative mission of the Southern Poverty Law Center to crush the beliefs embodied by JONAH has a systemic relationship to a view of the human being held by the SPLC. Instead of seeing the human being as a body and a psyche that incorporates a soul or conscience which must often struggle with impulse and perception, the SPLC and their allies see the human being as *only* body and psyche. The person, in their view, is condemned to act out impulse and perception. Struggle is neither desirable nor possible. This deeply deterministic and unfree view of the person is replicated in the authoritarian, coercive and punitive measures which they seek to accomplish through political and judicial means. Or, alternatively, this deterministic, constrained model of the person is promoted for the simple motive that no one should be able to call the indulgence of certain behaviours immoral since they "cannot be helped". They are like "skin colour" which cannot be behaviourally changed. The comparison is false: at Sinai, G-d did not command us to have a particular skin colour. He did, however, command us to contain certain sexual impulses and He does not command us in things that we cannot do. Where there is an ethical imperative, we have the freedom ultimately not to transgress it.

Just recently a therapist in New York, Dov Schwarz, mounted a challenge to a ban which the New York City Council had placed on such therapy even for adults. In the face of this challenge, the Council quickly took instructions from LGBT activists to repeal the act. They had good reason to suspect a Supreme Court ruling would overturn the ban on First Amendment grounds and they were afraid of the national ramifications from such a ruling[95]. The NYC ban was more radical than other state therapy bans which focused on children. Interestingly, however, the New Jersey case accomplished exactly that result. It bans responsible adults from engaging in therapy. But while the radical NY ban had plenty to be afraid of from a Supreme Court challenge, the New Jersey court ruling, which achieved practically the same thing, slipped under the radar. It could do this by interpreting the provision of therapy for unwanted same-sex attraction as a "consumer fraud". This was accomplished without presentation or scrutiny of evidence; as "consumer fraud," the rulings hide a wide range of constitutional rights and suppress basic human freedoms.

What is so insidious about violation of this particular freedom is that it chains religious freedom, not from without, but from *within*: to prevent the prisoner of one's own psyche from actualizing his or her own freedom and spiritual identity.

---

[95] More recently, the NY City Council came to a settlement whereby it agreed to pay US$100,000 in attorney's fees and other expenses to the Alliance Defending Freedom, which represented Dov Schwartz (reported in www.christian.post July 15, 2020).

Access to Therapy and Religious Freedom

From a Submission to the Australian Parliament on the Requirements of a Religious Freedom Bill with Professor John Whitehall

...The protection of religious freedom in Australia requires another override of actual or potential state legislation which would limit the access of patients to psychological services, which they require in pursuit of their religious beliefs.

Presently the Governments of Victoria and Queensland are preparing bills to criminalize the provision of psychological services to individuals who seek to overcome unwanted same-sex attraction in order to lead a heterosexual lifestyle; similarly, it will criminalize the provision of psychological services to those who want to allay experienced gender dysphoria and stay comfortably within their biological gender.

Why is the attempt to block patient access to these services a violation of religious freedom?

A basic tenet of religious belief is that the human being is not just a physical being, but also has a soul or conscience. This belief requires the human being to struggle if need be with impulses and perceptions, which, when actualized in conduct, are contrary to the values of conscience and belief. Religious belief further states that the human being is both free to modify his or her behaviour and obligated to do so. If a person, for example, has a psychological problem with kleptomania (an impulse to steal), the human is bound by conscience to struggle with that impulse, and to observe the precept upheld by religion, not to steal. If a person has difficulty in mastering that impulse, it is incumbent upon him or her to access counselling and psychological help to overcome that impulse.

Traditional Jews, Christians and Muslims, to name some faiths, do not believe homosexual or adulterous practices to be moral, and are bound by their faiths to overcome homosexual and adulterous impulses from materializing in practice. Their foundational texts point to the sanctity of heterosexual marriage. These faiths do not accept the ideology of gender fluidity in which there are no such binary entities as males and females, and that gender identity can be a changeable locus on a spectrum in between those poles. These faiths would promote the stability of gender identity in accordance with chromosomal directive and would encourage psychological support for the confused. In order to live with their faiths, they need psychological help to overcome gender dysphoria.

The political movements which have sought criminalize the access to psychological help, in cases such as these, reject these religious principles. They do not validate the conscience of religious people. They do not believe that the human being is free, or permitted, to struggle with impulses and perceptions at variance with conscience. They believe only in the dictation of impulse and perception, not the sovereignty of conscience and the right to struggle with impulse.

For them, all change can be a "one-way street" only. Thus, they will allow minors, without parental consent, to take puberty blockers and commence transitioning, but they will not allow minors to undergo counselling back to their biological gender. They will encourage children through school programs such as the "Safe-Schools", away from parental supervision, to embrace the ideology of gender fluidity, but they will prohibit any counselling to lead them back to a stable identity that accords with their chromosomes.

It is mooted also by such legislation to deny this autonomy of choice even to adults. They can get help to transition to another gender, but not to return to their biological gender; they can go to a "gay-affirming" psychologist, but may not go to a therapist who will help them with their desire to return to a heterosexuality.

Such legislation discriminates against those who believe, as do traditional Jews, Christians and Muslims, that it is conscience which is sovereign in the person, and that the person is both able and obligated to live in accordance with conscience.

The legislative criminalization of the provision of therapy, and hence of access to therapy, is an outright restriction of the religious freedom to live one's religion. In fact, it is a denial of the deepest religious freedom: to be able to live inwardly — psychologically and behaviourally — with oneself, according to conscience.

The ruse of "quackery"

The severe restriction of religious freedom in legislative plans to criminalize the above provision of psychological services to persons is hidden by the blanket denunciation of all such therapies as "quackery". This, however, intentionally suppresses the evidence of many successful such therapies, and the absence of evidence that all such therapies are harmful. The American Psychological Association has acknowledged this lack of evidence in its special Task Force Report on Sexual Orientation Change Efforts in 2009.

In respect of "quackery", the movements, which seek to criminalize therapies for the return to heterosexuality and affirmation of one's own biological gender, themselves espouse a host of techniques to which the very same charge can be made: "puberty blockers", irreversible sterilization and physical sex-reassignment — which have been associated either with serious side effects or a very high levels of morbidity (suicide) by those who have transitioned.

In other words, no scrutiny to detect medically and psychologically *sound* techniques has been allowed for those who wish to return. And no scrutiny to detect medically and psychological *unsound* techniques has been allowed for those who wish to leave.

Parliaments cannot legislate on how to remove tonsils. It is not for a Parliament to decide which therapies are medically and psychologically sound and which are not. Nor is it the role of a politically appointed "Health Complaints Commissioner" to do so. That is the role of an independent medical and psychological board, which dispassionately considers all evidence and determines what practices are "quackery" and what are not, in a case-by-case, therapy-by-therapy examination. Whilst Parliaments cannot assume medical or psychological expertise, they can make sure that the medical and psychological boards, which do make that examination, contain members of all persuasions, and that free and open enquiry is conducted in such boards (see Part 3, Division 2, section 16, of the draft legislation which requires that there be no religious discrimination in the conduct of qualifying bodies).

In conclusion

The Bill needs to establish a criterion for legislation that protects the religious freedom of patients to access therapies which enable them to live in accordance with their religious beliefs. What is "quackery" will be determined not by demagogy in the media or in Parliament, but by free and open, independent medical boards. Parliaments are, however, required not to deny the free exercise of religion, guaranteed by the Constitution, to which patient access to therapy is integral.

Chapter 8

Sexuality and Human Identity

In the sights of universal ethics, the human being acquires existence, purpose and identity through the family. The human being is born from, and nurtured and educated by, a mother and father and in turn goes on to unite in marriage with a spouse of the opposite sex to create new persons – their offspring – who extend their parents' ethical agencies in the world. The norm of marriage – and the family which it creates – set out by universal ethics, is the defining source of various dimensions of personal identity: the regulation of personal sexuality, the identities and relationships of male and female, husband and wife, mother, father and child.

This norm of marriage and the family serves first to define and direct sexuality for the individual as having its place in traditional marriage. This is important for the moral sexual education of the child and young adult. Without the regulative direction of human sexuality (and especially if it is actively deregulated as in much contemporary "gender-fluid" educational practice) it becomes, in the phrase of Sigmund Freud, "polymorphously perverse" – fluidly capable of any form, self-image, attraction and liaison. Secondly, in marriage itself as the legally and financially committed sexual bond of husband and wife, relations of identity, responsibility and security are accorded to the biological parent-child relationship. Finally, marriage as a biological reproductive union with its offspring, clarifies the identities of its parties as "male" and "female" (husband and wife, father and mother, son and daughter).

The pieces in this chapter relate to the progressive dismantling of traditional marriage as the normative goal and context of human sexuality, and with it the unravelling of the dimensions of human identity. The first piece, a conversation with Professor Patrick Parkinson, "Changes in Family law before Same-sex Marriage", continues themes treated in Politics and Universal Ethics concerning the first stage of the legislative dismantlement of traditional marriage. Marriage, then still understood as a heterosexual union, was impacted by new "relationships" legislation and the extension of reproductive technologies to unmarried couples and single individuals. The effect of this legislation was to weaken the normative framework provided in traditional marriage for the family as a whole – for father, mother and children. The second piece, "Heterosexuality and Human Identity", examines the second stage of the dismantlement of the traditional norm of marriage – "same-sex marriage" or the legislative overthrow of the normativity of heterosexual marriage – with its consequences for the identities of "parent" and "child". The third piece, "Transgenderism and the Dissolution of Identity", examines the third stage of the dismantlement of the traditional norm of marriage as form and context of human sexuality. With transgenderism occurs the final dissolution of human identity through deconstruction of the identities of "male" and "female". It completes the return of human sexuality to the primary formlessness and fluidity – the "polymorphous perversity" – of the child prior to any individual moral sexual education; and seeks to cultivate this fluidity as a model both for child "development" and for society at large.

Changes in Family Law before Same-sex Marriage
A discussion with Professor Patrick Parkinson

Shimon Cowen: In modern tims we have become accustomed to the modern, formal and legal act of marriage, which may be religious or in a secular mode. Nevertheless, it was once upon a time preceded by a common law notion of marriage, which was established essentially through some sort of stable cohabitation of woman and man; this is what we call nowadays de facto unions. At the same time, modern legislation has acted to give de facto unions the character of marriage.[96] *Would you care to comment on this?*

Patrick Parkinson: If you go back through the first millennium of the Common Era through to about the 1100's, 1200's, 1300's marriage was simply man and woman living together with the intention of it being a permanent arrangement. There may well have been local customs which surrounded and signified this intention. For example, in Wales, even as late as the late 1900's, there was a custom to put a broomstick in front of the doorway and the bride and groom would jump over to get into the house and once they had done that, they were married.

Notwithstanding such customs, basically it was a private arrangement: a man and a woman would decide to move in together and live together. Yet by about the twelfth century, problematic consequences of that became recognized in terms of law — that is, in terms of inheritance rights. The church became aware of the need to know if a couple was in fact married. They determined that a witness would be needed, and who better than the local priest? So, it was in Christian Europe — the practice became that people would be married outside the church in the presence of a priest. Why outside the church? Because in a typical English or German village, the church was the centre of the village. Everyone could see that you were getting married if you did it outside the door of the church and if any questions arose the Priest was there to witness. It was only in the fifteenth and sixteenth that the practice arose in the Catholic Church that a priest not simply witness the marriage but also celebrate the marriage and bless it. It wasn't until the English Marriage Act of 1753 that one actually had to have by law, a Priest or minister of religion perform the ceremony. This became the formal, legal contract of marriage. What we understand now as marriage as

---

[96] In your book, *Family Law and the Indissolubility of Parenthood*, you put it this way, "Historically, cohabitation gave rise to no obligation of support. Yet in Australia and New Zealand, cohabitation has been assimilated with marriage, so that once a court establishes that a cohabiting relationship of sufficient duration existed, the legal rights and obligations that flow therefrom in terms of property division and maintenance are the same as for marriages."

such with a distinct ceremony is only two or three hundred years old.

Shimon Cowen: Notwithstanding marriage laws, we see that de facto — non-formalized unions — continued and have grown greatly. In your book, you speak about a modern trend, which we see pre-eminently in legislation in Australian State legislatures, particularly in regard to "relationships registers" (such as the Victorian Relationships bill of 2008). Its intention is to give de facto unions essentially all the features — the rights and obligations of marriage — with regard to property division and spousal maintenance upon dissolution. In other words, even though the parties did not commit themselves formally, the State has made their relationship the equivalent — in terms of its benefits and obligations — of a contractual one. Would you like to comment on this?

Patrick Parkinson: This is a great question because, in actuality, in Australian tradition there is pretty much no difference in law between being married and living together outside of marriage. The status of marriage — with its rights and obligations — devolves upon the *de facto* couple once they have lived together for more than 2 years, or if they have a baby; or alternatively (without either of these) if they register their relationship. Now, if by about two years of living together you are considered as if you are married you can imagine the shock that people feel when, through the practical effect of the legislation, they realize it. Many couples don't want to be married. They are testing it out, they are living together in case they might marry. They might marry someone one day, but at the moment they are just living together — no ties. Yet, in the law they are treated as if they are already married once they have been living together for two years.

The law in New Zealand is the same, but it's not common around the world. In many other countries, living together before being married doesn't give you rights at all. In the U.S and Europe there is a specific cohabitation agreement for these obligations to ensue, or in the very least you have to register your relationship. For example, in the Netherlands you can register your *de facto* union, and that gives you the status of being effectively married.

With regard to the Australian and New Zealand legislation, I agree that once a couple has a child, they ought to be treated as if they are married in terms of property division and maintenance. This is because women typically bear the burden and pay the price if the relationship breaks up and we need to support women and children. However, in a situation where the couple is living together without a child, I strongly argued that we don't need to take away their freedom of choice because people should decide whether they want to be married or not. I felt that we should not impose those obligations upon them. I'm a voice crying in the wilderness here and I certainly lost that debate[97].

Financial commitments as an instrument of strengthening marriage

Shimon Cowen: In Biblical law, there is a view that in the formally contracted form of marriage, a man would make an explicit commitment to endow his wife in the event that he would divorce her or die during the marriage. At the same time, these applied under specific circumstances: they applied on the part of the husband where he divorced her "lightly", without good reason; and they could be forfeited where the wife was disloyal. In other words, they were used to, and applied to conditions which would, strengthen marriage. They were attached to conditions of what in modern times we would call "fault". In modern marriage, since 1975 in Australia, there is a concept of "no fault". Does the ability to collect maintenance without any fault in fact weaken, *not strengthen, marriage?*

Patrick Parkinson: I think it's a really difficult moral question. Because what the law used to be in Australia for divorce before 1975 was that it is essential that spousal maintenance be damages for the breach to the contract...you know that the couple has made a contract to live together for better or for worse, for richer or poorer, until their life's end and if the husband commits adultery, or is violent, or whatever it is — he has breached that contract, and the woman will then typically suffer financial loss as a result of the breakup of the marriage, and he should compensate her

---

[97] My understanding of the Noahide position, applied today, is that it is desirable that the ongoing sexual union of a couple should occur within marriage, which begins with formal legal and financial commitments (Shimon Cowen).

for that loss — that's what in some ways it was.

Because when you move to a no-fault system, it becomes problematic — what if the wife runs off with another man or it doesn't work out and, pretty much later, she's asking for spousal maintenance? She was the one who broke the marriage contract, she left. Or as it happens in many relationships, one of them becomes estranged from the other and wants a different or better life — should the other one than have to pay maintenance for that support? These are difficult moral questions and the law doesn't have any answers in an age of no fault divorce.

Marriage was a covenant, a commitment you each made to each other, for lifelong commitment and women rely on this, particularly those who leave the workforce for children or work part time. They are economically vulnerable if the marriage breaks up. So, this contract was foundational to raising a family; it was critically important. One of the problems with no-fault divorce is that it took away that foundation which was there.

Paternity and the care of children

Shimon Cowen. In one interpretation of the Biblical model, under the conditions of cohabitation or concubinage a child could be identified as the offspring of a father and would inherit him (or in modern terms receive maintenance from him). The second interpretation was that marriage took a more formal character, and that marriage established paternity and the obligation to support or to bequeath; or alternatively, where in the case of cohabitation or concubinage, the father would make an explicit acknowledgment of his paternity of a child. How has contemporary law established parenthood and the obligation of an identified parent to provide? Does the State now move to identify fathers?

Patrick Parkinson: I guess that, for a very long time, biological fathers have been responsible for supporting their children. This goes back to the English Poor Laws.[98] In a situation where they were not married and before the age of DNA testing or even reliable blood testing, one didn't know who the father was and so

---
[98] http://www.loyno.edu/~history/journal/1989-0/haller.htm

typically the responsibility for the mother and the child fell upon the community. But what has happened since the 1970's, and no-fault divorce and the rise of unmarried parenthood, is that the government has said we can't continue to bear this burden, we can't have tax payers paying more and more money each year to support all these mothers and children, therefore we have to have strong child support laws and so all over Western countries, in North America, Europe, Australia and New Zealand, we have seen enormous efforts being made to enforce obligation on the biological father, for no other reason than that his gametes were used to produce a child.

Prior to this, in establishing paternity, the first problem was getting from the mother who her partners had been. If she had no incentive to do that, if it was just the taxpayer who was worried who the father was, the first question was — how do you find out who the sexual partners were? But even if she said, 'I had sexual relations in that 3-month period with A, B and C', all you could do is take blood tests and it would show probabilities that it might well be B, but it couldn't be C. Nowadays, we all have certain blood groups and so on, there are certain tests that can be done. DNA has changed all of that and it means with DNA testing that you can say, not with complete certainly, but somewhere around 99% certainty, if someone is, or not, the father.

It's interesting to look at all the efforts made to enforce child support because very often it's like getting blood out of a stone. I chaired a child support review in Australia 2004/2005 and what we found is that 40% of fathers were on welfare benefits or income levels at or below welfare benefits. Many of the fathers are disabled or unemployed as well, and it's actually very difficult to get good financial support.

Certainly, there have been long periods of history where if the child was born outside marriage, it was only the mother that had responsibility not the mother and father, but there was still an obligation that the father could be chased. The point is that if the couple is married, then it's assumed that the husband is the father, in law, whether or not in fact he is, there are a fair number of marriages where children are born where, I'm afraid, the husband is not the biological father, but, in law, it's assumed he is.

A husband, who is not the biological father, can disclaim financial responsibility for a child, but he would then have to prove he wasn't the father, if he's presumed in law to be the father. And all the issues we've talked about, with different blood tests, which may say he probably is or probably isn't, they often couldn't say it's completely one way or the other. But in a situation where the husband has spent the last year in India, and Mum's just managed to give birth in Sydney without being anywhere close to the father, then obviously this is not the father.

There has always, in law, been an obligation on the biological father to provide for the child, but in terms of the actual serious efforts to purse the biological father, I can tell you exactly when; it was the 1980's, it was the 1980's in the U.S, where famously, a Senator in NY, said we must "hunt, hound and harass" these fathers who are not supporting their children. In Australia it was in 1987-1988, that we introduced the child support scheme of a child support agency. In Britain, it was the early 1990's. It's been a response to the enormous growth, in one parent families, the enormous growth of welfare bill and budget, that has led government to chase any father they can find.

Donor artificial reproductive technology and the abandonment of the classical biological model of parenthood

Shimon Cowen: Traditional marriage as the union of a man and a woman found its natural ("one flesh") expression in children. Marriage thus defined the parenthood of the children: it gave the child its (essential or existential) identity as the child of this father and this mother. It also defined a relationship of financial responsibility for the child. It made the child an heir and/or one entitled to maintenance from his or her parents. Today with artificial reproductive technology (IVF and surrogacy), it becomes possible for adults whether in a relationship or not, to "commission" the production of a child, which need not have any of their gametes — and to claim parenthood of the child. Can one replicate the "identifying" relationships of normal biological parenthood in this way?

Patrick Parkinson: The answer, *in law*, is we most certainly can. The answer in emotion, is maybe we can't and that's the confronting issue. The law has taken the view, for many, many years now, certainly going back to I think the 1930's in England, that I can recall, that if someone donates their sperm to help an infertile couple, that's a benevolent and altruistic thing to do, and if the couple want anonymity or don't want anonymity, the law protects the donor. And that's been the case for a long time. And, of course, there are the legendary stories of the medical student who donates his sperm and sees himself as helping the couple. That's the law — that there is no obligation to support the child if the conception was artificial. It's more problematic when you look at the children's needs, because children do have a great interest in where they come from and we know from adoption that many kids get to the point where they really do want to know who their biological father is and there may be health reasons why they want to know what their medical background is. And so, this idea of the anonymity of the sperm donor is certainly coming under some challenge now.

Shimon Cowen: The classical, millennial-long and biblical model of marriage and parenthood is that it is essentially a relationship of two people who together through their union produce a child. The marriage is the bond, the child is its expression. Parent and child have a reciprocal relationship of existential and material-economic identity. Although problems arise for heterosexual couples with donor gametes, the classic conundrum arises out of the concept of "homosexual marriage". This is a "union" which cannot biologically reproduce and is therefore outside the classical Judeo-Christian (and indeed universal) concept of marriage as expression the union of the two parents in the "one flesh" of their offspring. In addition to this, by seeking to commission the reproduction of children it raises a host of problems in the relationship and identities of parent and offspring. Could you comment?

Patrick Parkinson: One of the issues that has come up, quite often now, is homosexual men who donate their sperm to lesbian couples in order to help a woman in the partnership, have a baby and then they say, 'hey I want to see the kid, I want to be a father or uncle figure.' 'I want to see them regularly' or 'I want to be able to send birthday presents'. 'I want this child to know I am the father'. This has been the source of very considerable conflict and difficulty in the same-sex relationship community.

We've made an enormous mess of things by moving so far away from the foundational values, which have been formed not only by Judeo-Christian societies but by other societies around the world. We're now reaping the whirlwind that we have sown.

Heterosexuality and Human Identity

Heterosexuality and (pro)creation

This essay starts from the standpoint of the millennia-long biblical tradition, that the human being was created "in the image of G-d". What this means is that the human soul (which is what was made "in the image of G-d") resonates with Divinely instructed universal ethical principles. This spiritual endowment also makes the human the free and responsible agent of the implementation of the Divine purpose in Creation — namely, to refine the world through a life lived by these ethical principles. Heterosexual unions are alone permitted by this Divine ethics.

Human "heterosexuality" — that is to say, the complementary union of male and female, or masculine and feminine, with its procreative potential — has a metaphorical analogue in the Divine. Religious tradition[99] teaches that G-d Himself employs two kinds of powers to enliven and sustain the creation. One is a *transcendental* power which enlivens the creation into being in each moment from nothingness *(ex nihilo)*. The second is an *immanent*, delimiting Divine power which contains and articulates the transcendent G-dly life force in a way that delineates the manifold particularity of creation, and gives each detail its measured vitality. In the mystical tradition these are metaphorically denoted as "masculine" (transcendent) and "feminine" (immanent) powers of G-d.

---

99 This concept is elaborated at length in the work, *The Gate of Unity and Belief*, by Rabbi Schneur Zalman of Liadi. This work is in fact the second part of his comprehensive work, *Tanya*.

Human heterosexual reproduction parallels the Divine instruments of creation. The man provides the seed, the "transcendent" possibility, so to speak, of the child. The mother differentiates and articulates the fertilized ovum "immanently" within the womb into a whole human being with its multitude of distinct faculties. So too, after birth, the masculine/feminine division of labour continues: in the nurture of the child, the father is the more remote and abstract sustainer or provider, whilst the mother is the closer and more specific nurturer of the child.[100] Later, in the character- and moral-education of the child, the father models the abstract authority of ethical values, whilst the mother imparts these values with a warmth and application more specifically tuned to the temperament and developmental stage of the individual child. Thus, whether in procreative, nurturing or educative capacities, father and mother combine their distinct masculine and feminine characteristics, in a manner imitative of the Divine in Its complementary "transcendent" and "immanent" powers.[101]

These normative roles of masculinity and femininity are assigned by the Creator to the biological male and female respectively. If, in specific individual cases, physical, psychological or cultural factors have disturbed these potentials of masculinity and femininity in men and women, these are grounds, not for the rejection of these potentials, but for the attempt at their recovery. Homosexual behaviour is not within the Divine law or plan. The homosexual couple cannot themselves procreate, they cannot provide the complementary masculine and feminine dimensions of the nurture and education of the child and even as a unit in itself has a greater inherent instability.[102]

---

[100] Even though the balances in the roles of providing, nurturing and educating supplied by mother and father may change under social and economic conditions, this does not alter the fact of the endowment of father and mother with these unique – distinct and complementary – roles vis-a-vis the child, the value of which should not be lost.

[101] The analogy between "masculine" and "feminine" in the Divine creative powers and in the human procreative unit is not a strict or total one. The engendering role of the father in procreation is not *ex nihilo* – unlike G-d's transcendent engendering power – but from the father's seed.

[102] See S. D. Cowen, *Homosexuality, Marriage and Society*, Redland Bay: Connor Court, 2016, pp. 51-52.

Heterosexual procreation and identity: the psychic nexus

A homosexual couple cannot have a child which they can recognize as biologically fully their own. The artificial reproductive techniques upon which they call use donor gametes (one or both). The child thus "commissioned" conversely also cannot recognize itself as fully biologically their child. Procreation within a heterosexual married unit, on the other hand, does produce a child which they know as wholly theirs, and a child which knows and is raised by its own parents. What difference does this make, if the homosexual loves and rears the commissioned child as best s/he can?

The Bible relates in Genesis[103]: "Therefore a man shall leave his father and mother and cleave to his wife and they shall become one flesh". The "one flesh" which two people, a man and woman, become is their child. This says something very important about identity. The biological parents see *their* union in their child. That is what *they* become. Reciprocally, the child understands itself as the product of the union of *these* people, its parents. The parents know *themselves* in their child and the child knows *itself* in its parents.

On this biblical verse — which refers to the becoming one of father and mother in their child — a commentator[104] asks, why this is stated specifically with regard to the human being? Is it not true also of animals — that male and a female mate and from this comes the one flesh of their offspring? The answer he gives points to a subjective and psychological difference. The relationship of parent and offspring ceases to matter to animals beyond the initial phase of nurture. Parent and offspring walk away from each other — at least subjectively and psychologically — forever. With the human being, however, the relationship — the lineage and linkage — of parent and child continues to matter subjectively and psychologically to parent and child, *beyond* the end of nurture and rearing. Why is this so, in psychophysical terms?

---

[103] 2:24.
[104] The commentary *Gur Aryeh* on Genesis 2:24.

Procreation is the story of a human being's identity through time. My parents, from whose procreation I come, are my *past*. My relationship (my home) with my spouse (of the opposite sex, with whom I joined to procreate) is my *present*. My children, which result from my and my spouse's procreation, are my *future*. The lineage of generations is "my history" through time. The human psyche can grasp this sense of time — or personal history — as an important dimension of one's being.

Now, people in fact do adopt and raise with much love children who are *not* their biological children. If for some reason, a child cannot or will not be raised by its biological parents, it is certainly meritorious that others step in to care for the child. But this is of value, *after the event* that a child can or will not be raised by its own parents. It is not a situation, which should be set up *in the first instance*. Indeed, to create children *for* adoption — to create orphans — as artificial, donor and surrogate reproduction does for homosexual couples, denies children their full identity: their psychophysical lineage, with all the deep attachments, to the generations which constitute that lineage.[105] The loss is a deep one. To adopt an orphan is a good deed; to create an orphan is not.

Heterosexual procreation and identity: the spiritual nexus

Still the question arises of a yet deeper basis of the continuity of personal identity through and between biological generations — between grandparents, parents and grandchildren — when each of these generations are discrete bodies. If it doesn't matter to animals, who their parents and offspring are — for after all they *are* temporally and spatially discrete bodies — why should it matter psychologically to humans? What is this *continuous* intergenerational identity in humans made of, apart from the sense of time and personal history which humans have?

---

[105] Married heterosexual couples also sometimes use donor gametes in their own IVF procedures. This too raises similar ethical objections. The movement "Tangled Webs" which treats the identity difficulties of children born from donor gametes is well documented in Alana S. Newman, *The Anonymous Us Project: A Story-Collective on 3rd Party Reproduction*, NY: Broadway Publications, 2013.

As the possessor of knowledge of the Divine and a Divinely sanctioned morality, and as the free moral agent in creation, the human being is entrusted not only to carry out the ethical refinement of the world but also to create *further* human beings — children — who will continue that task after, and in addition to, them. To this end, there is a need for children not only to be born but also to be nurtured and educated in that moral code and mission. Human reproduction is not simply physical; it is also the generation of offspring as spiritual-ethical agents.

Humanity is thus generally bidden to have children, though there is no obligation *upon each and every* member of humanity to procreate.[106] There are also those who marry but are unable to have children, notwithstanding their desire to do so. Indeed, even without bearing children, individuals can carry out a certain kind of spiritual reproduction. Our tradition tells us that "one who teaches his fellow's son [the principles of an ethical life] is considered as having borne him". Our good deeds are also reckoned as "offspring": "The offspring of the righteous are their good deeds". Indeed, there have been very great human beings, with immense spiritual legacies, who had no physical children. But we are here speaking of spiritual reproduction through actual children: where children *are* born, why is it of spiritual importance that the generations be raised by their *own* biological parents?

In probing the spiritual content of the nexus of biological generations, it cannot be the souls themselves, for people of different generations and in different bodies have different souls. The answer must be that the spiritual "glue" of generations is the common spiritual-ethical legacy — the transmission and continuation of an ethical mission — for which and in which spiritually parents bore, nurtured and educated their children. This is a spiritual "relay" or transmission which travels through the nexus and conduit of biological procreation, nurture and education of the generations.

A famous saying of religious tradition illustrates this: "If one's

---

[106] See S. D. Cowen, *The Theory and Practice of Universal Ethics – the Noahide Laws*, pp. 232-234.

offspring are alive [that is to say, are *active* in continuing the moral tradition *they received from their parents*], so is one [the parent, after one's physical passing considered to be] alive". The essential need and entitlement of children to know and be bound up with their parents (and conversely, the desire of parents for children) is connected with the extension of the common spiritual-ethical life legacy and mission which was the *raison d'etre* of their procreation. Whether, in fact, parents themselves — or for that matter, the children — live up to that mission and legacy in their own lives, it is the enduring, redeemable potential and purpose for which there are successive, begotten generations.

In summary, the continuity of identity between biological generations as extensions of one another backwards and forwards in time is *both* psychophysical *and* spiritual. The parent needs the child and the child needs its parents for their own identities. And since the biological matrix of the procreation of the generations is built on heterosexuality, heterosexuality is built into human identity.

What then of persons who experience same-sex attraction? As discussed in my book, *Homosexuality, Marriage and Society*, the sources of homosexual attraction can be temperamental, psychological and cultural. But in all cases, these sources are extraneous to the essential person[107], the soul, made in the image of G-d, which (however unconscious) knows that homosexuality is not normative and has (whether alone or with the counsel and compassionate help of others) the ability to withstand or transform homosexual impulse. What of persons with hermaphroditism (or "intersex", a mixture of male and female genitalia)? To such persons, who can in no way help their situation, G-d has also commanded laws: the hermaphrodite can serve G-d within the matrix of possibilities granted it by G-d.[108] The individual who feels driven to identify with a gender, other than his or her own biological gender (the "transgender"), will work to overcome that

---

[107] See S. D. Cowen, *Homosexuality, Marriage and Society*, Ballan: Connor Court Publishing, 2016, Chapter 2.
[108] In universal – Noahide – law, a hermaphrodite is permitted to marry a woman, but not a man.

"drive" and will desist from surgical sexual re-assignment[109], and strive to carry out his or her Divine imperative and potential as the male or female he or she was biologically born. None of these conditions, challenging and difficult as they may be, can alter the Divine moral normativity of heterosexuality.

Let us say more than this. These people, with all their difficulties, had mothers and fathers. I once heard a homosexual say, "I had my own mother and father, and would not take that away from anyone". Let us pray that these people will, by their efforts and if necessary the help of others, and with G-d's help, themselves also become mothers and fathers, within the procreative bond of heterosexual marriage; that just as they possess a history out of the heterosexual biological matrix, so too they shall have a future out of the same matrix, in children who are wholly — psychophysically and spiritually — their own.

Transgenderism and the Dissolution of Identity
The objective definition of sexual identity

"Sex", as a classificatory system for human beings (at least) is defined by the religious tradition from Sinai, consists of male and female and a category traditionally known as the hermaphrodite and nowadays called "intersex". What is ultimately determinative is the actual reproductive organs and genitalia. The "intersex" person is one with reproductive organs and genitalia of *both* sexes.

In the tradition from Sinai, the (rare) phenomenon of the intersex person does *not* constitute a "third sex" or the possibility of other kinds of "sexes". Rather, it represents according to various views, a compounded or doubtful status arising from the male and female features in that individual. Thus, the tradition looks at which male and/or female obligations and prohibitions bind an intersex person in view of the complex-compounded male-female elements in that person. One conclusion, for various

---

[109] It is not permissible by biblical law to seek to transition to another sex, since this is in the category of "wounding oneself" and in any case does not change one's born biological status or the ethical imperatives associated with it.

reasons (which I will not go into here), is that, according to the tradition, an intersex person may marry a woman, but not a man.

In general, sexual identity — male or female — is significant because of the sometimes differing moral obligations which these different roles confer in accordance with the laws given to us by our Creator. The most salient of these has to do with marriage and procreation. For the purposes of procreation, a male is bound to join with a female, and a female with a male. Men are not permitted to marry men and women are not permitted to marry women and simply "outsource" the procreation. Marriage and procreation go together: only in this way is the identity of the generations protected and honoured — the parents know the child as the offspring of *their* union and the child knows *itself* as the child of its parents. Accordingly, with regard to marriage, a physiological male cannot be anything other than a physiological male with all the attendant obligations upon him; and so too a physiological female; and one of the opposite sex is needed to come together for marriage. The fact that certain societies have enacted "homosexual marriage" does not change the law of our Creator; it transgresses it.

The "subjective" definition of sexual identity

In recent times there has been an attempt to introduce a "subjective" concept of sexual identity, which has appropriated to itself the term "gender" and changed its meaning from physiological sexual identity to what it is that a person "feels" one is. This is part of a broad ideology which states that what the person "wants", the person may have, so long as it does not get in the way of another's enjoyment. It is part of a materialistic and hedonist world-view, which has brought with it the substantial collapse of the family and a culture of youth violence and drugs, which also expresses a spiritual and meaning void.

The religious tradition maintains that a human being should be guided not by impulse but by conscience; and that conscience makes reference to a Divine template of eternal values. It well understands the difficulty and suffering involved in the struggle between conscience or the soul and bodily passions, but it does not renounce that struggle. Conscience — the internal sense and resonance of those universal and eternal values willed and expressed by the Creator — constitutes us in the Creator's image. These play out in a society characterized by stability, cohesion and continuity. If one experiences an impulse of aggression or greed, one must contain, and hopefully transform. it. Similarly, if one experiences a sexual urge for a relationship which is prohibited to us by our Creator, one must work to contain and hopefully to transform it.

The desire for something contrary to the mandate of conscience with its Divine template is therefore either immoral, or, if it deeply and seemingly involuntarily takes hold of the person, it may also be a sickness, physical or psychological, deserving of help. In either case, desire, feeling and want do not define morality. Rather — and this can sometimes be hard work — morality needs to define our desires, feelings and wants. When a man therefore says "I feel like" or "want to be" a woman (or vice-versa), that person is saying I reject the obligations and prohibitions which the Creator has placed on me, created as a male. I want to redefine or reconstitute myself such as not to have those obligations or prohibitions. There is no subjective definition of sexual identity, just as there is no subjective definition of morality. Identity, and the obligations and prohibitions befitting that identity, are both designated by G-d.

What is the status of a "transgendered" person?

It follows that simply by calling, or dressing, himself as a female, a man does not become woman (or vice-versa). What of the situation where a male undertakes surgery to "become" a female or vice versa? The tradition from Sinai teaches that the identity of such a person does not change. He is a male as before and she is a female as before.

The difference is that such a man becomes a mutilated man, and the woman a mutilated woman. Self-mutilation is prohibited under universal ethics, where there is no benefit. Not only our lives, but also our bodies are not "ours" to harm. The psychological "benefit" which might be claimed by such a person is either immoral or the expression of an illness or disorder, and so does not count as a legitimate benefit.

Apart from self-mutilation, "sexual-reassignment" surgery will often lead to sexual sterilization. The person undertaking this has thus forfeited, for no just reason, the ability to procreate. Particularly, where a new culture has arisen, which encourages children (without parental control) to follow an impulse to change their sex and follow this up with surgery, a huge injustice is committed. The children are too young to be given a driver's licence or to vote, but it is suggested that they should be allowed permanently to mutilate their bodies and procreative capabilities.

The harm of transgenderism is not only to the "transgendered", who has been persuaded against his or her inner being, but also towards others. Men presenting as women and vice-versa can be a source of harassment or immorality. There is the bizarre case documented and sourced by Pat Byrne in his forthcoming book on Transgenderism, of Maddison Hall:

> Maddison Hall (born Noel Crompton in 1964) shot and killed hitchhiker Lyn Saunders at Gol Gol, New South Wales, in 1987. After being convicted in 1989, Hall began hormone treatment while in prison, and was transferred to the women's Mulawa Correctional Centre in 1999, where it was alleged that Hall had sexual relations with several female prisoners.

> After three months, Hall was alleged to have raped a woman and was returned to a male prison. Hall was charged with rape, but charges were dropped after the alleged victim was released, returned to New Zealand and refused to press charges.

> After being in male prison, Hall sued the state of NSW and received an out of court settlement for $25,000, which was used to fund Hall's sex reassignment surgery in 2003.

The consequences of a culture of transgenderism

A study[110] of transgender individuals (prior to or without surgery) reports a prevalence amongst "transgender" individuals (i.e. those who identify as the opposite sex) of suicide attempts at 41% alongside the national (North American) average of 4.6%. Another report states that people who have had sexual reassignment surgery are 19 times more likely to die of suicide than the general population. Whether or not the surgery is a factor in increasing the suicide rate in this group, we see that the condition is a profoundly morbid one. The salient point is that a culture which cultivates transgenderism, including amongst highly susceptible and impressionable children — the overwhelming mass of which would develop into normal male or female roles — *cultivates a high morbidity within its object group*. Instead of helping to a normal development and treating persons with gender dysphoria, the dangerously fallacious decision to make transgenderism co-normative with heterosexuality, compounds malaise in transsexuals and creates new ones. The first and deepest victim of an "affirmative" transgenderism is him- or herself, and then more individuals, who in effect are recruited into it in suggestible early childhood by this cultural programme. It is an illness which requires care and treatment, rather than being elevated to a cultural "norm".

The attempt to bend, blur and cross boundaries in the Creation is in effect a rebellion against the Creator, who fashioned the species and kinds, enjoined them to keep to their species and kinds, and endowed them with unique purposes. Here is another attempt, not only to dissolve the moral template — or compass — of humanity, but also to dissolve human identity itself. The Creator fashioned man and woman (and the rare intersex person) and charged them with their unique obligations.

The cultural dissolution both of the moral compass and of human

---

[110] https://williamsinstitute.law.ucla.edu/wp-content/uploads/AFSP-Williams-Suicide-Report-Final.pdf

identities themselves is captured by the parable of a recent Sage[111] in the religious tradition. It relates to the King of a principality and his adviser, which I'll modify slightly here. It goes as follows:

> There was a king of a small principality, whose top adviser had information that the grain harvested that year was tainted. Anyone who would eat from it would became insane (a human version of "mad cow disease"). "What can we do?" said the king. "It is not possible to destroy the crop for we don't have enough good grain stored to feed the entire population."
>
> "Perhaps," said the adviser, "we should set aside enough grain for ourselves. At least that way we could maintain our sanity." The king replied, "If we do that, *we'll* be considered crazy. If everyone behaves one way and we behave differently, we'll be considered the not normal ones.
>
> "Rather," said the king, "I suggest that we too eat from the crop, like everyone else. However, to remind ourselves that we are not normal, we will make a mark on our foreheads. Even if we are insane, whenever we look at each other, we will remember that we are insane!"

That mark on the king and his adviser's foreheads is the recollection that there *is* a moral compass. People of faith, true to the tradition which underpins our civilization, have that mark on their foreheads. It is the moral template which G-d imparted to the human soul, through which a person imitates G-d, and is able to carry out one's purpose, with good and G-dly behaviours in the Creation. It is the morality for which the world was created, and in accordance with which it operates harmoniously and with the ultimate goal of becoming a residence for the Divine.

The contrary worldview which is absolutely opposed to G-dly template for creation and the G-dly essence of the human being has arisen and gained a certain dominance in the last almost fifty years. I have called it hedonistic materialism. The materialism, which preceded it as the opponent of the human spirit, was that

---

[111] Rabbi Nachman of Breslov. See *A Greenbaum, Under the Table and How to Get Up. Jewish Pathways of Sp;iritual Growth*, Jerusalem: Tsohar Publishing, 1991.

of communism, called dialectical materialism. It came from a late eighteenth and nineteenth century doctrine which saw the human being — also "emancipated" from what it understood to be the chains of religion — as a promethean figure. The human being would become the master of nature, unlimited in his or her self-fulfillment. That vision left out G-d from the universe and the soul from the human being and produced the horror of communism, which only recently the Eastern European bloc threw off. Still it had a stable concept of the identity — if not the morality — of the human being.

The new materialism, I think, has its roots in Freud and Darwin. From Freud it takes the primacy of the pleasure principle and instinctual — primarily sexual — gratification. From the ideological overlay of Darwinism, it takes the concept of the human being as a mutant member of an animal kingdom. For both Freud and Darwin the human being is a *morphing* higher animal, unlike the human being in Marxist theory who was still a human being, something different from the rest of nature. It was simply that Marxism did not grasp the difference of the human being as consisting in the human soul modelled in the image of G-d.

Hedonistic materialism understands the creation of a vast animal kingdom in which the human being is only one — fluid — species. Indeed, the concept of a "Parliament" of nature has actually been formulated by some of the foremost exponents of hedonistic materialism. Because of the family affinities of humans, orangutans, chimpanzees and gorillas, it is appropriate that a Parliament should be constituted out of these species[112]. Ah — there is the problem that the orangutans, chimpanzees and gorillas do not make great political advocates and representatives. The answer provided by the Professors of hedonistic materialism is that they will be provided in this Parliament of nature with human spokespeople, just as disabled people have their spokespeople. One of the great chieftains of academia who espouses these views, has also found nothing ethically wrong with

---

[112] See Paola Cavilieri and Peter Singer (eds), *The Great Ape Project*, N.Y.: S Martins Press, 1995.

sexual relations between humans and animals, so one wonders whether — in the ultimate scheme of hedonistic materialism members of the animal blocs within this Parliament of nature could, in their scheme, also "marry" with the human bloc.

The fury and indignation with which this suggestion might be met by today's pundits does not prevent us from asking it. After all, we see a constant drift in the process of casting off a Divine template, etched within the human soul, and transmitted by tradition, in the definition of the human being. The first step in this was the degradation of the distinction between masculinity and femininity. Instead understanding the unique and complementary strengths of the mother and father within the family, a single standard of human actualization was urged: the ability to wield corporate power, amass wealth and to gratify personal desire. The unique and distinct qualities of the parenting roles of men and women — in raising up a new generation in transmitted, universal values — were repressed. But the normative heterosexual family unit was not repudiated.

The next step was that men and women were no longer bound to heterosexual relationships. As noted in the essay "Heterosexuality and human identity", the heterosexual procreative unit of the family was the way through which human beings produced offspring which were theirs and which knew themselves, as we have noted, as the product of that union. It was the bond of generations. "Homosexual marriage" throws off that bond. According to our tradition and the laws of G-d, homosexual unions are wrong — wrong both to homosexuals themselves and to the children who are artificially commissioned for them — notwithstanding any compassion which is due on account of the psychological, physical and cultural pressures which work to produce homosexuality. For homosexuality is extraneous to the human essence, to the soul (including the soul of the homosexual) which knows and wants to follow G-d.

Yet, for most of those who mistakenly — in the spiritual darkness of our times — wanted to afford the opportunity to men to marry men and women to marry women, and for most homosexuals themselves, men were still men and women were still women. They simply wanted to throw off the *obligation* which behooves men and women, namely to procreate with a member of the opposite sex, and to produce children who are truly theirs.

Now, as noted above, we have come one step further. It is not only that men no longer have the obligations incumbent upon men and women upon women with regard to procreation within the heterosexual family with its needed identity of generations. In transgenderism we are revising the concept of what a man, and what a woman, is. In fifty short years, this society progressively degraded masculinity and femininity within the family, then threw off the concept of the distinct moral obligations which behoove men and women, and then proceeded to disintegrate the very concept of what a man and woman are. This is the ultimate dissolution of the boundaries: the eclipse of G-d, who planted those boundaries and obligations, and of the human spirit or soul, which knows it.

The politicians, pundits and academicians who advocated and achieved homosexual marriage will have to answer to a generation of manufactured orphans, children created not to be raised by both of their biological parents, for homosexual couples. The politicians, pundits and academicians who have advocated for transgenderism and who seek to implement. through programmes such as the so-called "safe schools" programmes, a culture which encourages children to follow impulse to mutilate and sterilize their bodies will have to answer to a generation of boys and girls, who after "transitioning", whether surgically or psychologically, are still boys and girls, but now physically or psychologically mutilated boys and girls. If they succeed in their plan, G-d forbid, they will have driven children and adults against themselves, against their own souls and hence innermost being.

I conclude with another parable from the same modern Sage:

> There was once a prince who took ill and decided he was a turkey. Stripping off his clothes, he crouched naked under the royal table, refusing to eat anything but crumbs which had

fallen to the ground. The king was greatly upset. Many doctors were called to the palace to examine the prince but none could offer a cure.

One day a wise man came to the king and said, "Let me live in your home that I might befriend your son. Be patient and I will make him well again." Immediately the sage approached the royal table, stripped off his clothes and sat down naked next to the prince.

"Who are you and what are you?" demanded the king's son.

"I am your friend, a turkey like yourself," the wise man replied.

"I thought you might be lonely and decided to come and live with you for a while."

Some weeks passed. The "turkeys" grew accustomed to each other and soon became good friends. They ate crumbs, drank from tin plates and discussed the advantages of being domesticated birds rather than men.

One night, when the royal family was having dinner, the wise man signalled to the king, whose servants brought two silk robes and cautiously placed them under the table. The sage quickly donned one of the robes and before the king's son could utter a word proudly announced, "There are some dumb turkeys who are so insecure that they believe putting on a silk robe might endanger their identity." The prince thought for a moment, nodded his head and began to clothe himself.

Some days later the wise man once again signalled the king. Broiled beef, baked potatoes, and fresh green vegetables were brought and placed on the ground near the sage. Looking quite pleased with himself, the wise man bit into his food and exclaimed, "Absolutely delicious! It's good to be a turkey sophisticated enough to enjoy the food of men." The prince readily agreed and hungrily ate his fill.

Eventually, the wise man called for some silverware and asked to be served from the king's good china. "After all," he explained to the prince, "why shouldn't intelligent turkeys want the best for themselves?"

Finally, after many months the sage came and sat by the table. While eating and drinking with the royal family, he called down to the prince and said, "Come join me. The food is the same but the chairs make an appreciable difference. Besides, we turkeys have a lot to offer. Why should we restrict ourselves by remaining aloof? Certainly our ideas can benefit the minds of men."

This story has a strange relevance, not only because of the thought that the mutations in human identity embraced by hedonistic materialists might also come to fruition — if not in ghoulish human-animal genetic hybridization then — in macabre surgical sculpture. Our story of the prince who thought he was a turkey (species dysphoria) is like transgenderism (gender dysphoria), because it has to do with *subjective* delusion. We know that transgenderism is a dysphoria, a delusion, because it is contrary to the plan which G-d has established, and which, once freed, the human spirit — the *real* human dimension — at once ratifies. People were supposed to be people, turkeys turkeys, men men and women women. The delusion is possible only as long as G-d is shut out of our society and the human soul eclipsed. Not only is transgenderism morally wrong (whatever its causes), it leads to personal misery, social havoc and decay. Our society will surely revolt at the mixing of bathrooms and shower and changing rooms. The madness will become self-evident.

To cure this situation we need to bring back G-d and the human soul into our culture. We need psychiatrists and psychologists, who themselves know the difference between right and wrong, and who know of the human soul, which knows that distinction and wants its casing — body and mind — to live accordingly. With G-d's help and with their help, we can, as one writer once put it, get the turkey back up from under the table.

Chapter 9

Issues of Justice

Three issues in the conduct of justice — from the courts down to responsible citizens — are discussed in the pieces in this chapter. The first relates to the background ethical framework which, from the standpoint of universal ethics, should inform all legislation and judicial decision-making. This idea is treated initially in the essay "Universal Ethics and the Australian Constitution." It was written in response to legislation in Victoria in 2008 that compelled doctors, notwithstanding their conscientious objection to abortion, to participate in abortion through having to refer clients to doctors known to have no objection to it. The question was whether there was any constitutional recourse of voiding a law which enforced complicity in killing. The enquiry led to consideration of the Preamble to the Australian Constitution, which seems to imply an ultimate moral authority, and background ethical framework, for the law. This importance of the background framework of universal ethics for the law receives confirmation in the second piece, a conversation held with a former Chief Justice of the High Court of Australia, the Hon Murray Gleeson, entitled "Universal Ethics and the Courts".

Justice — whether it is pursued in the courts, public debate or by the individual — involves not only the application of valid norms. It is also about the *judgment* itself. It requires impartial hearing and critical examination of all the "facts" and "arguments", unswayed by raw sentiment and unfiltered "feeling". The last essay in this chapter, "Drugs and the Culture of Responsibility", looks at the impact of drugs on individual responsibility and "judgment".

Universal Ethics and the Australian Constitution
Searching the Constitution for Limits on Abortion

The letter of the Constitution

Where does the name of G-d appear in the Constitution? It is found, not in the Constitution itself but, in the Preamble to the Act of the United Kingdom Parliament, which enacted the Australian Constitution (Commonwealth Of Australia Constitution Act, 1900). This preamble of course was formulated by the drafters of the Australian Constitution. It states:

> Whereas the people of New South Wales, Victoria, South Australia, Queensland and Tasmania, humbly relying on the blessing of Al-mighty G-d have agreed to unite in one indissoluble Federal Commonwealth...

Here we have a secular State with a Constitution prefaced by a recognition of G-d. What does this amount to? Is it just a piety? Or does it have some actual constitutional significance and impact?

The significance of the Preamble to the Commonwealth of Australia Constitution Act with its reference to G-d becomes apparent when we look at what the Australian Constitution internally (i.e. after its Preamble) cannot rectify. This is a law enacted by the Parliament of Victoria in 2008, which some have called the worst abortion law in the Western World.

The Victorian Abortion Law Reform Act first of all provides for abortion on demand for foetuses up to 24 weeks for any reason or for no reason whatsoever. It also facilitates abortion up to birth, where two opinions can be found to support it — something not difficult in contemporary culture and society. Not only this, it also has a set of extreme further provisions. One is that if a baby is aborted alive, it is left to die. To place a vulnerable new born human being in a situation which hastens its death is clearly associated with homicide in Noahide law. But the most egregious evil of this law is that it forces doctors against their conscience to participate in what in Noahide law is forbidden killing, in a circumstance where there is no danger to the mother's life.

This last point is the content of section 8 (1) of this law, which states that a doctor who does not want to abort, where there are no circumstances threatening the life of the mother, must refer the client to another doctor whom the first doctor knows to have no objection to performing the abortion. Now recently the case came up under this law, where a couple came to a doctor and said that the wife was pregnant with a foetus which is female, that they did not want a female and wanted the doctor to abort it. The doctor said that he would not abort the baby and would not refer to another doctor: he would not be a party to such an act. By saying that under the Victorian Abortion law, he faces arraignment before a medical tribunal and losing his registration to practice as a doctor.

Now this is an incredible situation. The tradition shared and carried forward from their root (where it is known as the teaching of the Noahide laws) by the great faiths, including those which form the social and historical background of our society, prohibits abortion on demand. It is classified with forbidden killing. There are circumstances in which it is permitted: where there is danger to the mother's life; or possibly after rape and incest, if the abortion is performed within 40 days of conception, or possibly also where there is a foetal deformity so great that the baby has no prospect of survival beyond birth. But that abortion could be an unquestionable routine — and that beyond that one can force doctors to be a party to it against their will through the complicity of referral — is clearly forbidden by universal Noahide law.

So, we are left with a law which forces doctors to be complicit in acts of killing which Noahide law manifestly forbids, and which various faith communities — Jewish, Christian and Muslim — have all found to be contradictory to their own traditions and have communicated this to the Parliament. Not only is the killing wrong, but complicity in it is also wrong. It could be added that while this relates only to *abetting* a forbidden killing, outright killing of the innocent is something in which Noahide law requires a person to give up his or her life, rather than perform it, even under duress.

How could such a law be permitted by the Australian Constitution? Yet, when one explores the different avenues which might limit it *within* the Australian Constitution one comes up against one dead-end after another. I wish now to indicate some various thinkable avenues of challenge against this law within the Constitution and to show how each fails; and here we are assisted by a writing of the Chief Justice of the High Court of Australia, His Honour Justice Robert French, on "Religion and the Constitution".[113]

Section 116 of the Constitution amongst other things provides that the Commonwealth shall "not make any law ... for prohibiting the free exercise of any religion". Ostensibly this should protect a doctor, whose religion forbids him or her from carrying out abortion on demand, for a reason not justifiable under Noahide law and the faith of most traditional religions. It would seem also to offer protection from coercion to participate in it by referral. But this avenue is blocked by the fact that section 116 protects individuals only from laws enacted by the Federal Government which infringe the freedom of religious practice by individuals. The abortion law before us was enacted by State Government, to which section 116 does not apply. Nor, as the present Chief Justice French has said, does it "create an justiciable individual right to the free exercise of religion"[114] which could be exported to a State jurisdiction, but only freedom from Federal laws which offend it.

Another possible recourse against the coercion of conscience of doctors by the Victorian Abortion law is the fact that Australia is a party or signatory to international treaties, such as the International Covenant on Civil and Political Rights, which in its Article 18 guarantees freedom of conscience and religion. This, one would hope, would provide succour for the Victorian doctor who does not want to violate his or her religious conscience by performing or having any truck (by referral) with an abortion forbidden by religious law. Here again we are foiled by the

---

[113] Chief Justice Robert French AC, "Religion and the Constitution", a speech presented to the WA Society of Jewish Jurists and Lawyers Inc on 14 May, 2013.
[114] *Ibid.*, p. 1.

constitutional rule, that only by enacting a law at a Federal level through the "external affairs power" conferred by section 51 of the Constitution can a provision of an international treaty become part of Australian law. Only then, by virtue of section 109 of the Constitution, which specifies that Federal law shall override a State law inconsistent with it, could such a Federal law (once enacted) embodying the principle of religious freedom impact the anti-conscience clause of the Victorian Abortion Reform Law. Similarly were the Federal Government to enact a law disallowing discrimination on religious grounds, by section 109, this could also override a State law which discriminated against doctors (forcing them out of their profession) because of their religious objections to various kinds of supposed grounds or groundlessness for abortion. Yet as the present Chief Justice points out the Commonwealth has never legislated such a law.[115]

There appears another possible avenue within the Constitution which might assure the Victorian doctor the right to resist forced complicity in an abortion which revolts his conscience. This is in the concept of "implied rights". "Implied rights" are those rights which can be argued to be implicit in certain provisions of the Constitution. Thus the High Court of Australia has developed a doctrine of an implied right of "political communication". The problem here is that the only implied right which has been deduced from the Constitution by a majority decision of the High Court of Australia is that of "political communication". Others, such as freedom of conscience, have not. In conclusion, therefore, *within* the text of the Australian Constitution, there seems to be little succour for the doctor who does not want, and yet is forced by this law, to participate in an abortion, which violates universal Noahide law.

The "envelope" of the constitution

Having pursued all these "dead-ends" *within* the Constitution, it may be that a solution can be found in the "meta-doctrine" which

---

[115] *Ibid.*, p. 7.

envelopes the Constitution from *without*. This is to be found in (and perhaps is the significance of) the wording of the Preamble of the Australian Constitution Act which enacts the Constitution. It states that "permission" — a "blessing" — has been presumed to write and promulgate the Constitution. Who gave permission for the Constitution of Australia to be written and promulgated? The answer is, in the words of the Preamble, "humbly relying on the blessing of Al-mighty G-d [the States] have agreed to unite in one indissoluble Federal Commonwealth". In other words the constitution proceeds upon the humble assumption of, and "reliance" upon, G-d's permission — His "blessing".

One of the great commentators on the law of England, from which our law derives, William Blackstone in the eighteenth century, wrote in his great classic *Commentaries on the Laws of England* that there are two kinds of laws. There are laws of G-d, sometimes termed laws of nature, and there are laws enacted by society, known as "positive" law. He states that no positive law can override a law of G-d, the content of which, Blackstone further writes, is made known in Scripture. In other words nations have sovereignty, but their sovereignty is subordinate to G-d's sovereignty and the laws and rights which G-d bestows upon the peoples of all nations. We have seen this in recent history. The Germans had a sovereign Parliament under Hitler, but some of its laws were voided, and the acts performed in accordance with them punished, as crimes against humanity. Crimes against humanity are in fact crimes against the laws of G-d. There is a higher sovereignty which voided those laws. This applies also, we could argue, in regard to the Victorian Abortion Law Reform Act.

One of the laws of G-d is the entitlement of a human being to protection of his or her life and the prohibition of killing. As both Noahide law (and Blackstone) state, a liability for killing begins also in relation to pre-natal life. This law of G-d informs us that pre-natal life is not freely disposable. It doesn't mean, as mentioned above, that there are no grounds for abortion. But, the law of G-d, as revealed in Scripture (and expounded in commentary) is plain that abortion on demand, and the compulsion upon a doctor to participate by referral in abortion on demand (i.e. where there is no danger to the life of the mother or other compelling ground) are prohibited.

Indeed, the philosophy which upholds this law, to the extent of coercing doctors to comply with it, inverts the law of G-d, by postulating an unfettered right to kill unborn life. It has been formulated as a so-called "reproductive right" which reduces the child to little more than a corn in its mother's foot which no one can prevent her from removing and beyond that, which one can force another to remove, as a service to which one is entitled. The foetus becomes, in this view, a mere thing.

The G-d Who prohibits the brazen claim to an unqualified "right" to destroy prenatal life, the G-d of the Constitution, is the G-d of all peoples — not specific to any one religion. The words "Al-mighty G-d" in the Preamble are neutral and universal to all religions. Even though the majority of persons who participated in the framing of the Constitution were Christian, the term does not have a specifically Christian connotation. The words are and have proven to be acceptable to Jew, Christian, Muslim, Hindu and Buddhist alike.

This is not just the view of religious people. We find that even persons, such as a former Prime Minister, Julia Gillard, who described herself as a non-believer, could also recognize the role of Biblical values in our society.[116] My interpretation of this goes along the same lines as Viktor Frankl. He stated that every person

---

[116] The *Daily Telegraph* of 21 March, 2011 carried the following story: Ms Gillard said she was "on the conservative side" of the gay marriage issue "because of the way our society is and how we got here", *the Daily Telegraph* reports.
"I think that there are some important things from our past that need to continue to be part of our present and part of our future," she said. "If I was in a different walk of life, if I'd continued in the law and was partner of a law firm now, I would express the same view, that I think for our culture, for our heritage, the Marriage Act and marriage being between a man and a woman has a special status.
"Now, I know people might look at me and think that's something that they wouldn't necessarily expect me to say, but that is what I believe.
"I'm on the record as saying things like I think it's important for people to understand their Bible stories, not because I'm an advocate of religion - clearly, I'm not - but once again, what comes from the Bible has formed such an important part of our culture."

is capable of self-transcendence and finding a higher purpose of life. The key ingredient of this self-transcendence is humility — which is to ask whether there something bigger than I and than what I want. Frankl said that to come to this you do not have to be religious. He stated that even the "non-believer" who begins the process of self-transcendence is in fact *en route* to G-d, and consequently, I would add, tends to share the same values of the believer, which are G-d's laws. I dare say that the humble non-believer is closer to G-d than the arrogant religionist. The gun-toting jihadists talk about G-d, but when they say that word, they mean themselves. Humility is the road to G-d. Both the 70% of Australians with a religious affiliation and many non-believers (the humble grass-roots, not the "doctrinaire" ones) can and have lived with the Preamble to the Australian Constitution and its G-d. It took its place in 1901 and has been left in place.

In it is the reference to a G-d who permitted us to write a Constitution, but not to violate His laws. The anti-conscience clause of the abortion law is particularly abhorrent to all decent and reasonably straight thinking people, even to the otherwise pro-abortion *Age* newspaper. The Victorian Abortion Law Reform Act works to create a culture in which life is cheap and life is disposable. If the Australian Constitution was based on permission by G-d, how can a law be promulgated within its ambit which so negates the laws of G-d? The suggestion that there is an unfettered right to kill pre-natal life is a rebellion against G-d, Who has told us to protect life.

For a good reason G-d was put into the Preamble of the constitution, and in a Preamble which is not even part of the Constitution, but a Preamble to the act which enacts the Constitution. Its position teaches us that there is a radical break and a transcendent separation between G-d and the Constitution. He is not part of it; He is the enveloping condition, within which it has permission to exist. No constitution and no system of Government crafted by human beings can guarantee the decency and morality of its "positive" laws. No "bill of rights" is secure against perverted interpretation. Only the knowledge of the laws of the "King of all kings", the Creator, can guarantee that.

It may be that, as raised in the following discussion with the former Chief Justice of Australia, no judge can disqualify the law of a Parliament by reference to universal ethics. A judge can only resign, if the law given to him or her to apply violates conscience. For law-makers, who can remake laws, and for judges who are asked to innovate doctrines, not previously in the law, the reference to universal ethics and to G-d, must be real and actual.

The Courts and Universal Ethics

Conversation with a former Chief Justice, the Hon Murray Gleeson

Shimon Cowen: There is a concept of "universal ethics" which ultimately arbitrates ethical human conduct. This concept is treated both by "natural law" thinking and also by the tradition of the Noahide laws, going back to Sinai, and before that to Abraham and Noah. How does the adjudication and application of "positive" law (law made by judges and by statute) take these universal ethics into account?

The Hon Murray Gleeson: The idea of a level of justice over and above the positive law is widely accepted, but its practical implementation requires care. The enforcement of the law by courts is subject to an obligation of legitimacy. The law cannot rise above its source. The authority of judges cannot rise above the Constitution pursuant to which they are appointed. Problems in this regard come up from time to time. For example, in Fiji, to take a country in our region, as a result of activities in recent years, judges had to decide whether they would continue to sit in the courts and implement the law — and if so, what law? This was a society in which citizens were complaining that authority had been usurped. The judiciary in Pakistan, to take another example, has had to respond to changes in power raising questions as to the validity of the appointment of judges and the exercise of judicial authority.

I think the way most Australian judges would approach the question of universal ethics is not that there is some higher law, which authorizes judges to overthrow a positive law or to refuse to implement a positive law which they do not like, with which they disagree. Most judges would say that if they can't apply the law according to their consciences they ought to resign.

The approach of judges here is rather how universal ethics *inform the content and the practical application of positive law*. In our positive law, whether it is judge-made law or statute law enacted by Parliament, there are many values from the tradition of universal ethics, that inform the law and are taken into account by judges when they interpret and apply the law.

In the implementation of criminal justice, for example, respect for human life informs the content of the criminal law. All societies have a law against homicide. Respect for life and human dignity inform sentencing laws. In some societies the law permits capital punishment. In our society it does not. In some societies the law permits corporal punishment. Our law does not. But all civilized societies have a respect for human life and a respect for human dignity which they implement in practice, perhaps in different ways.

Similarly, all civilized societies have said that public access to justice is an ideal that ought to be pursued. All societies try to make the civil justice system available to the citizens for example by minimizing cost and delay. All civilized societies enact what they regard as appropriate sentencing laws, though they reach different practical conclusions as to what is appropriate.

With regard to the way universal values inform the application of the law, it could be noted that the American Declaration of Independence begins with a declaration of universal values, which looks like a statement written by a natural lawyer. We know as a matter of historical fact that the authors of that statement were not believers in natural law. We know that some of the authors of the statement that all men are born equal were men who owned slaves. But they began their Declaration of Independence with an appeal to universal laws because of the nature of the Declaration of Independence. It is framed as an indictment of the King of England. It makes allegations of contraventions of universal principles of law by those who had authority to make positive law. Why did the authors do that? What else could they have done? If you overthrow the legitimate Government and you are appealing to the universal public, the world, for recognition and legitimacy, you have to base your legitimacy on something. They based it on a declaration of principles of natural law or universal ethics. It is natural for people to appeal to universal principles to justify what they are doing in the conduct of their positive law.

How do you tell the difference between a good law and a bad law except by appeal to some value or standard outside the law which you are judging? How do you tell the difference between a good tax law and a bad tax law? You might say, one is inefficient, you might say, it doesn't raise revenue; it discourages incentives. There are pragmatic criteria by which you might distinguish a good from a bad law. But suppose you had a tax law which unfairly discriminates. To what standard of fairness would you be appealing? It would have to be to a concept of fairness outside the Income Tax Assessment Act. People could say, a tax is a tax. If it is in accordance with the Income Tax Assessment Act you have to pay it, if not you don't have to pay it. People complain from time to time that tax laws are unjust laws or unfair laws, and when they do that they can only argue their case by reference to some standard which must exist outside the law.

In conclusion, our positive law is suffused with values and principles that come from universal standards, universal ethics. And whether you find them in natural law, in Noahide law or more recently in declarations of universal human rights you are appealing to some standard outside the positive law. When Governments enact statute law, they often appeal to universal principles to demonstrate that the law they are enacting is just law. When courts interpret positive law that stands in need of interpretation or to develop the common law they often appeal to these universal standards to justify their interpretation.

Thus, from the point of view of an Australian judge, universal values, universal ethics of the kind discussed here, are reflected in the content of the law and in the practical implementation of the law. But they are not seen as something justifying a court or a judge overruling the law in refusing to implement the law or bending the law to the will or the moral perceptions of the judge.

A case in point of law and universal value: marriage

Shimon Cowen: There are areas of crisis in the values of society. I think of the law in Sweden which allows half siblings to marry, a case of incest. How do we identify values? In Australia there are legislative attempts to introduce homosexual marriage. How can the law here be related to universal values?

The Hon Murray Gleeson: Because of the decline of the influence of organized religion, which is the biggest single change in society in my lifetime, people now seek alternative sources for much the same values. G K Chesterton said that "when people stop believing in G-d, they don't believe in nothing — they believe in anything". And other religions or quasi-religious beliefs for many people have supplanted religion as the source of their values. The human rights movement is the most obvious example. Perhaps, the conservation movement is another example.

Canadian writers on jurisprudence have coined a very apt description of the kind of society we live in. They refer to a culture of justification. By that they mean that people are no longer uncritically accepting of authority. They require authority to justify itself, and when people in authority, including judges, justify their exercise of authority, they seek to legitimize their legislation and their judgments; and still the most common way of justifying legislation, decisions, use of power is with reference to universal principles.

The common law and statute law enacted by the Parliaments of Australia is full of values of the kind that Rabbi Cowen has mentioned and it is amazing and sometimes alarming to see how little that aspect of the law is appreciated. Rabbi Cowen mentioned a development in Swedish law on marriage. The area of marriage provides a good example of the astonishing lack of reflection upon how and why the law of marriage got there. We have a definition in the Marriage Act which defines marriage as the union of a man and a woman to the exclusion of all others voluntarily entered into for life. Where does that come from? There is another provision in the statute which is practically unmentioned. In any discussion about changes of the law with respect to marriage I would have thought it ought to be mentioned. The Family Law Act 1975 of the Commonwealth provides that the marriage is an institution, and the courts have the obligation *to protect* the institution of marriage as the union of a man and woman to the exclusion of all others voluntarily entered into for life. The Commonwealth Parliament in the Marriage Act has declared that marriage is an institution that needs to be *preserved and protected*. Again, where did that come from? Well, the answer, as a matter of history, is obvious. Until the nineteenth century, family law, the law of divorce and other aspects, was not administered by the ordinary Courts. It was the concern of ecclesiastic authorities, the Church court. That definition of marriage and recognition of marriage as an institution came into our law from Rome and it was the Church and the ecclesiastical courts which administered it. The Church took it from the Judaic tradition and the Judeo-Christian approach to marriage. This has entered into our law and is now described as an "institution" that needs to be preserved and protected.

How often do you hear reference to that provision of the Family Law Act in the context of proposals to change the definition of marriage in the Marriage Act? One aspect of the definition of marriage in the Marriage Act is that marriage joins a man and a woman exclusively. There are societies in which polygamy is currently practiced, and some people from those societies are now coming to Australia. If polygamists were a more active political force, then people would be forced to have another look at the definition of the institution of marriage and to ask where those values come from and what in those values may be threatened and if the nature of the institution is altered. That seems to me to provide a textbook example of a value that has come into law from a universal value, and that has not been widely appreciated. Many of our laws have come from religious sources and this, like the respect for human life, is an obvious example.

I append here a note written to me earlier by the Hon Murray Gleeson on marriage as a legal institution.

'The phrase "de facto" has no grammatical function unless, either expressly or by implication, it qualifies a noun. Its antonym is "de jure". The expression was commonly used in the past to qualify the noun "marriage" (or "husband" or "wife" or "spouse"). Over time, people came to drop explicit reference to the noun, but "my de facto" meant "my de facto (husband or wife)". It never meant "my de facto friend", because "husband" or "wife" signified a legal (de jure) status; "friend" did not. A relationship can only be de facto (or de jure) if it is one that has a definable legal status. In the past a man's de facto wife was a woman he wanted, for practical purposes, to have the status of his wife. The typical reason she would not be his de jure wife was that there was some legal or religious impediment to marriage (such as another subsisting marriage). As divorce became more common, and religious prohibitions were relaxed, impediments to marriage became less frequent. However, relationships between people who might have chosen, for any reason, not to marry, or who might simply not have contemplated marriage, became described as "de facto". De facto what? Once the concept of a de facto relationship is cut loose from the defined legal status of marriage, what has it become?

As to marriage, if it is not the union of one man and one woman for life, then what is it? So far, the religious idea of marriage has provided our law with the conceptual frame of reference by which a status is defined. That status has a host of legal consequences. If the religious idea of marriage is to go, what is to replace it? What will be the de jure status by reference to which our understanding of a de facto relationship is formed?

If marriage ceases to be a status defined by law according to a principle derived from social and religious tradition, and becomes a status people can confer upon themselves by acknowledging a certain commitment, what kind of commitment will suffice? Will exclusivity be a necessary feature of the commitment? Why? Self-evidently, care of children will not. If reproduction and marriage are unrelated, why should sexual attachment be any more significant than physical or emotional dependence, or commonality of interests? There could be many good reasons, having nothing to do with sex, why people would wish to "share their lives".

The institution of marriage was not devised to cater for sex, but for the consequences of the procreative potential of sex. Specifically, it was a means of obliging males to take responsibility for their offspring.[117] The family unit was considered the optimal environment for the care and nurture of children. If society is to sever, formally, the relationship between procreation and marriage, why should it retain the institution at all?

Dame Leonie Kramer was once reported to have said (with particular reference to the word "disinterested") that when the meaning of a word is corrupted, society often loses a value. I can think of no better example than the word "marriage".'

Drugs and the Culture of Personal Responsibility

A question of human responsibility

Our evaluation of drugs — as with most of the big issues of our day, from same-sex marriage to euthanasia — have to do frequently with "consequences": what will be the consequences of taking a particular policy stand on "medical marijuana" as these ramify to persons and situations outside the focus of the policy in question? Or, how will it differently affect other areas of society and culture? Without question, drugs have dire

---

[117] As the Hon Murray Gleeson wrote in his judgment as Chief Justice of the High Court in Magill v Magill (2006) 226 CLR 551 at 564 in paragraph 24, "The Family Law Act 1975 (Cth), in s 43, speaks of "the need to preserve and protect the institution of marriage as the union of a man and a woman to the exclusion of all others voluntarily entered into for life". As Jacobs J explained in *Russell v Russell* 51), the institution originated, at least in Western society, partly as a means of involving males in the nurture and protection of their offspring. Blackstone, in his Commentaries, described marriage as "built on this natural obligation of the father to provide for his children". The structure of marriage and the family is intended to sustain responsibility and obligation. In times of easy and frequent dissolution of marriage, the emphasis that is placed on the welfare of the children reflects the same purpose."

addictive consequences impacting the health and psychological wellbeing of those who take them. They impact families and the relationships of drug-takers. For society, the most obvious and alarming consequence is their generation of spiralling crime to pay for, and supply, the needs of the addicted. "Milder" drug habits lead to more and more serious and destructive ones and so on.

Whilst the consequences which flow from drugs are unquestionably drastic and sufficient reason to ban their use, I prefer here not to focus on arguments against drugs because of their *consequences*. Rather, I would like to explore the concept that any taking of a consciousness-altering drug — even a single, isolated (and supervised) taking of drugs by a supposedly justified consumer (on medical or other grounds) — is, in and of itself, wrong.

The reason for taking this tack is twofold. First, I think that bad flows from bad, i.e., the consequences are bad because the initial act, as I wish to argue, is bad. Secondly, if we separate the act itself from the consequences — suspending judgment on the act itself and concerning ourselves primarily with the consequence — then we become drawn to all sorts of proposals, arguments, plans and promises to contain and avoid the disturbing consequences, and could be "trapped" into endorsing implicitly the act itself, which, however, is morally flawed.

Thus, following a "consequences"-only argument, people can be led to argue for euthanasia because they have a bill which is the most "conservative" and "safeguard-laden" one in the world. But this carries the immensely problematic assumption that in an "ideal case" euthanasia is acceptable. They will argue for the limited use of "medical" cannabis, because with all the restrictions on cannabis use designed to stop it spreading, there is nothing really wrong, in their view, with the use of cannabis in a specific situation. In fact, however, with all the slippery slope arguments, we risk sidestepping the essential ethical reality that there is no justifiable candidate for euthanasia (because life is Divine property). Similarly, I want to argue here, the taking of consciousness-altering drugs *is wrong in itself* — there is no acceptable or justifiable circumstance for it.

The explanation of this is to be prefaced by the consideration that the true hallmark of the human being is moral responsibility and answerability in every moment of his or her existence. This is understood by reference to the make-up of a human being, as a composite of body, mind and a higher faculty, which we could call conscience and which in traditional religious language is called the soul. The conscience or the soul has the ability to apprehend — or at least to ratify and resonate with — objective universal values. That is what the Bible means when it says the human being is made in the image of the Creator: it relates to a moral compass. That soul or conscience however resides in the person alongside body and mind, which can draw the human being in directions contrary to that moral compass. This struggle or tension between conscience and psychophysical impulse is the source of human freedom: the freedom to choose whether to follow the moral compass or to follow contrary persuasions — be they bodily, psychological or ideologically cultural.

Our faith tradition teaches us that we are mandated to choose good and to follow that moral compass. It is within our ability to do so because conscience or soul is ultimately the sovereign power within the person and has the ability to win its internal struggle. Viktor Frankl stated, that as long as a person is alive and intellectually conscious, there are no limits to the human freedom and responsibility to find meaning and moral purpose and to respond accordingly. Even in the most drastic circumstances, such as where a person is hemmed in by paralysis or physically constrained by others, he or she has the freedom and ability still to take up an attitude towards — a meaningful stance towards — one's predicament.

The instrument of responsibility

The role of mind is central in the life of responsibility. The power of intellect, properly used, has two sides. On the one hand, the power of mind is the power of analysis, review and restraint —

to calculate the consequences of acting on a particular impulse and on that basis to decide whether to desist from, or to permit, so acting. Intellect submits unruly emotion to a reality check.

The second side of intellect — that is, of healthy and honest intellect — is its recognition that the *principles*, upon which it decides to admit or reject certain desires or impulses, are *beyond* itself. The ultimate criteria of "good" and "bad", "right" and "wrong" transcend, and transcendently inform, intellect. The culture war we have today — over whether the human being is solely a material, sentient being (for whom pleasure and pain alone exist) or whether the human being also has a spiritual dimension with an absolute moral compass — is about such first principles. This does not leave us with a relativism of ultimate assumptions. For the *truly* self-transcending intellect, as Viktor Frankl pointed out, leads to that which is beyond the interests of mind and body — to the Divine, to that which is greater — whilst hedonistic materialism is tied to the interests of mind and body. Hedonism is incapable of self-transcendence: its first principles are not beyond, but below, mere predilections.

Now the problem of drugs is that the instrument of responsibility — namely, intellect — becomes disordered at both ends. The regulative and analytic function of the mind, with its unique ability to review and check experience and feeling, is weakened. In the words of the report on "The health and social effects of non-medical cannabis use" (World Health Organization, 2016) the factors of "cognition, attention, emotionality and motivation" all become impaired under the use of cannabis. But not only has the *lower* regulative function of intellect broken down. In, *and because of*, its hedonistic self-directedness, the taking of drugs also impairs the *higher* function of intellect in a *self-transcending* opening to values beyond itself.

Here is the difference between consciousness-altering drugs and other stimulants such as nicotine, caffeine and alcohol. Whilst (especially) alcohol in an extreme measure can remove the function of intellect in responsibility — regulating action in accordance with higher values — a controlled, moderate amount (and certainly with nicotine and caffeine) does not. With drugs, even a small quantity can introduce *qualitative* degradation of rationality and hence of responsibility. As noted by David W. Murray,

> Alcohol... is eliminated in a few hours, there is little or no evidence for carcinogenicity or teratogenicity [producing abnormalities] ... psychotic phenomena only occur after heavy and prolonged dosage ... it escalates only to itself; the price paid for overuse is paid in later life. Cannabis is taken specifically for its psychic action; it is cumulative and persistent; its tar is carcinogenic ... experimentally it is teratogenic; psychotic phenomena may occur with a single dose; it can predispose to the use of other drugs; the price for its overuse is paid in adolescence or in early life.

In summary, the difference between alcohol and drugs is that the same "moderate"—*quantitative* intake of each produces *qualitatively* different results. Consciousness-altering drugs generically put out of function the instrument of human responsibility. For this reason, not even a person in great pain or suffering, should be "stoned" — should lose the power to relate meaningfully and responsibly to his or her circumstances, however hard they are. For that is a deprivation of a person's essential humanity — his or her power responsibility, the ability meaningfully to *respond*. The same applies to "safe injecting rooms" for heroin addicts. The act of injection of heroin is humanly wrong, in and of itself, whatever the addict's circumstance.

The culture of responsibility

For the higher function of intellect and responsibility — the ability to access those values upon which we act — to operate, we need the cultural conditions which permit and favour self-transcendence. The sensitivity to, and appreciation of, religious belief is the nurturing culture of self-transcendence. Religious belief is not the only, but it is the greatest and most central, expression of human self-transcendence.

As both the religious — and the enemies of religion — know, the capacity for, and knowledge of, religious experience is primarily conveyed within the family. But ours is a society in which the bulwark of the family — marriage — has been fractured. About one-third of all children in Australia are born out of wedlock, and amongst those marriages, which were contracted, there is significant breakdown. This impairs the transmission of religion and the culture of self-transcendence.

The second vital support for religious transmission — religious education — has also been greatly weakened. The former President of the European Union, Herman van Rompuy, asked poignantly with regard to so much of contemporary European youth "How can one find G-d when one has never heard of Him..." Much of our youth — in Australia — does not even know of their legacy of the knowledge and experience of faith, to claim it for themselves.

To restore, or indeed even to offer, to our youth their unclaimed religious inheritance, the first thing we can do is to face up to the aggressive attempts to remove it from education in our society today. One such successful aggressive move to dismantle religious transmission was accomplished within the Victorian Department of Education under the present Victorian State Government. A resolutely atheist organization — protestations of non-hostility to religion per se notwithstanding — called FIRIS ("Fairness in Religion in Schools") managed successfully to lobby the Labor Government to exclude from school hours even one lesson of optional religious education provided by Jewish, Christian and Islamic agencies. The Victorian Education Department supposedly "compensated" this removal of religious education with something which in fact contributes further to secularization. It established a new compulsory stream throughout the school curriculum which teaches not religion but "about" religion. Setting up a comparative study of religions, which includes secular humanism as an alternative to religion, is however not an education *in* personally experienced and confirmed religious belief and practice. Rather it is a comparative study of beliefs and non-belief which *relativises and neutralizes* religious beliefs, both amongst one another, and alongside the religious *non-belief* of secular humanism. The educational model comes from Sweden, possibly the most atheistic society of the West (without a communist background) which has pursued a secularization of traditional values to the extent that it permits siblings with one common parent to marry — incest. The fundamental rationale of this subject is that religion is the problem, not the solution, and it can only be neutralized through comparative, relativising study which teaches "tolerance" and "respect". It seems that FIRIS plans to work on other State education departments, focussing now on the New South Wales Department of Education, with the same objective of removing optional religious education from State schools.

The secularist attack on religion — as "the problem" which produces conflict — is born of a deep ignorance of religion. The authentic heart of religiosity is self-transcendence. The violent movements, such ISIS, which claim a religious veneer, are crude idolatries, which may speak of a Creator, but in fact mean themselves. Today, as traditional values are assailed by hedonistic materialism, we find the great world religions delineating the true common ground, which they possess and want to save. This is the set of common ultimate values, which are ratified by every self-transcending soul, and the authentic element of self-transcendence in every faith. Interestingly, the great psychologist Viktor Frankl wrote that when the non-religious person embarks upon genuine self-transcendence, he or she is actually on the same trajectory as the religious person — and will ultimately resonate with the same transcendently anchored universal values.

It follows that a sensitive religious education is ultimately a force for social harmony and the common apprehension of ultimate human values. It is aggressive secularism, which undermines self-transcendence and breeds social disintegration. Its focus is primarily on the diverse flux of individual hedonistic gains, the opposite of a rallying to common values and spiritual ideals. It has largely produced the "existential void" which has become the lot of a spiritually orphaned generation (or perhaps we could say, generations — those of both young adult youth *and* of their parents today).

An existential void of meaning predisposes towards hedonism and escapism. Viktor Frankl wrote many years ago of sexual hedonism as a reflex of existential void:

> ...we see how precisely where the will to meaning remains unfulfilled, that the will to pleasure serves to anaesthetize the existential unfulfillment of persons, at least as far as their own consciousness is concerned. In other words, the will to pleasure first appears when a person's will to meaning is unfulfilled. Sexual libido only runs wild in an existential vacuum. The existential disappointment of the person in the struggle for existential meaning will be vicariously compensated through a sexual anaesthetization.[118]

I believe his words apply equally to the culture of drug-taking.

When religion, the model and mentor of all self-transcendence, atrophies in society, so too does self-transcendence. And, so too, do meaning and motivation in life atrophy. There dissipates the sense of, and addressee for, responsibility — that, and to which or to Whom, we need to answer. In a recent editorial of the grass roots mass media tabloid, the *Herald Sun* of 14 August 2017, headed "Drug Deaths Hit Statewide", the newspaper said:

> ... education and rehabilitation are the major tools to be used in the fight to stop people using dangerous drugs and help them kick addiction.
>
> In the end, individual responsibility, danger awareness and comprehensive support must all form part of the response if we are to turn the tide of these awful losses.

The ingredient, which the newspaper listed first, "individual responsibility", is nurtured, above all, by our spiritual tradition. FIRIS managed to have the Creator shown out of the classroom, but it opened the door to the Ice Age.[119]

---

[118] Viktor E. Frankl, *On the Theory and Therapy of Mental Disorders* (transl. James Dubois), N.Y.: Brunner-Routledge, 2004, p. 159.

[119] The allusion here is to the widespread use amongst youth of the drug "ice", methamphetamine.

Chapter 10

Recovering the Sanctity of Life

Since the publication of *Politics and Universal Ethics* — which witnessed and discussed the legislation of abortion on demand in Victoria — Government sanctioned killing has extended to "assisted suicide" and euthanasia. The word euthanasia is avoided by the legislation which speaks instead about "assisted dying". The legislation, however, makes it clear that if the patient is unable, with the proffered means, to kill him- or herself the physician may do it, that is, perform euthanasia.

One of the most disturbing features of the "assisted dying" legislation in Victoria is that it requires that the request for assistance to commit suicide be made in a state of mental competence. This implies that suicide is not necessarily an expression of a mental illness, depression or otherwise, but can also be a *rational* decision. The legislative ideas that suicide may be facilitated as a "rational" choice and that unborn babies may be aborted on demand for any or no reason, together eliminate the sanctity of life as an absolute principle of society. The sanctity of life can only be recovered when we remember and re-experience the principles in universal ethics which make life sacred and which make killing bad.

The following pieces seek to retrieve what contemporary legislation has excised from the concept of a human being, namely, the spiritual aspect of the human being. Within the legislation's truncated concept of the human as an exclusively psychophysical organism, one's own or another's life may be disposed of as a mere burden, when pain or difficulty and, with abortion, even inconvenience arise. It overlooks or suppresses or has forgotten the ever "healthy" and sovereign part of the human — the soul or conscience — which defines the essence of the human being; and that this is a Divine agency and Divine property, which can be removed only with the permission of its Creator.

This culture of killing moreover corrupts care of the sick and suffering as a social value; and undoes the ethics of healing for doctors, who are coerced, despite their objections, to participate in killing, by an obligation to refer to doctors who have no qualms in doing so. An essay in this chapter address the *nihilism* of the culture of killing. By sanctioning the killing of humans, it removes the very concept of moral agency, which is the purpose of human existence. It annihilates in advance the good which the slain foetus or sick adult could do or could elicit from others. A further essay addresses the *contagion* of the killing culture. Once the absolute value of life is gone, there are no limits in deeming a life worthless. A baby born with Down syndrome or a depressed teenager or adult all become candidates for extinction. It is not a matter of a "slippery slope": either life has absolute value, or it has none. The culture of killing threatens to destroy civilization which is based on the lives of human beings, who were born to *live* for an ethical purpose.

Compassion for the Whole Person

A Letter to the Members of the Tasmanian Parliament on the "Voluntary Assisted Dying Bill"

May I share the following thoughts with you? The compassion for human suffering is a very noble quality. So is compassion for the suffering of animals and even the concern not to ravage non-living things, such as natural resources and environments. The compassion for the human being, however, has an extra dimension. A human being is not only sentient flesh, which can experience physical pain and physical pleasure. The human being also possesses a soul. Assisted suicide, euthanasia and abortion on demand, therefore relate not simply to the cessation of physical life. They are about extinguishing the operation of a soul within a body.

The "soul" could be understood both religiously and in a secular vein. From a religious point of view, the soul is a spark of the Divine. From a secular point of view, it has been understood as that which seeks higher meaning and purpose for its vehicles — body and mind — in life. Even in suffering and even in extreme suffering, Viktor Frankl (author of *Man's Search for Meaning*) has written that this highest human faculty is free and active. Hemmed in by the most frightful physical suffering, it is still free: to take up a meaningful attitude towards its suffering. This highest faculty of the human being — call it soul or conscience — is always whole and intact: it never becomes diseased or morbid and it is always potentially in control. The human being as a union of body, mind and soul is a composite agency endowed, under all circumstances whether expansive or profoundly hemmed-in, with the ability to spread goodness in the world, whether through action, speech or even thought alone.

In the tradition of universal ethics at the root of the world religions we are told that a person does not have dominion over his or her own life — body, mind and soul — to harm or shame it and surely not to destroy it. These were entrusted to us by the Creator for a purpose. To destroy it is to affront the Divine, to respect it is to respect the Divine. There are special circumstances when life can and even should be taken, such as in self-defence. However, the notion that a human being can *actively intervene to dispose* of life at will because of physical pain is part of a doctrine which teaches that the physical and material happiness is "all there is" and that the human being has no other — spiritual — purpose above and despite that suffering.

The materialistic worldview focused exclusively on pain and pleasure shades into a comprehensive view of the disposability of life for reasons of material or physical interest. It favours not only euthanasia, but also abortion on demand (even to allow a person to abort simply because a boy is preferred to a girl or vice-versa), to a culture of voluntary suicide and, for some "ethicists", to infanticide of living infants up to one month old, judged "unworthy" of life because of physical or mental disabilities.

We must do everything we can to alleviate suffering, but a policy which makes killing a reflex to pain is a false and treacherous compassion. It erodes an ethic of care and compassion for the vulnerable at the beginnings and end of life. It forces older people, who are perceived as "burden" on families and society, to struggle to defend their existence. It fuels abortion on demand for the most capricious reasons. It has, as we have seen in legislation, set up a regime of coercion to compel others — pre-eminently doctors and others of the *caring* professions — to be complicit in killing, against their own conscience. And it seeks to impose a total cultural silence over that part of the person, the soul, which mirrors and quests its Creator. This through-and-through materialistic culture can, if permitted to establish itself through euthanasia laws, become an instrument of ultimate cruelty towards the human body and the human spirit. The *complete* compassion is for the *whole* person, body and soul, and so-to-speak for its Creator, Who entreats us to actualize (not to cancel) the human being, through the heights and depths of life, as an agency of light and goodness.

Speaking on behalf of the Abrahamic religions, of which the Judeo-Christian foundations of our society are a key strand, I ask you reject to the bill for "assisted dying" before the Tasmanian Parliament.

What Life is and Why Killing is Wrong
A Victorian Bill for "Assisted Dying"

The heart of the matter: the inviolability of life

We live in times when those anchor values of society, which were once shared by both the centre-right and the centre-left of politics, are being forgotten. The most basic of these is the sacredness and inviolability of life and the eternal prohibition on killing. This means that although there are extreme circumstances where life may be taken — as in self-defence or war *to protect life* — we cannot otherwise actively take a life, neither another's nor our own. Yet the overturning of this basic value is what is proposed in the forthcoming Victorian Euthanasia Bill — euphemistically rendered as "assisted dying".

Very many of the arguments against euthanasia deal validly with the abuses of euthanasia, like the claimed 1000 persons euthanised in Holland "by mistake". Or by reference to the argument of a "slippery slope", the bottom of which has already been reached in Belgium where a child can request euthanasia. Others point to the general cultural damage of a bill which makes suicide a contagion — an acceptable option in general and so gives huge impetus to destructive impulses in depressed youth and others. All of these are true, but we need to know what is *essentially* wrong with euthanasia even when it is administered to what is thought the "best candidate", i.e., with "consent" to a terminally ill patient in great pain.

Why does traditional morality, the morality of millennia of human civilization, of which the religious traditions seem to be the main custodians, prohibit killing, whether of others or of oneself? Why does pain not provide grounds for killing a person or for the self-killing of a person? To answer the question, why life is inviolable, we have to ask what life — the life of a human being — is. A human being has a body and a mind, both of which are capable of happiness and suffering. But the human being also has a faculty, which has been forgotten by many. Some terms for this faculty are "conscience" or a "self-transcending" or "meaning-and-purpose-seeking" faculty.

The religious tradition calls this essential faculty of the human being the "soul". The Bible refers to it as made in the image of its Creator, capable of knowing and resonating with the eternal moral laws of the Creator. It is this faculty which leads one to an eternal moral compass. Bearing the Divine stamp, this essential faculty makes human life Divine property or a Divine agency, which is not ours to dispose of — whether in ourselves or in others — at will. So, when it comes to talk about "personal autonomy" and euthanasia, there are two ways to respond: One is that I have no autonomy to dispose of my soul, my essential life. Or, secondly, that my real, autonomous self *is* this Divine self. This essential

"I" is not sick or in pain. Rather it is *located* in a body and mind, which may be sick or in pain. Even there it retains the ability to fulfil its mission. Its value and significance remain unchanged.

Suffering calls for a response not extinguishment

In other words, there is a higher self — call it soul or conscience — which one can and must separate from the predicament of both body and mind. That higher self is not the body with its joys and suffering; it is also not the mind, with its pleasures and anguish. It *has* the body and mind, as its vehicles, and it is ethically responsible for their conduct. It has to act morally, notwithstanding — that is to say *despite* — the pressures of body and mind. This pure self is the true autonomous, responsible, and essential human self. It is not driven by body or mind against its moral obligations, but rather is the sovereign director within the human being.

The great psychologist Viktor Frankl reaffirmed the centrality of this faculty in the human being. He crystallized his teaching in the Nazi concentration camps, the greatest, continuous day-by-day suffering of body and mind, for its victims, in human history. There, the constant question for everyone was "why not commit suicide", and the answer, which he enshrined in his psychological teaching, was that the human being is capable of — and humanly responsible and obligated in — finding and actualizing meaning and purpose in any predicament. Our autonomy consists in giving life meaning, not in signing it away.

The dynamic of caring

Not only are we supposed, in life's difficulties and challenges, to direct ourselves to meaning and purpose, which means embracing, valuing and utilizing our life however hard it has become. We are supposed also to care for the lives of others. Part of the purpose of the existence of the well and the sick, is that the sick should be cared for by the well. This is like the dynamic of rich and poor in the matter of charity. It is within the ability of the Creator to sustain all in plenty, but He desires that the portion of the poor be augmented by the rich. And that is of benefit — in terms of personal refinement — for the rich themselves. Thus, a caring society is of as great value for the carers as for the cared for. A regime of euthanasia undermines the ethic of caring. The existence of an ever-present possibility of removing the burden of care through euthanasia, diminishes the sense of obligation of the carer and places pressure on the cared for to eliminate the burden of care by agreeing to "go".

There is no cessation of the ethical value of the human soul, the receptor of the knowledge of good and bad, even when it is housed in a body or a mind that suffers. Even in the midst of great suffering, by virtue of the soul, one has yet the power to take up a redemptive and meaningful stance towards one's suffering. With whatever powers of thought, speech and action which are left one, one can still effect good. The carer finds strength in knowing that one is assisting the mission of the life for which one cares.

The falsehood that life is only pleasure and pain

The view which forgets the soul — and understands the human being as only body and mind — runs towards pleasure and flees pain. Life has a myriad of challenges, of which a number can be painful. It is painful to grow through and overcome a difficulty in a relationship. It is painful to exert the effort necessary to master a skill. But the overcoming and the response to challenges, whether in deed, experience or resolution, is what makes a human being — human. This is the space of true human autonomy and freedom. A person who is impelled in decisions by pleasure and pain is not autonomous: that person is *driven*, not free and responsible. The essential self — conscience or soul — has been locked down, repressed. The truly autonomous, responsible human being is the one who *examines* one's own impulses, perceptions and reactions The advocates of euthanasia include those who have argued for killing children who have born with Down syndrome. Since, they argue, this person's pleasures, whether physical or intellectual, are limited, their life is not worth living. This is only because they understand the human being only as body and mind, and only as pleasure and pain. But they have lost sight of what the human being essentially is — a soul, a conscience, a higher purpose — and this is not adjudicated by pleasure and pain, but rather adjudicates and *morally* decides what pleasure is acceptable and what pain may be avoided.

One choice that a person, even with much suffering, may not make, according to the universal ethics of the fully actualized conscience or soul, is to request an active intervention to end his or her own life. We do not want pain; indeed, we seek its amelioration. By the same token we do not have to pursue aggressively new interventions to prolong life amidst great suffering. We may even pray that one be released from one's suffering through death. The decision to *end* life, however, can be made only by the Creator, who placed the soul within that life and alone can end its mission.

Endorsing killing undermines all morality

What, in short, euthanasia or "assisted suicide" is, is the understanding of the human being as a soulless, pleasure and pain organism. Instead of resolving and dealing with suffering, it eliminates the sufferer. And in so doing it disregards the deepest prohibition of which civilization knows, the prohibition of killing. In snuffing out the human soul, made in the image of G-d, it extinguishes the receptor of all morality. It makes way for a barbarism across the board. Its purported "compassion" is corrupted. Those who argue that if a pet can be put down, a person should certainly be allowed this, forget the difference between a human and animal: the human soul. They reduce the human being to an animal. On the *whole* human being — body mind *and soul* — there is no compassion.

The Nihilism in Euthanasia

A bill is shortly to come before the Victorian Parliament to legalize "assisted suicide", and where the patient is unable to do this by him- or herself, to require a physician to perform euthanasia. The Rabbinical Council of Victoria has issued a statement against this bill, explaining that Judaism prohibits both. It refers to further serious concerns: that this bill undermines a societal ethic of care; that it corrodes medical ethics and particularly the age-old Hippocratic oath to do no harm; that it pressures vulnerable sick and elderly persons to see themselves as a burden on their families and to agree to euthanasia; and that legislative condoning of suicide impacts depressed and disabled persons, young and old, sapping hope and the will to live. Others point to the "creep" of legal euthanasia, whether by "mistake" to unwilling patients, or simple policy drift to include those who experience psychological or "existential" pain. In Belgium, where euthanasia is legal, the percentage of deaths from euthanasia rose from 1.9% in 2007 to 4.6% in 2013. Today, a child can request euthanasia in Belgium.

Instead of contemplating all this real collateral damage of euthanasia legislation, let us rather consider why our tradition prohibits the intervention to end the life even of the supposed "best" candidate for euthanasia, a person in great pain at the end of a long life. This question is best answered in comparison with a leading philosophy of euthanasia.

This pro-euthanasia philosophy understands the human being as no more than mind and body — in the words of Viktor Frankl, a "psychophysical" organism — for which *alone* pleasure and pain count. On this basis, this philosophy of euthanasia argues that infants born with Down Syndrome could also be euthanized because of their diminished own capacity for physical and intellectual enjoyment as well as their burden on others (paining them also), just like the elderly person dying from a terminal illness.

The religious tradition is profoundly concerned with the suffering of body and mind. But it also sees in the human being a third dimension, the human soul. It is the soul or conscience, which, by reference to a higher set of values, does not merely react to, but rather adjudicates pain and pleasure: it decides which pleasures should be accepted and which rejected, what pain should be avoided and which endured. It seeks meaning in, and takes up an attitude towards, suffering. Its reference framework is that of the laws of our Creator, one of which is that we may not actively end a life, even in great pain.

A reason adduced for that law is that the soul of a human being — in regard to which the Bible calls the human being "made in the image of" its Creator, knowing moral right and wrong — partakes of the holiness of its Creator. Bearing the Divine stamp, and on a Divine mission, it is Divine property that may not be disposed of at will. A major philosophy of euthanasia, on the other hand, equates human and animal within the one dimension of "sentience" — capacity for pain and pleasure. Just as it finds no soul in the animal, it finds none in the human being. Even in the soul's ascendency — at the summation of its mission in an elderly dying person, or in the soul's radiance (as our tradition makes us aware) in a Down syndrome child — this philosophy of euthanasia is blind to the spiritual. Looking only at pain and pleasure levels, rather than seeking to alleviate suffering through care, love and meaning, it proposes extinguishment.

Were euthanasia legislation to become universal — at the current death rate from euthanasia in Belgium, and with the proposal of some of its proponents for infanticide of children born with severe disadvantage — a "legal" killing greater than the size of the Jewish holocaust could well occur over the same time interval of the holocaust. "How can you compare the two?", one could ask. "Euthanasia proceeds from 'consent', whilst the Holocaust proceeded from persecution". In answer, I quote the words of the great psychologist and Auschwitz survivor, Viktor Frankl: "I am absolutely convinced that the gas chambers of Auschwitz, Treblinka, and Majdanek were ultimately prepared not in some Ministry or other in Berlin, but rather at the desks and in the lecture halls of nihilistic scientists and philosophers". The same philosophical nihilism — the unhinging of "reason" from higher, objective, spiritual values — that sprouted the Holocaust, operates in the culture of euthanasia, which understands the human as no more than a psychophysical organism, whose morality is derived solely from a calculus of pain and pleasure ("hedonistic utilitarianism").

The religious tradition sanctifies human life as the seat of the soul, which — with its objective knowledge of good and evil — seeks meaning and response in suffering. Rejecting the soul and objective moral knowledge, hedonistic utilitarianism wants, in one of its proponent's words, to "unsanctify" life and make it, in conditions of pain, as disposable as any piece of physical property. The religious tradition knows that one does not always have to cling to life through undertaking new treatments, which could simply prolong life in pain; but it knows equally that one may not then intervene directly to take life. Hedonistic utilitarianism sees no difference. Hedonistic utilitarianism wants to gratify what Freud called the "death instinct", a desire to "return" to an "inorganic state". In response to pain, it markets oblivion. Our tradition embraces the meaning and purpose of a soul placed in us by our Creator, which only He can take back to Himself when He deems its mission concluded.

The Contagion of Euthanasia

With Arthur Goldberg

In Canada, "natural death" must be "reasonably foreseeable" before a doctor may euthanize a patient. In spite of such statutory language, in *A.B. v. Canada*, a case decided this June, the Court judged that the anticipated natural death need not be "imminent"; it need not even be "connected to a particular terminal disease or condition." Rather, Justice Paul Perell concluded, "what is a 'reasonably foreseeable death' is a person's specific medical question to be made without necessarily making, but not precluding, a prognosis of the remaining lifespan." Physician-assisted suicide may go forward as long as a medical professional considers "all of a particular person's medical circumstances."

One wonders in what sort of case death would *not* be reasonably foreseeable, under this loose standard.

The foundation for this decision was an earlier Canadian Supreme Court case, *Carter* v. *Canada*. It overturned the law that criminalized both the assisting of another's suicide and the consenting to one's own death, on the grounds that the law "unjustifiably infringed" upon the rights and freedoms of "competent adult persons."

The slippage is part of a common pattern. A strong element in contemporary secularism sees human life as the personal property of its person. When suffering renders life burdensome to self or others, it can and may be disposed of; this is, for such secularists, the "compassionate" thing to do. But — as Canadians and others have by now found, again and again — the contagion of assisted suicide, once the command "Thou shalt not kill" is set aside, quickly spreads elsewhere.

The push for assisted suicide is really a corruption of compassion. True compassion requires recognizing what followers of the Abrahamic faiths have long recognized: human life is animated by the soul, fashioned by G-d in the image of G-d. Life has been given to the human in trust, and it can only be protected and respected by following the universal ethical values of the Noahide Code, a set of principles at the root of the world religions.

The contagion of euthanasia

Regimes in which euthanasia prevail create a *contagion* of killing, which travels far beyond the "limits" initially intended by its proponents. Early experience with assisted suicide laws indicates how these laws can easily be extended.

One vector for the contagion of euthanasia is the vagueness of the terms in which the conditions for termination of life are expressed. Alex Schadenberg, International Chair of the Euthanasia Prevention Coalition, provides a couple of examples. *A.B.* v. *Canada*, the case cited above, arose because the petitioner's doctor was unwilling to execute a woman with excruciating osteoarthritis, fearing that if he did so, he might be charged with murder. If the requirement that death be "reasonably foreseeable" is supposed to rule *anything* out, it probably should rule out killing someone with painful, non-terminal arthritis — yet the court found some way to justify the killing. Schadenberg also points to a case of a young man in a Vancouver nursing home who was diagnosed with a neurological disease and struggled to "find a cure with massive doses of vitamins." Nowhere near dying, this man was nevertheless killed by a Vancouver physician.

The spread of the contagion is facilitated by financial motives also. Insurance companies, trying to save money, often seek to replace *sanctity of life* with so-called *quality of life*. Dr. Brian Callister, an associate professor at the University of Nevada School of Medicine and former head of the State's Medical Association, attempted to transfer two patients to hospitals in other states, so that they could receive potentially life-saving treatments unavailable in Nevada. His patients were denied insurance for their transfer and treatment. The insurers asked: "Have you considered suicide?" Speaking from personal experience, Dr. Callister says, "Assisted suicide changes the way we care for patients. It creates a dangerous segue to perverse incentives for insurance companies and there's no going back from that."

The psychological contagion of suicide

Humans do not live in isolation. The more our culture sends messages that some lives are less valuable than others, the more some people will internalize messages to end their lives. A psychological contagion of suicide is unleashed by euthanasia and assisted suicide laws. Condoning suicide in one circumstance implicitly condones it across the board. The wrong of suicide is no longer absolute: death is made a reasonable — even the expected — response to pain, misfortune, and sadness.

On his *Fox News* show, Tucker Carlson highlighted the negative effect of *13 Reasons Why*, a Netflix show, on two teenage girls in California. According to their parents, the girls committed suicides after "binging" on episodes of the show. They blamed their children's deaths on the show's glamorization of suicide, its presentation of suicide as a response to the stresses of teenage life.

It is perhaps no accident that Oregon, the first state to legalize assisted suicide, has a general suicide rate some 40 percent higher than the American national average. Whether legal "assisted suicide" fuelled the State's culture of suicide, or was fuelled by an otherwise existing culture of suicide, the Oregon experience at least suggests that suicide as a culturally accepted "value" and legislation permitting "assisted suicide" go together.

The culture of suicide, given its imprimatur by the state, confounds the efforts of parents and caregivers. There's something patently contradictory in a state's provision of, on the one hand, a suicide hotline and, on the other, assisted suicide. The depressed and disabled need our care and encouragement.

Conscience rights

Permitting euthanasia does not just harm those who are killed. It also harms those who are forced to kill, or else suffer legal consequences or be forced from a profession. Legislation implemented in Ontario — and similar legislation proposed in Victoria, Australia — forces physicians who oppose personal involvement in euthanasia or "assisted suicide" to "effectively refer" their patients to another physician who will kill. "Effective referral" is defined as a referral to carry out the purposes of the Act. That means a specific referral either "to someone who will do it or someone who will arrange it. Either way," EPC Chair Alex Schadenberg explains, "it's a referral for the purpose of death." It thus denies conscience rights to medical professionals who do not understand killing their patients to be part of their craft.

In the view of Larry Worthen, executive director of the Christian Medical and Dental Association of Canada, when doctors are told they must send their patient to an executioner, "we are being forced to violate our deeply held religious beliefs. Effective referral and participating in assisted death are morally and ethically the same thing. This forces people of conscience and faith to act against their moral convictions and threatens the very core of why they became physicians, which is to help to heal people."

Dr. Mark D'Souza, a palliative care physician and board director of Concerned Ontario Doctors, indicates that as a "conscientious objector," he objects to killing a patient. As a result, he and several other doctors he knows will no longer accept patients needing palliative care. The palliative care system in the community in which he practices (Scarborough) is grossly underserviced. The effect of these retirements is to worsen available care for patients in severe pain. In addition to contradicting the very concept of palliative care, the availability of euthanasia also tends to undermine its practice; where euthanasia is available, funding for palliative care falls correspondingly.

True compassion

The very expression "mercy killing" is an oxymoron that sets on edge the conscience of anyone with a background in the world faiths and the universal Noahide ethics incorporated within those faiths. People frequently request euthanasia when they are emotionally and/or psychologically distraught. Evidence from Oregon demonstrates that assisted suicide is overwhelmingly requested and granted based on misguided "compassionate" concerns such as burdening family and caregivers. It is prompted by fears of the loss of autonomy, of control over bodily functions, and of the ability to participate in enjoyable activities.

Euthanasia therefore abandons people at their most vulnerable. Rather than providing compassion and support for people in their suffering, euthanasia presents a callous and insensitive "alternative." As Viktor Frankl points out, the essential human dimension is neither body nor mind, but rather a soul or conscience with both mind and body as its vehicles and challenges. The task of soul or conscience is to respond purposefully and ethically to the predicaments of mind and body.

A "compassion" that extinguishes life on account of suffering practices cruelty against this essential person, which is itself *higher* than suffering but still must *deal morally* with suffering. According to this view, the response to suffering cannot be to simply extinguish the sufferer. True compassion balances kindness towards suffering with respect for the boundaries and purposes of persons as defined by their Creator. The most important boundary drawn around life is to protect it. The highest of purposes is to find ethical meaning and purpose in the mission of life, as long as life is sustained within us by G-d, not to throw off that trust and escape into oblivion.

We can see a shining example of true compassion in the case of an Oregon resident, Jeanette Hall. After receiving a terminal diagnosis of cancer, she requested lethal drugs, thinking it appropriate to "do what our law allowed"— a law for which she voted. Her doctor, however, encouraged her not to give up, even though medical diagnosis gave her six months to live. A decade later she is still surviving.

Inalienable rights and obligations

America's founding fathers specified that our [American] society is premised on certain inalienable rights given by our Creator that are beyond manipulation by a legislature or the courts. The American Revolution was based on a religious belief that crucial fundamental rights and obligations derive from G-d, not from government. But more than 200 years have passed since that epic event, and secular humanists have developed a dogma that now places the state above G-d. Without the foundation of inalienable rights and obligations granted by a Creator that are *beyond* the influence of government, what we have is a dictatorship of ever-changing popular opinion.

If we are to be loyal to our [the American] Constitution and the Bill of Rights, we must understand and implement the universal moral ethics given to us by G-d though the Noahide Code, a set of values recognized on a bipartisan basis as the ethical and moral underpinnings of America. By ignoring this foundation, secular humanism has attempted to establish legislative and judicial fiats whereby G-d is replaced as the final moral arbiter of life and death.

In a previous *Public Discourse* essay, we spoke about the conditions required to achieve restoration of the political-moral centre. One essential ingredient is to overcome a culture of sanctioned killing, to re-anchor our contemporary culture towards the protection of life, rather than its disposal. To do this we must crystallize into our collective consciousness the principles of the Noahide Code, the moral root of our great religious traditions and our civilization.

Chapter 11

Universal Ethics in Economic Life

The claim to universality of certain ethical principles in economic life is manifested and demonstrated both through their resonance within, and their applicability to, a variety of economic systems. For economic systems arise out of diverse historical, cultural and social conditions and choices. The concept of universal principles which can be manifested in diverse and particular forms of economy removes the ideological "heat" from the contrast between different economic systems and shifts the focus to universally achievable ethical ideals.

The essay in this chapter, "Universal Ethics and Economic Life", distinguishes different forms or systems of economic organization from a universal ethical norm of voluntary (free) and reciprocal economic exchange. It seeks to show how different forms and structures of economic activity (whether centralized, individualist or "cooperative") do not of themselves preclude or guarantee free and reciprocal exchange – but can incorporate them. The criteria for the operation of these principles, which are given different weight by different systems, are also provided by universal ethics.

Universal Ethics and Economic Life

This essay explores the concept of universal economic ethics as both independent of, yet applicable to, the variety of specific types of economic systems. Different economic systems arise out of distinct political, cultural and historical choices and conditions. What matters, from the standpoint of universal ethics is whether and to what extent within these systems universal ethical economic principles can and do operate.

In the first part of this essay a nuanced principle of "free and reciprocal exchange" is elaborated as a universal ethical principle for economies.[120] The essay goes on, in the second section, to consider a typology of economies. The typology is constructed and the types distinguished from one another by their application of the distinct features of freedom of exchange on the other hand and reciprocity or mutuality of exchange – having to do with equality of consideration of needs – on the other. The resultant "pure" or "formal" types are centralized (such as socialist) economies, individualist (such as laissez faire capitalist) economies and a third model which mediates between them, "distributist" or "cooperative" economic structures.

Finally, the essay looks at the conditions under which each of these types of economic system or structure does or does not exhibit a "hue" of the norm of voluntary and reciprocal or exchange.

Voluntary and reciprocal exchange

Economic activity consists of individual – and the aggregation into a total economy of these individual – acts of exchange. A customer exchanges money for goods from a shopkeeper; a worker exchanges his or her labour for the wage provided by the employer. Through a price system, the values of all economic exchanges come to expression.

> The price system organizes economic activity primarily by coordinating the decisions of consumers, producers and owner of productive resources. Million of economic agents who have no direct communication with one another are led by the price system to supply each other's wants ... Prices are an expression of the consensus on the values of different things, and every society that permits exchanges among men has prices.[121]

---

[120] See S. Cowen, *The Theory and Practice of Universal Ethics – the Noahide Laws*, chapter12.
[121] "Price System", Encyclopedia Britannica, Macropedia, Vol. 14, p. 1004.

The key terms here are "decisions" and "wants". An economic act of exchange is a free decision to exchange one's money, labour and so forth, which brings about the fulfilment of wants on both sides of the act of exchange.

Of the seven universal Noahide laws at the root of the world religious traditions, the one which provides the implicit criteria for ethical economic activity is the prohibition of theft. For theft is the very antithesis of a freely decided exchange of money, property or labour in return for a reward or good of some kind which would satisfy a need. The thief may take money without consent of the owner, or it use labour or a service rendered by someone without paying for it (to take some examples of theft). Theft negates the freedom of the person to own and decide what to do with one's property or money and labour. Theft, secondly, is absolutely indifferent to the needs of the victim, whether the needs served by the money or property stolen, or the needs which could have been satisfied in return for the exchange of that money or labour. The thief considers his or her needs only, not that of the other. There is no reciprocity. It is ethically speaking a "non-exchange", or the negation of ethical exchange. From this we can learn that for economic activity, which is about exchange of money, goods and labour, to be ethical it must be both "free" or voluntary and evince "reciprocal" concern for the fulfilment of the needs of the parties.

The "reciprocity" concern for needs in the exchange relationship can take one towards a concept of "equality" in the sense of the "equality" of actual needs satisfaction among the economic agents in a society. But it need not do so. They need not push towards a concept of identical satisfaction of needs – equal income, housing etc. – but instead a notion of equality of consideration for the other, of what constitutes satisfaction for the other. notions of fulfilment of needs which are unique and distinct between individuals as far as is practicable. Similarly, "freedom" does not necessarily imply complete freedom of decision and complete ownership of the resources with which one deals. An individual is also free, when one freely assigns and authorizes one's decision-making and one's property to others. An economic system or structure as a whole will be assessed ethically in the way it provides systemically for (variously nuanced) free and reciprocal exchange.

Formal types of economy

The three systems or types of economy to be considered here can be set out in terms of the dimensions of the act of exchange set out above: (1) the free agency of individuals to make decisions with regard to the exchange of their money, property and labour and (2) the consideration of reciprocity – the equality of consideration of the needs satisfied on both sides by the exchange. The classic distinction here is between the two systems which place primary emphasis on one vis-à-vis the other of these two considerations.[122]

The classical laissez faire capitalist model[123] stresses the primacy of the freedom of the economic agent. Paramount is the right of the individual to own property and to make decisions in his or her own interest in regard to his wealth and labour. In so doing it rejects the interference of the State or regulatory bodies with regard to ownership, excessive taxation and the regulation of prices and competition.

At the same time this theory must answer to the claims of the other aspect of the exchange relationship, namely the equality of consideration and meeting of the needs of the others. The classical individual free enterprise model answers to this criterion in the words of its classic exponent, Adam Smith in the Wealth of Nations:

> It is not from the benevolence of the butcher, the brewer, or the baker, that we expect our dinner, but from their regard to their own interest. We address ourselves, not to their humanity but to their self-love, and never talk to them of our necessities

---

[122] See the essay by Rabbi Jonathan Sacks, "The Economy of Liberty" in *Covenant and Conversation,* Jerusalem: Koren, 2015, parshas Behar.
[123] Preceded by historically earlier and more limited market economies.

but of their advantages.[124]

Thus, Smith writes, the "invisible hand" of the market to accommodate the basic needs of all.[125]

An opposite emphasis in the exchange relationship is posited by the centralized economy of the classical socialist type. Its primary concern is with the equality, or equal consideration, of the needs-satisfaction of the population of economic agents as a whole. For this it sought to remove property from private ownership and enterprise from the personal decision making of individuals and vest that ownership in the State. The State, then, in the interest of its grasp of the needs of the population, makes decisions concerning production, pricing and consumption and employment.

As for the consideration of the free or voluntary aspect of exchange, the centralized economy may be able to claim that the citizens have voluntarily assigned their property and ownership rights to the State, that the State is indeed run by the "Party of the People". They may also claim that freedom cannot exist where there is poverty and that economic systems under private control in fact represent forms of subjugation and "enslavement", as was the argument of classical Marxism. The very fact that a centralized economy (with its corresponding political order) is "legitimate" in the eyes of the population is an expression of the freedom of the economic agents in conferring in legitimacy[126] on

---

[124] *The Wealth Of Nations*, Book I, Chapter II, pp. 26-7, para 12.

[125] [The rich] consume little more than the poor, and in spite of their natural selfishness and rapacity…they divide with the poor the produce of all their improvements. They are led by an invisible hand to make nearly the same distribution of the necessaries of life, which would have been made, had the earth been divided into equal portions among all its inhabitants, and thus without intending it, without knowing it, advance the interest of the society, and afford means to the multiplication of the species". *The Theory Of Moral Sentiments*, Part IV, Chapter I, pp. 184-5, para. 10.

[126] Other historical forms of (pre-socialist) centralized economy, which Max Weber termed "traditional" societies, had a similar basis. Thus "patriarchal and patrimonial" economies "showed an inherent tendency to substantive regulation of economic activity. This derived from the character of the claim to legitimacy and the corresponding interest in the contentment of the subjects". Max Weber, *The Theory of Social and Economic Organization* (transl. A. M Henderson and T. Parsons), NY: The Free Press, p. 357

an order which has taken over their property and makes decisions for them.

There is a third model, which mediates between the typically socialist centralized economy under State control and the individualist laissez faire capitalist model. This is the model of "distributism" set forth over a hundred years ago by the Catholic Church and elaborated in the writings of G. K. Chesterton and Hillaire Belloc. It was intended to steer between what it regarded as the twin "evils" of the concentrated State ownership of socialism and "run-away" individualist capitalism. It would do this through the "diffusion" or "distribution" of ownership within cooperatives. Workers would themselves become owners in cooperatives, each with a share in the capital and the profits. They would conjointly make economic decisions in respect to the operation of the co-operative within a consultative and participatory framework. Needs would be jointly met and often there were associated with the cooperative secondary educational and child-raising supports, with housing and banking assistance. The Israeli kibbutz is a classic model of the cooperative. The focus is on meeting the needs of all, whilst maintain the freedom of all in governance and decision-making. Wage differentials were capped. The formation of the cooperative was essentially voluntary, unlike the agricultural collectives organized under Soviet communism, which were compulsorily formed and directed by the central State apparatus.

In short, the goal of the cooperative or distributist model is to achieve an equilibrium between the freedom of the individual economic agent and the reciprocal consideration of needs-satisfaction for all. Cooperatives exist as "islands" within wider economies though the distributist model has also been envisaged on an economy -wide scale when, for example, "Indonesia gained its independence in 1945, [and] the cooperative was explicitly incorporated as the basis of a nation-based economy, based on article 33, paragraph one of the 1945 Constitution."[127] In reality, it appears that no society has developed an economy-wide or, as some have called it, a "cooperative commonwealth".

The ethical ideal in differing economic systems

Let us now consider practically and historically the ability of the universal ethical norm of voluntary and reciprocal exchange to operate or not operate in each of the economic systems set out in the forgoing section. This involves the invocation of some further ethical criteria drawn from the Noahide laws.

As noted, modern socialist orders are examples of a centralized "top-down" administered economy, but they have much earlier historical exemplars such as the "patriarchal and patrimonial" economies mentioned by Weber. A biblical instance of such an economy was that administered by Joseph, the viceroy of Egypt, who devised the plan of storing up state reserves of grain during the years of famine. When the famine arrived and the Egyptians found their private supplies depleted or spoilt and could no longer afford to purchase grain from the state, Joseph, upon the voluntary request of the people organized the sale of their land and their labour to the State in return for food and agricultural capital. This involved no violation of Noahide law. Whilst, under Noahide law, one cannot own the body of another person, an individual may voluntarily make over his or ownership of land and property and also one's labour to the State. The Bible records that this is what the Egyptians freely did. Secondly, Joseph actually supplied the material and the spiritual needs of the Egyptian population successfully, and in a way which produced no recorded discontent. The Egyptian population assimilated an economic order of free exchange of their labour and property (including land) in return for the supply of food and agricultural capital, under which they remitted to the State a portion of their productive output. Their needs were ostensibly met.

---

[127] A. M. N. Syechalad, I Hasan and M. S. A. Majid, "The Role of Cooperative in the Indonesian Economy", *International Journal of Humanities and Social Science Invention*, Vol. 6, Issue 10, Oct 2017, p. 43.

What will disqualify a centralized economy is where the State appropriates property and labour in a way which is not legitimated by the population. In that case the people have not made the State or its leader "their master" and the transfer of their property or labour is not free. Even in a centralized political and economic order, which was once legitimated by the people, where the State acts arbitrarily and capriciously – inconsistently with its own purported rules – through, for example, nepotism or corruption, the economic order is unethical. For then the State itself is a thief, and the people its victims. Without corruption and caprice, a centralized system, which does not strive to meet the needs of the people is also unethical.

Liberal capitalist or private enterprise orders, with their precursors in historical market economies prima facie meet the criterion of "free exchange" better than do many central economies, which can only claim that they are freely legitimated by their subjects. At the same time the fact that the discrepancy in wealth which can arise in such systems arguably creates poverty and need, which diminishes freedom. Especially when the economic power of the economic agents, whether it is customer and corporation or businesses amongst themselves is so asymmetrical that oppression and exploitation becomes a feature of economic life. Anecdotally, I would personally recount that, in the liberal capitalist society in which I live, my shoe repairer and my bank were on opposite sides of the same street. They were also often on opposite sides of a moral divide. When I walked into the shoe repairer, we greeted each other with a smile. He was gratified by my customer loyalty to him and I by his discounts. We had an economic, but also an essentially human, relationship. On the other side of the road in the branch of my bank, the tellers were being monitored to assure their "friendliness" to customers, whilst the bank hierarchy were hatching plans to scalp new profits from their client base. I wrote to the bank executive at one point:

> On several occasions the bank debited cheques of mine twice and I had to spend hours at the bank having the errors corrected. When I complained about this to ... Management,

> I received an answer that [the bank] offers no compensation for my time wasted by its mistakes. When however, with debit card purchases, my account was unintentionally overdrawn, I (like many others) was hit with $50 penalties (until, upon outcry that was pulled back to a $9 fee). The bottom line here is that there is currently little reciprocity – equality and mutuality – between the bank and its customers … The customer would be punished for his or her mistakes, but not the bank.

These exploitative penalties were a significant source of profit for the bank made possible by an oligopoly of four huge banking corporations in Australia. My relationship with the shoe repairer and the bank represented the equal possibilities of humane and inhumane economic relationships within capitalism.

Whilst, as the cold-war competition between communist and capitalist states indicated, capitalism had a better record in supplying needs – consumer goods – than did socialism, this need not necessarily be so. Especially, when a chasm arises between the earning power of different groups. Life can become intolerably expensive and debt-ridden.

The commune, co-operative or other "distributist" forms of economic organization, were consciously built to maximize both free participation and reciprocal fulfilment of needs. Inasmuch as the distributist or cooperative model was designed as a "hybrid" of socialism and capitalism – centralized and individualist economy – its ethical success or failure in practice depend on it ability to fulfil the criteria of each of these components of the model. The "command" character of the collective may or may not be oppressive to the individual members of the cooperative. It may or may not fulfil their individual needs, especially in collective living arrangements such as in the communal raising of children in the kibbutzim. So also, the cooperative as a "corporation" in the wider economy may act ethically or unethically with regard to all the ethical pitfalls of capitalism, price rigging, collusion and the abuse of market share, where the cooperative is a powerful unit. Within its own operation, it can also fall prey to endemic problems of capitalism: abandonment of limited wage differentials, drawing in expert managers who themselves disdain the cooperative "idea", with a resultant loss of autonomy of participation of the individual members of the cooperative.

Chapter 12

The Environment

Religiously Conscious and Secularizing Environmentalism

The proper treatment of nature, both animal and non-animal, is the subject of one of the seven biblical universal laws of Noah, the root and core common denominator values of the world faiths and cultures. The American Congress in 1991 affirmed these universal laws as the ethical foundation of civilization in the following terms:

> Whereas Congress recognizes the historical tradition of ethical values and principles which are the basis of civilized society and upon which our great Nation was founded.
>
> Whereas these ethical values and principles have been the bedrock of society from the dawn of civilization, when they were known as the Seven Noahide Laws.[128]

This Noahide law takes the specific form of a prohibition of a particularly cruel treatment of animals — the consumption of the limb of a living creature — yet it provides a general framework for the ethical human treatment of nature as a whole. I have set out the content of this basic law of civilization at some length in my book, *The Theory and Practice of Universal Ethics — the Noahide Laws*[129] and will not reiterate its detail here. Basically, it is concerned with removing unnecessary suffering in the human utilization of animals and unnecessary destruction in the human utilization of physical resources.

---

[128] Public Law 102-14, 102d Congress, 1st Session, H.J. Res. 104.
[129] Chapter 13.

This unchanging, millennia-long concern of core religious tradition for what is now termed the "environment" is to be contrasted here with a salient doctrine of contemporary environmentalism. It arises from the writings of Peter Singer, the intellectual architect of the Australian "Greens" political party and from the teaching of "Deep Ecology" in the work of the Norwegian philosopher, Arne Naess. From these emerges a comprehensive ideology, which ramifies into a political and social movement, of which the Greens are the flagship. The programme militates against traditional religious belief, against traditional sexual norms and revises traditional norms of the sanctity of life, advocating instead abortion on demand, euthanasia and "assisted suicide". It has also mooted infanticide for children born with disabilities.[130]

Singer's work is clearly anti-theistic, and in this respect, of course, stands in opposition to the spiritual tradition of the Noahide laws as G-d-given laws. Deep Ecology is also opposed to traditional religion — the teaching of and about a transcendent Creator — though it fashions a "New Age" religion of nature of its own. A great many people, who do not share their principled rejection of traditional religion, are yet swayed by the environmentalist zeal of the Greens and are drawn into affiliation with their wider ideology. One could even say that, apart from a number of small, consciously religiously or traditionally anchored political parties, the Greens' comprehensive ideology has influenced most of the political spectrum: the mainstream centre-right and centre-left parties in Australia are different "shades" of Green.

Many on both sides of the political centre, who trail in the wake of the Greens, do so with little rigorous reflection on the ideology which underlies the Greens' attitude towards nature. They might ask, What difference does it make, if one takes up environmental activism with this or that background world-view. Isn't the deed — to act with concern for nature — the main thing? The answer, which this essay seeks to elaborate, is that the wrong foundation of environmental action can both produce major collateral harm

---

[130] P. Singer, *Practical Ethics*. Cambridge: Cambridge University Press, 1979.

in many spheres of social policy *and* affect the practical efficacy of "environmental action". No legislation has more aggressively prosecuted the mistreatment of animals than the Reich Nature Protection Law of 1935, enacted by the Government of Adolf Hitler, which also covered the protection of forests. Yet these ostensible expressions of concern for nature were parts of a political ideology and movement, which bewilder the historical imagination by their unrivalled cruelty and horror.

The crux of the difference between the environmentalism of the spiritual tradition of the Noahide laws and the secularizing environmentalism of the Greens is in the stance towards the relationship of humanity and nature. It reduces further to a fundamental point: whether humanity may at all distinguish itself from nature and take up a distinct role within it. For the spiritual tradition, the answer is that the human being has a moral agency, which it receives from the Creator of nature. For this secularizing environmentalism, there is no Creator of nature and consequently no "privileged" role of the human being as the bearer of a transcendent, Divinely given moral template. I have called it a "secularizing" environmentalism rather than a "secular" environmentalism, because it is not simply indifferent to the religious tradition's stance in social policy; it seeks to negate and remove its influence.

The two — religious and secularizing — views differ, as is to be discussed in this essay, in respect of (1) the understanding of suffering and destruction in nature (2) the relationship between the human — as what I call a "vertical" dimension — and nature — as the "horizontal" dimension — in relation to the phenomena of suffering and destruction in nature and its overcoming of that and (3) the dimensions of environmental action.

Suffering and destruction in nature

The secularizing environmentalism discovers suffering and destruction in nature solely in, and to the extent of, human action in and towards the environment. It would seem to maintain that, aside from acts of human "aggression" and despoliation in nature, there is no suffering or destruction in nature which should concern us or be within our ability to alter. Thus, in the animal realm, Peter Singer sees a history of human domination, rapacity and cruelty towards animals. This is underpinned by what he regards as the unacceptable notion of the "superiority" of the human being, which he calls a "speciesism", that is, the tyranny by one — the human — species over other, in this case animal, species. Aside from egregious acts of cruelty to animals, he maintains that the very act of killing animals to eat their meat is an act of violence. The only remedy to this infliction of unjustifiable suffering, for Singer, is to reduce the status of the human being to one species of animal — a "human animal" — among others with no legitimate claim to superiority or dominance over "other" animals. As such the human enters into a utilitarian calculus of pleasure and pain on a footing of equality with animals.[131]

Where Singer's original focus, as the title of his book *Animal Liberation* suggests, is on animal nature, the movement of Deep Ecology takes in the entirety of nature. This includes vegetation and inorganic nature as parts of an order — an "ecosystem" — which, it holds, rightfully exists *for itself* independent of human interests. Consequently, in its view, the appropriation by humans of any natural resources, other than for the most minimal, vital needs, violates the independent integrity of the ecosystem. A model of Deep Ecology in practice, it is claimed, is found in the practice of indigenous Australian, who are portrayed as living in pristine harmony with the "land". The "deep ecologists" see the work of what they call "shallow ecologists", who advocate recycling and the development of renewable energy sources, as insufficient, because the latter's focus remains on human needs: the preservation of resources *not for their own sake*, but for the sake of humans. The human consumption of natural resources in systematic, technological industrial processes is grasped

---

[131] Experimentation on animals could for Singer be justified only on the basis of a utilitarian calculus, which achieves the greatest sentient gratification of the greatest number: for example the introduction of Parkinsons disease into 100 monkeys to improve the lives of 40,000 people. https://www.bbc.co.uk/blogs/ni/2006/11/peter_singer_defends_animal_ex.html

by Deep Ecology as a travesty, a wanton *destruction*, of nature. Their remedy is that humanity desist to the utmost degree from utilization, appropriation and consumption of natural resources. The destruction and consumption of nature can be rectified only by the greatest possible retraction of human utilization of it.

In the tradition of the Noahide laws there is also a sense of suffering and destruction in nature. This, however, is found not solely in acts committed by the human being which directly afflict animals and destroy natural resources. More so, suffering and destruction is a systemic characteristic of nature *itself*, even where there is no direct human action upon it. The human being — Adam and Eve — were placed in a space of the natural world termed the Garden of Eden. It was an idyllic condition in terms of the relationships between humans, between humans and nature, and within nature itself. The human being was not threatened by the elements, by animals or by need or scarcity. The world had the peacefulness and orderliness of a "garden". Nature spontaneously offered its bounty to the human being which the human being received without technical exploitation. Strikingly, there was also no suffering or disorder in nature itself. Amongst the animals there was no predation, no struggle with one another. The animals were all herbivorous. They did not kill one another.[132]

In the biblical account, there occurred, in the midst of this ideal state of humanity and nature, an event, which is called the sin of the Tree of Knowledge. It was an event of cosmic importance. With this sin was actualized the potential of the human for moral evil. The human being could choose between good and bad and made a bad choice and from now on would be engaged in a life of inner moral struggle.

From the human choice of evil in the sin of the Tree of Knowledge there ensued a systemic corruption within the whole of creation. This played out dramatically in the next generation of humans, the children of Adam and Eve, when the first murder occurred. Cain killed his brother, Abel. The moral corruption

---

[132] See the commentary of Nachmanides (Ramban) on Leviticus 23:6.

also disturbed the relationship of the human and nature. Adam, the human being, as a consquence was told by the Creator that from now on, nature would be his antagonist: "cursed is the earth because of you...thorns and thistles will it sprout for you...by the sweat of your brow will you eat bread."[133] Pain entered human life. The woman was told that gestation, childbirth and child-rearing would be difficult. And finally, *within* nature a struggle arose, as noted above in the phenomenon of predation.

There are two important points to be drawn from this biblical account — the Noahide Laws' standpoint — on the "environment". The first is that humanity does impact the environment practically and directly, but most significantly in terms of a moral and spiritual nexus and dynamic with nature. Secondly, nature, by virtue of its spiritual nexus with the human, falls, but also *rises*, with the human being. Thus, the human being is essential to the redemption of nature — the repair of its own suffering and destruction — as discussed in the next section on "the vertical and the horizontal" in nature. So too in the processual elicitation of desirable environmental "outcomes", the human must turn not only to material, but *also* to spiritual dimensions of the nexus with nature, as discussed in the final section on the "dimensions of environmental action".

As noted, neither Singer nor Deep Ecology appear to acknowledge any disorder or dysfunction in nature itself (that is, apart from points of human intervention). And yet the palpable reality of much of the animal world, in and by itself, is the terrible cruelty of its members to one another. This is the world which Darwin — whether or not one accepts his evolutionary theory — described accurately as a universal struggle for survival; the state of nature, which Hobbes saw lawless and unformed society modelling, namely that of "continual fear, and danger of violent death." The picture of a lion pack tearing living flesh from their prey merely illustrates this. So too the non-animal world is similarly convulsed by chaotic and disruptive behaviour. The explosive eruption of a volcano or the consequences of an earthquake with

---

[133] Genesis 3:17-19.

their disruption of the "ecosystem" are no idyll. The materialism of Singer and Deep Ecology has no concept of the potential ideal of spiritual harmony within nature and hence has no grasp of the disorder that actually manifests within nature itself.

The biblical concept of the pre-eminence of the human being as the directing subject of nature, bidden to rule and subdue nature, was not, as the secularizing environmentalists would have it, a pretext for mere "domination" over nature. That is a purely materialistic view of the interrelationship of nature and the human levelled to the one plane of physical existence. When, however, the whole of creation is grasped as a spiritually enlivened existence — a creation fashioned, enlivened and constantly renewed by G-d — one is open to the concept of the human and nature also as elements of a spiritual dynamic. It is then understood that the human being *did* bring suffering and destruction upon nature — but in a much deeper sense than the practical subjugation of animals and the practical consumption of physical resources. Rather, the human being spiritually *altered* and corrupted the *inner* character of nature. This produced the *abnormality* of nature, which Singer and Deep Ecology, without any concept of a spiritual norm, regard as *normal*.

Just as the spiritual nexus of humanity and nature brought about the corruption of nature through human moral failure, so, we have noted, it is the vehicle for the "redemption of nature". This is the deeper meaning of the biblical imperative to the human, placed upon the earth, "to serve and to keep it".[134] Contrary to much modern misunderstanding of these words, it does not mean that the human being was intended to minister, or to function as a "steward", to nature *as it is*. Their real meaning is "to *serve* [G-d's moral injunctions] and to *keep* [from what G-d has prohibited"] whereby nature through history would be transformed and restored to inner harmony.

The redemptive end-state of human history, as set forth in the tradition of the Noahide laws is thus the restoration of the

---

[134] Genesis 2:15. See Rabbi M. M. Schneerson, *Likkutei Sichos*, NY: Kehot, Vol. 20, p. 262.

harmonious state of Creation, that existed at the beginning and its elevation to an even higher level. The prophecies of Isaiah, speak not only of peace between human beings, as the verse from Isaiah on the wall of the United Nations — "They shall beat their swords into ploughshares and their spears into pruning hooks"[135] — declares, but also of peace *within* nature:

> The wolf will live with the sheep and the leopard will lie down with the kid; a lion whelp and a fatling [will walk together, and a young child will lead them. A cow and bear will graze and their young will lie down together; and a lion, like cattle, will eat hay. A suckling will play by a viper's hole; and a newly weaned child will stretch his hand towards an adder's lair. They will neither injure nor destroy in all of My sacred mountain; for the earth will be as filled with the knowledge of G-d as the waters cover over the ocean bed.[136]

The prophet Zechariah[137] speaks also of the purification of the oceans, and the revivification of agriculture — vegetative nature. And the prophet Isaiah speaks further of a "a new heavens and a new earth", free of rupture and decay.[138]

The vertical and the horizontal

The phenomena of suffering and destruction in nature are not inherently good and the goal of redemption, in the world-view of the Noahide laws, is to remove them. Yet the way to their transformation is through a form of human service and involvement with nature which proceeds with, and through, the fact of suffering and consumption-destruction: in a process that uses — whilst removing unnecessary and gratuitous — suffering and consumption-destruction to bring about the transformation that will eventually abolish them. It is a process of *refinement* of nature.

---

[135] Isaiah 2:4.
[136] *Ibid.*, 11:6-9.
[137] 14:8. See also Joel 4:18 and Ezekiel 47.
[138] Isaiah 66:22 with the commentary of *Malbim*. See also Rabbi M. M. Schneerson, *Likkutei Sichos*, Vol. 20, p. 265, fn. 29.

This process of refinement can be seen in the very form of the commandment which frames the Noahide treatment of nature — the prohibition on the consumption of the limb of a living animal. Such an act is clearly one of gross cruelty and with it was intended the removal of unwarranted suffering. It has, however, also a deeper, spiritual significance. Up to the time of the biblical Flood, the human being was prohibited to kill animals in order to eat, or make other use of, them. This can be understood. The animal is a particularly sentient being, which feels the pain of slaughter, and moreover it is possible for a human to live without eating meat. Yet it now became permissible for the human to slaughter animals to eat their meat and a commandment was given placing conditions on this permission.

The reason[139] why it became permitted to slaughter animals to eat their flesh was that, along with the general corruption of nature caused by the sin of the Tree of Knowledge and subsequent human moral decline, the animal world itself experienced its own inner corruption, as we have described. The way in which the animal realm could be "repaired" spiritually was through being elevated to the spiritual world, a Divine realm, accessed by an ethical humanity. This concept of the human's taking up and connecting nature (in this case the animal) with a spiritual realm is a "vertical" ascent through nature. Through that vertical dimension, the animal realm not only ascended towards the spiritual, but the spiritual could in turn also be drawn down into it, spiritualizing and transforming it. Accordingly, the consumption of the animal by the human being — who ate it with the purpose of incorporating the energy derived from it in an ethically purposeful human existence — is instrumental to the spiritual rectification of the animal species. It is an ascent for which the animal needs the human, and which animals themselves cannot accomplish. According to some views, this would lead to the refinement of the animal world and the removal of the need and

---

[139] See *B'er Mayim Chayim* on Genesis 9:4.

permission to eat meat as existed at the beginning of creation.[140]

The process of incorporation, elevation and refinement of the animal by the human, in eating it, has conditions. It involves *selection* of that aspect of the animal, which can be elevated, and *rejection* of that aspect which cannot. The stilled flesh of the animal after slaughter can be elevated; the degraded raw vitality of the animal, as it has become and *lives,* cannot. This meant the human was not permitted to ingest the *living* animal, that is, the severed limb of a living creature in which its living vitality had been captured and stored. The Noahide prohibition of the consumption of the limb severed from a living animal models three points in the normative human interaction with nature: the consumption has a spiritual (as well as a practical) purpose for nature itself; the consumption should be carried out with sensitivity to nature; and it is to be carried out in a discerning and transformative way, incorporating that which can be elevated and rejecting that which cannot.

This is a model for the Noahide treatment of the whole of nature, including vegetative and inorganic realms: the "vertical" elevation of these realms to the Divine, via its incorporation in the life of an ethical and spiritual humanity, with the reciprocal drawing of the Divine down into the natural realm bringing about the eventual transformation of its disorder. The elevation of the animal realm is to be purchased with a measure of its suffering — the slaughter, consumption and other utilization of animals.. So too the elevation of non-animal nature — the burning of a log of wood to produce fire to take a simple example — is purchased through consumption and destruction. Here too a stricture is placed by religious tradition on the unnecessarily wasteful consumption and destruction of physical resources.

Viewed "horizontally", creation discloses at every level — inorganic, vegetative, animal and human — the phenomena of

---

[140] See Rabbi A. Y. Kook, *Chazon HaTzimchonus v'haShalom,* cited in D. Sears, *The Vision of Eden,* Spring Valley, NY: Orot, 2003. It may also be noted that Chassidic philosophy explains that "eating" is a metaphor for the process of refinement of nature *("avoidas habirurim")* and that in final stage of the redemptive transformation of creation – the resurrection of the dead – there will be no eating or drinking.

suffering and destruction-consumption. Vegetation "feeds" upon the nutrients of the inorganic level below it, minerals, water, gasses (carbon dioxide). Animals consume vegetation, water, air, and the predators, other animals. Some plants consume insects. The omnipresent consumption extends to the human beings. Like physical nature we are consumed. From birth onwards, a medieval Sage wrote, a baby begins to "dry out", our bodies are consumed through life's stresses. Like machines made of inorganic parts, humans also "wear out".

The vertical spiritual dimension intersecting both human and physical nature elicits the redeemable aspect of suffering and consumption. Good relationships are often built through "suffering", through the struggle for self-control and enduring and learning from difficult experiences. Good ideas and artworks are developed through suffering — through strain and exertion. Purposeful work is "hard"; we are worn and gradually "used up" from it. We do not embrace suffering and consumption, and properly seek to ameliorate them in our own and others' lives, but they are necessarily involved in the repair of our moral and social selves. In order properly to "consume" and elevate the rest of creation, the human being must first be "consumed" in the process of moral and spiritual self-repair.

Although the serried "horizontal" levels of nature — animal, vegetative and inorganic — find their rectification through "vertical" incorporation in the human being who is "above" them all, they are not thereby "inferior" or relatively valueless. Indeed, the mystical aspect of the core religious tradition of the Noahide laws teaches that the fact that the "lower" level — nature (food and resources) — nurtures and "powers" the level — the human — above it, indicates in some ways its higher spiritual source. It is simply that those more elemental and pristine powers — energies and beings of nature — need to be housed within the forms, identities, structures and purposes known from the ethical template of the Noahide laws: so that their powers are channelled into harmonies, rather than chaos. Each thing in nature has a Divinely created identity and purpose — a "name" — which the spiritually informed human being has the ability to connect to its Divine purpose and Divine source. In a mystical sense, the things "know" this. If not a "soul", like that of a human being, each thing possesses a Divine vitality or spark, through which G-d gives it its form and continued existence. The Divine spark or vitality in a rock, plant or animal possesses, so to speak, a spiritual awareness (a "spiritual" [if not physical] sentience) and "desire" to be incorporated in the Divine purpose. It "waits" for proper incorporation — through the ethical-spiritual human — into that purpose, and through it is *gratified*.

The secularizing environmentalism of Peter Singer and Deep Ecology, as we have noted, knows only of the suffering and destruction imposed by humans on non-human nature. They are focussed solely on the horizontal dimension of nature itself, in which they alone grasp the interaction of the human and nature. In this view, nature should not be made instrumental towards human concerns. The animal world and non-animal nature are considered goals in, and unto, themselves. Singer requires that no suffering be inflicted upon an animal by humans for human purposes simply because they are human purposes. The Deep Ecology of Arne Naess holds that all of nature including the vegetative and inorganic realms requires independence from human interests and needs. As noted, even the concepts of recycling and generation of renewable energy are mere "shallow ecology" — because they are focussed ultimately on *human* interests, minimizing the depletion of resources for the sake of humans. Deep ecology opposes the *very concept* of the consumption of natural resources for human utilization (other than in the most minimal degree, essential for bare human survival) by persons.

The dismantlement by Singer and Deep Ecology of the vertical dimension, which thereby prohibits nature the bond with a spiritual realm, not only mistakes and perpetuates the disorder of nature itself; it also degrades the human being to the horizontal dimension of animal nature. Singer equalizes the human being with animals. In this horizontal "commonwealth of nature", as I would call it, the human being has no more than one vote, and indeed Singer has endorsed in the book he co-edited, *The Great Ape Project*, the concept of a "Parliament" of primates, in which humans, orangutans, gorillas and chimpanzees would all participate. The disability — or the inability — to speak which the apes have in this Parliament would be rectified by providing them with human spokespeople or aides, who are presumed to know their best interests.

For Singer and Naess, nature is "fine": the human being must simply be held at arm's length from, and forbidden any dominance or superiority over, it. Core religious tradition in the Noahide laws disagrees. Nature is not fine: it is itself characterized by predation, suffering, struggle and destruction. The spontaneous cooperation it once exhibited, and could exhibit, with the human, is held back. It is only the human being, armed with a Divine moral and transformative agency that can redeem nature from its own degraded "state of nature". The most serious consequence of the denial of the vertical dimension by secularizing environmentalism, however, is the ethical degradation of the human itself, as we shall presently discuss. This is harmful not only for the human, but for nature itself.

The dimensions of environmental action

Any "environmentalism" wants to *act* in a way that produces a desirable environmental outcome. The human being necessarily has a practical relationship to nature. There is almost always a "science" involved in the human interaction with nature, from the simplest science of the farmer by which one knows how to prepare the earth and sow it with seed, to that of the most advanced industrial technologies which systematically utilize natural resources. Properly, these sciences will have an eye to the future — the farmer's land should continue to yield and the advanced industrial utilization of resources will seek to secure sustainable resources for the future. Yet, a basic question remains. Is it *solely* the practical "science" which assures that environmental "future"? Are there further dimensions of action required to "secure" that environmental future?

The tradition of the Noahide laws put the answer this way almost two thousand years ago in the Jerusalem Talmud: "The human believes in the Life of all worlds [that is, in G-d] and sows [the earth]".[141] This human being seeks sustenance — and *continued* sustenance — from nature, and knows that it involves "science", in this case a rudimentary science of agriculture with its methods of preparing and sowing the earth with seed, resting the earth at times and so forth. However, that same human being knows that the *yield* of nature "in consequence" of those required efforts *actually* depends on the transcendent G-d of nature. The apparent "laws" of nature are not autonomous or independent of G-d. They "function", or in circumstances "misfunction", and are attended by non-foreseeable conditions, according to G-d's will. Knowing this, and especially in relation to the climate — typically, historically, the rains — the believing person has always prayed to G-d that the practical science should actually work and be accompanied by all the conditions requisite for its continued success. This applies to all realms of human endeavour. Thousands of years after the adage of the Jerusalem Talmud was said, I sat in a taxi, which in sweltering heat and bumper-to-bumper traffic, inched its hours-long way from an airport into New York City. I cannot forget the words of the perspiring black driver who would probably have to do several such trips to make the day's living: "I'm workin' hard and I'm hopin' to G-d".

The religious world-view states, that it is not only practical conduct undertaken by humans with nature that produces results, but also and fundamentally the relationship of the human being to the G-d (that is to say, to the transcendent Creator and day-to-day Renewer) of nature. G-d gives the human being the ability — and requires the human — to act, but G-d's Providence forms the consequences of those actions, even despite those actions. In a broader sense, the "future" of nature, whether tomorrow or later, depends on Divine reception of the human being's prayers and deeds. For this reason, the human being needs good deeds and the power of prayer that G-d grant the advantageous conditions

---

[141] Cited in *Tosafos*, Babylonian Talmud, Tractate *Shabbos* 31a.

and desired outcomes of one's work, one's practical "science".

If success in the outcomes and attendant conditions of our agriculture and industry depends on G-d, why then do we have to do anything? Why do we need a "science", a practical-technical engagement with nature, at all - cannot the blessing come from G-d without our efforts and "science"? The answer to this question, from the standpoint of core religious tradition, is that G-d wants us to engage with the world in such a way as to refine both it and ourselves. The farmer should act ethically in the context of his work, treat livestock and resources considerately, use the earnings from the work for a worthy family life and give from them to charity, believe in and ask G-d for assistance amidst the hardships. This improves the farmer, the human, and spiritually elevates that sphere of nature drawn into his productive efforts. The success of the crop and tomorrow's weather conditions are no less a consequence of the farmer's moral merits and prayers than they are a consequence of the farmer's "science". The practical science — the work of engagement with nature — is in fact the *opportunity* for those merits and prayers. The farmer needs both the science and G-d, Who can grant it success. For this reason, paradigmatically, the farmer *first* "believes in the Life of all worlds" — entreats the Creator and Renewer of nature — and *secondly* "sows the earth", engages with the practical means.

The Noahide laws teach us an ethical environmentalism, but it is not through these actions that *I engineer* the future. The care that one takes not to treat a resource wastefully does not cause it to be preserved. It is because one recognizes the resource as a something purposefully created by G-d, and fulfils G-d's injunction to treat it without heedless destruction, that, along with prayers and other good deeds, one merits that *G-d* maintain that resource, or create fresh resources of this or of another kind. And if G-d grants efficacious results presently (or even for a long time) to those who have no belief in G-d and disregard His commandments, that too is willed on account of His kindness or patience or for other reasons known to Him.

The secularizing environmentalism recognizes no transcendent

Creator of nature and, *as a corollary*, rejects the primacy of the human in nature, for the human has that primacy only as an agent of the Divine, being made in the image of G-d, and being privy to His ethical will. Thus, in *Animal Liberation*, Peter Singer (though he seems sometimes to be asking for, and not merely rejecting, "proofs" for G-d)[142] excludes a transcendent Creator of nature. Deep Ecology to some extent replaces the concept of a transcendent Creator with a pantheism of nature. Pantheism, which makes nature G-d, however, in the sights of the Noahide laws, is idolatry. Idolatry involves taking something which is a creation of G-d, and making it absolute, in place of G-d. Pantheism accords this absolute status to physical nature.

The abolition by the secularizing environmentalists of the distinction between culture (or humanity) and nature — between the vertical and the horizontal — and the assimilation of both into the one "horizontal" plane of nature, has broad consequences. For it is from culture — by which is here meant the culture informed by the knowledge of the Creator and His moral template — that we know the essences, boundaries, orienting values and purposes of the entities of nature, including the human body.[143] If humanity appears to have forfeited its claim to primacy because of its own disconnection with the spiritual, this does not negate the reality of its task of moral agency, but rather points out only its failure to take it up.

Singer's reduction of the human to a "human animal" means that the principal criterion of personhood becomes an animal one: the satisfaction of "sentience". Sentience, the common denominator or common animality of the members of this commonwealth of nature, is the "capacity for suffering" or pain and equally the capacity for pleasure. The regulatory ethical principle which

---

[142] In his biography of his grandfather David Oppenheim, entitled *Pushing Time Away – The Tragedy of Viennese Jewry*, there is a sad paradox, which Singer does not recognize. David Oppenheim's own grandfather was the sixth in a chain of generations of Rabbis. His grandfather's detachment from traditional Judaism (which may have begun with David's father), was to embrace the very culture which – to his bewilderment – gave birth to the Nazism that destroyed him.

[143] Thrown into confusion by current "gender fluidity" theory.

Singer applies to this animal commonwealth is a "hedonistic utilitarianism" — the greatest amount of pleasure for the greatest number of animals (human and animal). Or similarly, the removal of pain for the greatest number of sentient beings. Without the vertical dimension. which reaches to the moral template outside and above nature and confers moral agency on the human, there is no principle by which qualitatively to evaluate responses to "pleasure and pain" other than their crude utilitarian maximization and minimization. Other than this, Singer has no principle on the basis of which to decide *what* pleasure may morally be indulged or must morally be foregone; and *what* pain may morally be escaped or morally should be endured.

Thus, Singer has sought to justify bestiality ethically on the basis of the pleasure of the parties. He has intimated also that incest between adult siblings could be ethically justified. These are travesties of the Noahide law of prohibited sexual unions. Similarly, on the basis of his rejection of the Divine and its imprint in the human soul and life, and by dint of his "hedonistic utilitarianism", Singer in his own words proceeds to "unsanctify" life. This provides permission for abortion on demand, since there is no consideration of a soul in the foetus, without which the foetus is a mere "potential" life, that is to say, a mere potential of the developed, conscious pleasure centre which for Singer defines the person. For the ill and disabled, in his doctrine, voluntary euthanasia becomes a favour — the pleasure of oblivion from pain and suffering. Because of their limited prospects for "pleasure", he has advocated infanticide for Down Syndrome newborn babies.

Naess' Deep Ecology also demolishes the norms known to humanity from a transcendent Creator outside and above nature. Rather, for him, all beings are "constituted" out of the shifting "nets" of their relationships. There are no fixed identities or norms and this applies also to human nature. Naess, states one writer,

> ...entirely cast away moral blame or praise, even the very existence of moral agents. If the borderline between me and

the beings that surround me vanishes, then there remains no one for me to harm or benefit.[144]

The removal of identities and norms, supplied by a spiritual human culture, from nature is extended by "Queer Ecology" to validate fluid sexual identities and unions, amongst human beings, grasped as part of the fluid body of nature.[145] It has been further suggested that Naess' principle of human population reduction (to retract human dominance over nature) and an emphasis on the "quality", as distinct from the sanctity, of life brings Deep Ecology to favour voluntary euthanasia.[146] This, too, is part of Deep Ecology's dissolution of the "moral agency" of the human being, coming from above and outside nature.

The environmental action program of the secularizing environmentalism is a science with no spiritual dimension. Indeed, it promotes idolatry, forbidden sexual unions and killing — hardly merits for a desirable environmental future. By contrast, with all due environmental circumspection, the Noahide laws promote the fulfilment of valid human needs and thereby the transformative incorporation of animal and non-animal nature by an ethical and spiritual humanity. This works for the removal of suffering and destruction in nature, which secularizing environmentalism cannot see, in a redemption of nature, which it cannot imagine.

---

[144] Evangelos D. Protopapadakis, "'Supernatural Will' and 'Organic Unity in Process': From Spinoza's Naturalistic Pantheism to Arne Naess' New Age 'Ecosophy T'' and Environmental Ethics', p. in George Arabatzis (ed.), *Studies on Supernaturalism*, Berlin, Logos Verlag, 2009, p. 193.

[145] "A queer interpretation of ecology blurs boundaries of identities and opens the possibility to theoretically reconstruct ourselves and the world around us". C. M. Doak, "Queering Nature: The Liberatory Effects of Queer Ecology", Honours Thesis at Dickinson College, https://scholar.dickinson.edu/cgi/viewcontent.cgi?article=1229&context=student_honors

[146] See P. Carrick, "Deep Ecology and End-of-Life Care" in J. Pierce and G. Randels (eds), *Contemporary Bioethics – A Reader with Cases*, NY: Oxford University Press, 2010.

PART 4: MANIFESTOES

Chapter 13

There is more than this…

Four Lectures in Advance of the Victorian State Elections 2014[147]

Introduction

Re-establishing the Political Moral Centre

A crucible of world directions for culture and politics could be witnessed in the elections of the Australian State of Victoria, held in November 2014. Whilst for many, the election was simply about personal benefits — public transport costs and further education places, and that may have decided the actual result — there are those who know that it was also about a conflict between two ways of seeing the world and the values which flow from them: a world of values based on common faith traditions, and another cut loose, or at least drifting, from those traditions. In terms of the Government formed, the result may look like a defeat for one world-view — that which relies on tradition, faith and values. In fact, the real result is a reconfiguration of politics, which hopefully will ultimately correct the moral drift of the major parties in Victoria, and encourage a similar, wider trend to restore the moral centre of politics in other parts of the world. It will also pose the ultimate choice between the two opposing world-views, in the starkest terms.

Until recent years, it was unthinkable that the major parties of the right and left (in moderate democracies, centre-right and centre-left) would operate outside the periphery of traditional, universal ethics which have prevailed for thousands of years. It was unthinkable that either of them would promote same-sex

---

[147] Four lectures, held under the auspices of Campion College, Australia before the Victorian State elections in 2014, and dedicated to the memory of Sir Zelman Cowen on the third anniversary of his passing. The author is grateful to Eleni Arapoglou for editorial work on the text of the lectures.

marriage or institute abortion on demand, backed with punitive compulsion on doctors to comply. It was also inconceivable that one of them (the Labor party) would ever force a religious institution to employ only staff with values and practices at variance with the religious ethos of those institutions. Only a fringe party could hold such views.

And yet in the Victorian elections of 2014, the major "right" party supported one and a half[148] of these positions and the major "left" party supported all three. Major parties had, with respect to the universal values of civilization, become in moral terms fringe parties.

How did this happen? The simple answer seems to be that a world-view, which is fundamentally atheistic, materialistic and geared to a pleasure-and-pain calculus alone, has gained substantial ground in our society. Its primary political home is the "Greens". Having started as a party, with legitimate concerns such as protecting the environment, it was philosophically reengineered into a movement that sees the human being as another animal within nature. In this commonwealth of nature, there is no distinguishing soul within the human being and no G-d within or beyond nature. There remains only sentient flesh, the pleasures of which should be gratified by morphing sexual morality and the pain of which should be fled through euthanasia, abortion on demand (which alleviates the pain of adults, not babies) and "assisted suicide". The Greens are the "purists" of this world-view, and they go one step beyond the major parties, which in various policies they have already towed significantly into their waters. They seek to prohibit all — even optional — religious education in State Schools; and they want State partial funding for religious schools to be ended, notwithstanding that 70% of Australians are religiously affiliated and they also pay the taxes, of which an allocation is made to

---

[148] The Liberal-National Party Coalition funded the "Safe Schools Coalition of Victoria" program to introduce students to a "norm" of homosexual lifestyles, on an optional (school chosen) basis (half support of the principle); whilst Labor announced a policy to make it compulsory in all Victorian State Schools (full support). The Liberal-National Party coalition also failed to amend the abortion law with its compulsion on doctors to comply by referral. Labor, under which this law had been brought in, was opposed to its amendment.

religious schools. This political movement knows that traditional morality has its root in religious tradition and education, and wants to eradicate this root.

This world-view was philosophically and politically elaborated in direct opposition to the Judeo-Christian ethic, or I would prefer to say, the Abrahamic ethic, which includes, alongside Judaism and Christianity, Islam. The Abrahamic faith tradition knows of the soul, in addition to the flesh, of the human being and of a G-d within and beyond nature. It knows of G-d-given moral imperatives from Mount Sinai that set the fundamental compass of the human being in fulfilment of his and her mission on earth, to make the world a more human and G-dly place.

Providence has it, however, that the Greens, who have culturally and electorally towed the major parties out of the periphery of universal values, will be countered by another new pole in politics. A plethora of small, mainly traditionally minded parties have been elected in the Victorian Upper House. The trend exists also in the Federal Parliament. Both of these Upper Houses are based on electoral systems which reflect minority opinion better. Yet, even if this is dismissed as a quirk of the electoral system, it still points to a populism of the human spirit which is currently if somewhat haphazardly represented by these small parties. The Labor party cannot govern in Victoria without the support of these crossbench "micro-"parties. European populism (even if there the issues are slightly different) has also shown that if the major parties do not find the true centre of the society and align themselves closely on either side of it, they will cease to be able to function as major parties. In addition to this, the more Labor validates the policies and world-view of the Greens, the more it enhances a world-view which pulls it away from the moral centre and from elements of its traditional support base. The role of the small, populist traditionalist parties (which take hold in the moral centre, increasingly abandoned by the major parties) will hopefully be to bring the major parties back to the true moral-political centre, where they can again function as major parties, representing right and left *but within the perimeter of universal values.*

I originally subtitled these lectures "a new view from the university" because I am proud to deliver them under the auspices of a courageous tertiary institution of learning. This is so, particularly at a time when the arts and sciences have never been as politicized in a supposedly democratic society as they are today. The world-view of hedonistic materialism ultimately takes root and is cultivated in universities, where academics are marshalled by political correctness on pain of withheld research funding, academic contracts and advancement, and generations of students are educated in it on pain of failing or doing poorly if they do not conform. Our journalists, teachers, bureaucrats, health practitioners, counsellors and psychologists, lawyers, economists, scientists, artists and graduates at large have been indoctrinated by their teachers in the universities in this world-view. They either believe it, or are afraid on account of sanctions to speak up against it. We live in times where the *least* free forum of speech and openness to a genuine exchange of ideas is the university. Therefore, I welcome the auspices of Campion College for these lectures. It is a tertiary institution that is not afraid to stand up for its values — the values of tradition, which come ultimately from Mount Sinai — and understands that clearly representing this ethical tradition not only enhances the spiritual good of its students, but also the wholeness of intellectual enquiry.

The themes of these lectures have to do with major issues that were mostly *not* contested by the policies of the major parties in the Victorian elections of 2014. Yet, they are matters of global concern and highlight the differences between the materialistic world-view that has increasingly dominated politics and the spiritual world-view of the Abrahamic religions which it challenges.

The political arena is the one in which human lives are concretely changed and society is remade, for better or for worse. The purpose of these lectures is to clarify the moral centre and periphery of politics in terms of *universal conscience and its ethics* found at the root, and in the moral common denominator, of the world faiths which have shaped our, and most of world's, civilization. May this moral centre be re-established by politicians of universal conscience.

First Lecture

Culture, the Divine and Happiness

Culture

We are living in a time of culture wars. This is most unfortunate, because war is not the best form of communication. One of these wars is about the word "G-d". When I say the word "G-d", I mean a whole world of spiritual experience that is most fundamental to my life. This word, in much of the mainstream press, is uttered with resentment by journalists who associate it with the so-called "religious right". "G-d" and the "religious right" conjure a mythic spectre or ideology used to back up what is believed to be a repression of purported "freedoms". We are certainly not talking about the same idea, engaging in a common theme or exploring a common "phenomenon". What features is essentially zero-engagement. Each side stands behind its ramparts, one struggling to defend a religious tradition, experience and its values; the other attacks it in defence of its own world-view.

Sometimes what is mainly religious defence moves to the offense and sometimes what is mainly secularist attack moves to the defence. But there is no communication, no attempt to compare the two world views in basic terms so that the mass can see what the argument is really about, experience what the sides are fundamentally claiming and then decide. There is little or none of the closeness that allows friends or kin with natural bonds to open to each others' perspectives. This could be achieved through *real* tolerance. This, as Viktor Frankl explained, does not mean moral relativism which is an abandonment of truth. Rather, the real spirit of tolerance is love, that is, openness and closeness to another human being. It also comes hopefully with the benefit that this open up a better communication and resolution.

Though rare, there have been genuine attempts to achieve a discussion between the fundamentally opposed perspectives of religion and secularism. An example is found in the published attempts of a prominent contemporary European philosopher, Jürgen Habermas, to engage with Catholic theologians. One of these dialogues, published as *Dialectics of Secularization*, was held with the previous Pope, while he was still Cardinal Joseph Ratzinger. Another was with a group of Jesuits, published in a work entitled *An Awareness of What is Missing*. Habermas embarked in good faith on both of these encounters. He acknowledged the "unexhausted" strength of religion, its power to muster solidarity around values and to motivate conduct. But he simply could not let himself into the world of the human spirit and the sense of the Divine. He concluded, like much of contemporary thinking, with an insistence that discussion avail itself solely of "public reason", i.e. only that which intellect based on the evidence of the physical senses can discuss. The secularists' argument is simple, "Everyone, including you, has a mind and physical senses (that is, 'public reason'). Use them exclusively and don't bring into the discussion your personal spiritual or soul experience (because that is merely 'private reason')." But it did not occur to Habermas — and I don't know if it was even put to him in these dialogues — that it is equally valid to draw upon and discuss *spiritual* experience, because that is equally "public". For everyone has a soul. Certainly that is the evidence of human history, of which religion is perhaps the most salient and persistent feature. Could I therefore suggest to Habermas, "Perhaps, you too have a soul, a capacity for spiritual experience. Explore and *exercise* it and don't restrict discussion to the material veneer of reality, which is all your physical senses can access".

Anticipating this challenge, Habermas has written, citing the words of Max Weber, the great sociologist of religion, but who was not a believer: I am *"religiös unmusikalisch"* ("religiously unmusical"). That translates plainly as: "Spiritually, I am tone deaf". The rejoinder to that of course is, "Work on your spiritual hearing, exercise your spiritual faculty". But Habermas was not asked and was not induced to do that. Even if the dialogue failed, at least there was the commendable good will on both sides — a practising and highly reflective religious thinker and a most proficient, but atheistic secular thinker sat down together and tried to communicate.

I chose for this first lecture, and these lectures as a whole, the title, "There is more than this...", based on something I heard from a psychiatrist friend of mine. He spoke about a young depressed patient, whose father had said to him about the world the boy found himself in, "This is all there is, there is nothing else". Fundamentally, this is what the contemporary culture wars are all about. The religious world-view states that the material world is a glove on the much greater reality of the Divine. The secularist world view states that the material world is all there is. The ramifications of this disagreement reach into the struggle over social values. If the material world is all there is, and no Divine reality stands behind it arbitrating how we should act, then grounds can be found to mutate social institutions, marriage, life issues, based on considerations that arise only from the material perspective on humanity as sentient flesh — that is, pleasure and pain. How else does one find happiness in a material world? If, however, if there is a Divine reality and a Divine moral template and human beings who follow it manifest the Divine into the world, then that Divine template is clearly a great human good that we must pursue. Taking this viewpoint does not abdicate reason; rather, it gives reason a different starting point and brief.

So the question for us all is — very simply — when looking at the material world, "Is that all there is, or is there more than this?" We do not want to reproach those who are unaware of anything more. The former President of the European Union (European Council), Herman van Rompuy, rightly wondered in his book *Het Christendom een modern gedachte*, how we can reproach a person for not knowing G-d, when he or she has never heard of Him. In the age of education, paradoxically so many of us are utterly illiterate in the realm of the spirit. So I want to present some exercises in spiritual perception — which might help some to come to see that "there is more than this".

This will not begin with logic, but will be about the basic assumption or perception that we *give* to logic to work with. Before proceeding, I would like to draw attention to a problematic program being offered as an alternative to religious instruction in schools in the Australian state of New South Wales. As a "rationalist" program, it claims not to impart moral instruction, but rather to help children discover reasons for deeming views as right nor wrong. The difficulty is that "reasons" themselves proceed from basic assumptions, ways of "seeing the world". There is no way in which *reason* can arbitrate between the basic alternative assumptions. Its supplementary requirement (in addition to the use of "reason") is to show "respectfulness for others". This is good but it will also not help children to discover the true ultimate principles that underlie moral reasoning. These are matters of belief. The rationalist program asks:

> *Are some things just wrong?* Different cultures have different moral codes. What underlies these differences and is there an independent way to judge the moral values of other cultures?

Reason cannot adjudicate between the two fundamental belief choices given to the child by religious tradition on the one hand and a secular materialist one on the other. It is a question of which metaphysical foundations to choose. The program claims to steer between moral relativism and blind acceptance of authority, between moral instruction and reasons for moral positions. The problem is that the arbitrating criteria are always reducible to first principles. Is there more to reality than meets the eye? Is there a Divine impulse and a Divine Providence in reality? Or, is the material world all there is? That is a matter of basic, supra-empirical perception or as Peter Singer, the architect of the Greens philosophy and hedonistic materialism at large acknowledged to me, a matter of belief. He *believes* that the physical world is all there is. I *believe* there is more. That is what the culture wars are all about, but at least Peter Singer and I, have sat down together to talk. Maybe he will one day see what I see (I once saw only what he sees; but then became aware of a spiritual reality). He was skeptical about that but did combat the possibility.

The Divine

We speak of a Judeo-Christian ethic — though it would be more appropriate to speak of a wider Abrahamic ethic (which includes Islam) — that forms the basis of our society. What goes with this, is that certain values, associated with that ethic, shape our civilization and society. But even more fundamental to it is a belief in G-d. For without the G-d of Abraham, we do not have the values of the Abrahamic heritage. This is because G-d is their source and it is through belief in, and orientation to, the G-d of Abraham that we resonate with and ascribe authority to these values.

Belief in G-d is a very native thing. Children believe readily in G-d. But does that mean that it is naive? No. Children readily believe because theirs is an unclouded spiritual faculty. Adults are equipped with more advanced intellect and intellect becomes more refined as we grow older. And precisely for this reason there is a danger that a hubris of intellect can obscure the vision of the soul. Who can appreciate intellect and yet have the humility to understand the limits of intellect and the general finitude and dependency of our existence? There is a well-known saying that there are no atheists in the trenches. Everyone in the trenches (including great intellectuals) senses finitude, vulnerability and dependency. The problem arises when the bullets stop overhead, and we climb out of the trenches and believe that we are absolutely in control again.

This is an experiential approach to belief in G-d through "crises". We have all probably experienced moments — crises that dissolved our egos and our sense of "self-madeness" — when we experienced our dependency on something much greater than ourselves. The occupational hazard of our prowess as human beings is that we can forget that we are creatures (i.e. created beings) until a crisis reminds us of the fact. That is why children so readily believe: they have not tasted the sense of sovereignty and the feeling of control that the older individual, with an advanced intellect and an estate in life, which tends to suppress the awareness of personal finitude, has. The truth is, however, that the soul's knowledge or experience is of a different order altogether from that of intellect. It can come into intellect, but it does not start in intellect, because the intellect is finite (a sophisticated piece of nature, but sharing the finitude of nature) with finite perception, whilst the soul as a mirror of G-d can truly sense and apprise the infinite. Belief begins before understanding is able to start (using belief as its fundamental assumption or starting point) and picks up again where intellect exhausts its limits.

The sense of dependency, the sense of our boundedness before the infinite, however, is only one avenue to G-d. It is associated with a sense of the awe of G-d. There is another meditation (again spiritual in essence) which brings to the love of G-d. This occurs when I sense that the entire Creation is sustained and renewed into being in every moment by G-d. I am aware of myself as a living being, but that the ultimate foundation of my life is the ongoing creative act of G-d. A person is energized by a human act of kindness — a considerate word, a gesture of help and encouragement, appreciation, a smile, financial assistance when it is needed — and how much more so when one senses that one's *life* — one's entire being — is sustained day by day and moment by moment by the kindness of G-d. Love arouses love. The ability to see and feel this is part of the *spiritual* contemplation of the religious life. It involves the *engagement* of a soul faculty that dwells in all. It becomes the ability to *see* a deeper reality: that all is animated and enlivened by the Creator.

The sense of a personal G-d is also facilitated through the experience of Divine Providence. Not only is creation in all of its manifold detail sustained and renewed constantly, it is also *providentially* renewed. That means that G-d, Who is the essence of goodness, crafts our situations, individually and collectively in such a way as to elicit responses from us, which draw the world closer towards redemption. No one is alone. More than our family, friends and community, our most intimate, powerful and constant associate is G-d. It is He who sets life as a series of challenges and gives us the strength to meet them well and redemptively. For the individual attuned to Providence, G-d is experienced as setting up the stage for our choices and nudging us towards the right ones. For the more secularly minded person, but who is still open to a little self-transcendence, this can be put more neutrally, in terms of the beckoning of existence: "What does life ask of me?"

Finally, a spiritually experiential path to G-d is the sense of attachment to G-d through the ethical precepts mandated by Him. This comes from the idea of the "imitation of G-d": just as G-d is merciful, you should be merciful; just as G-d is kind you should be kind and so forth. The universal ethics, known as the Noahide laws, the root of the Abrahamic faith, translate into action the imitation of G-d's attributes. This gives us our moral benchmarks. Not only belief in and respect for G-d flow from the imitation of the Divine, but also sexual morality and the way in which traditional marriage bears on the Divine likeness in the human being. From it we derive the parameters of the proper treatment of the persons and property of others, of a justice system, the concept and guidelines of the protection of life and the proper treatment of animals and physical nature. All of these values and their contours express the imitation of G-d. We need tradition to inform us of their details, but we know that when we observe these G-dly universal ethics, we are close to G-d.

Conversely, an ethics cut loose from G-d, takes us away from the experience of, and attachment to, G-d. The belief in G-d and G-dly ethics are one piece. Through living by Divinely mandated ethics, the human being actualizes his or her deepest self, the soul. The spiritual is not something less than reason. It is the envelope or the space within which reason operates. It is the encompassing framework of reason, which reason itself cannot "establish", and to which it necessarily refers when it is concerned with ultimate truths. It is the repository of the moral inheritance of humanity.

The materialistic and hedonistic secularism of the present age is the inverse of this world-view. It starts with a G-dless nature and a soulless human being. Searching for an ethical principle in a purely material universe, it finds this only in material enjoyment. Naturally it has no knowledge, love of, or respect for, G-d, because that is out of the picture. Its sexual morality morphs and mutates, because it does not relate sexuality to Divinely mandated concepts of procreation and the lines of biological identity and continuity between generations. In matters of justice it is open to all kinds of "novelty", wholly unconstrained by universal ethics. When finally it comes to the protection of life, it does not even know what life is in order to protect it. By not recognizing a soul in the human being but only a capacity for enjoyment in a physical sense, the foetus and the terminally ill are downgraded lives. A religious view changes this. The soul shines in these dependent and frail existences, full of potential and potencies with which the soul within endows them. The soul is the "more than this" of the physical body. These perceptions or beliefs are the legacy of culture and civilization. They are taught and transmitted experientially, made familiar and internal, to each new generation, when religious transmission is strong. When the transmission is weakened in the home and school, and the secular culture enters through every pore to contradict that transmission, the spiritual experience is naturally further attenuated in the next generation of children. How much harder is it for a child placed by "enlightened" parents in a rationalist secular humanist ethics to class discover G-d by "reason" alone?

Happiness

The German philosopher Nietzsche wrote in *Thus Spoke Zarathustra*, "Indeed, all joy wants eternity — wants deep, deep eternity". The word in his original German for "joy" is *Lust* and I think, with my own experience of German, that the better translation and truer to the spirit of Nietzche's thought, is that *Lust* should be translated as "pleasure". I would like eventually to contrast this with a wholly different sense of "joy".

As noted, in today's world view of "this is all there is", we are largely left with the concern of sentient flesh, human and animal, which is with pleasure and pain. Pleasure is the culture of happiness we have today. But as a mentor of mine, Rabbi Chaim Gutnick, said, "Young people today have a lot of pleasure, but little happiness". Pleasure means gratification of flesh. Sometimes it takes in intellectual pleasures, too.

Now, the United States Declaration of Independence contains the words:

> We hold these truths to be self-evident, that all men are created equal, that they are endowed by their Creator with certain unalienable Rights, that among these are Life, Liberty and the pursuit of Happiness.

Whatever the word "happiness" meant in that Declaration 238 years ago, for contemporary culture it now means, or must include, the pursuit of pleasure. This principle has become embedded in our culture as the supreme principle that overrides all other considerations.

Thus, all Australian State Departments of Education appear to follow a rule that children have a right to sexual pleasure and sexual activity. The idea that children are not psychologically ready for it, particularly young girls; the possibility of sexually transmitted diseases; or that sex could result in unwanted pregnancy and abortion, let alone the traditional concept that sex should be within the context of marriage, which is that of commitment and responsibility: all of these considerations cannot outweigh the posited primary right to sexual pleasure. What remains is collateral damage control: making sex "safe", providing abortion on demand, instruction on minimization of infection by sexually transmitted diseases. None of these ills could possibly outweigh in consideration the undoubted primary right to sexual pleasure of children.

So it is also when we come to cohabiting adults. I remember reading in 2008 a *Time Magazine* leading story which quite shocked me. It found that one in two children in the United Kingdom was born out of wedlock. It also noted that British children had the highest rates of teenage pregnancy, substance abuse and violence in Europe. A great authority, a senior Professor from the London School of Economics was asked for an explanation. His response was that it seemed that the children were lacking in adult role models. In simple words, which do not require an LSE professorship, they had minimally functioning parents. In subsequent years, I have found that some Scandinavian societies beat this figure with up to 60% being born out of wedlock, whilst in Australia "only" one out of three is born out of wedlock. But would anyone dare say that cohabitation is bad and irresponsible, especially with regard to children? No, for that would violate the supreme right of people to pleasure, including sexuality without inhibitions — such as formal commitments to partners and offspring. The pursuit of happiness as an absolute human right has come to mean the unfettered right to pleasure with an equal consenting other.

Just as the supreme quest for pleasure comes to endorse "polymorphous [formless and fluid] perversity" — from diverse sexualities to gender indeterminacy — its other side, the flight from pain leads our society into widespread killing: abortion on demand for the legions of unwanted babies, euthanasia for unwanted life, suicide for unwanted suffering. All of these lives have pain — either for those who would otherwise have to care for them, or for the sufferers themselves — which it should be everyone's "right" to escape, without any deeper sense of responsibility.

But I would like to explore another "take" on happiness — one that has to do with the word "joy", rather than "pleasure". The characteristic of "joy", the way I want to employ it, is not immersion in one's own pleasurable experience of something, but rather of the sense of transcendence which one has from an uplifting experience. Joy is a kind of illumination, which comes from the palpable experience of the goodness of something. This illumination, this clarification, transports an individual. It is the experience of an elevated joy that creates the extraordinary ability in a person to unite with others and to change and improve oneself. True joy taps into real transcendence — the soul and the Divine — and is found in what manifests these.

That is why the culture of desperate material pleasure paradoxically has its root in the Divine, though ends up being its inversion. It seeks transcendence — of which one feature is the feeling of eternity — in pleasure. It wants to get "high" that is, to be free of, itself — but it can find this only in physical pleasure. This could be the pleasure of drugs, sex, the distorted pleasure of violence, but it is all a bitterly derailed quest for transcendence.

We live in a time of unparalleled self-harm and suicide among youth. The rates keep on ascending. It has been remarked that the smile of stranger (and certainly a friend) can stop a suicide. If people cannot find comfort in the life of the spirit, because it has been eviscerated, why can't they find it in the common humanity of other people? Why can't people smile at each other? Or more pertinently, what does it take to smile at another person?

One answer to this would be simple compassion. If you saw a wounded or crying animal, would you not be moved? How much more so seeing a wounded, crying or simply depressed human being? Yet the fact is that flesh has little compassion for flesh. Operating on the material plane we tend to be concerned overwhelmingly for our *own* material wellbeing. Material interests often conflict: Why should I actually care for or love another human being or creature if it doesn't benefit me? On the material plane, we do not find our common humanity.

Where then do we find our true commonality, our true kinship? What unites us is the human spirit — the human soul, which we all possess. The reason for this is that within the soul resides a Divine capacity and quality. In this, all souls have an affinity with one another. Unlike the bodies, they are united in their common orientation to G-d. It's interesting that the materialistic world of divergent material interests can at best speak of tolerance of differences, whilst the spiritual dimension speaks of unity. I have found this in interfaith too. If we focus on our differences, then the best we can do is to ask for tolerance. Tolerance establishes a limited solidarity. But when the faiths see what they have in common, belief in G-d and a basic set of shared values, then we are actually united, we are brothers and sisters, not merely tolerant strangers.

So it is when we look upon another human being as a spiritual potential, as a soul, it suddenly becomes possible to smile, because spirit is drawn to spirit, (whilst, as mentioned, flesh is not necessarily drawn to flesh, except where there is a particular interest or need to be met). The same applies to the non-human world. A wounded animal, a ravaged landscape deserves our concern because these have value as things, like ourselves, created by G-d and endowed by G-d with purpose and for that reason should not be treated heedlessly.

What I am saying here is that real happiness has to be more than pleasure; it has to connect with the human spirit and with something higher. But that doesn't mean that it is bloodless, disembodied of all physical pleasure. To the contrary, we were equipped with bodies with all their passions, in order to refine and direct those passions as motors for good ends. There is nothing wrong with the enjoyment of eating, when it is done a spirit of wholesome conviviality or simply to have the energy to pursue our tasks, but it should not be an exclusively self-absorbed activity. The pleasure of sexuality is a good thing when it enhances the love for one's spouse. In short, the material is good when it is wedded to the spirit, not when it becomes an end in itself.

We all want joy. But the real prospect for joy and not mere pleasure laced with despair, is when we open ourselves and our youth to the world of the spirit. That is to say, when contemplating the material veneer of reality, we know and say, "there is more than this".

Second Lecture

Homosexuality:
What does Sex have to do with G-d?

Homosexuality as a claimed cultural value

At the time of writing there was in the State of Victoria a programme, supported by the Coalition Government in some 152 schools, to educate school children in the legitimacy of homosexual behaviour. The Labor party had undertaken, if elected, to extend this program to every State School in Victoria. Nothing could indicate more clearly that homosexuality as a "value" — whether for "marriage", adoption, provision of IVF services or simple moral approbation — was no longer a personal matter. The debate is about the role it is to assume in the conscious and collective culture of our society. There is a drive to install it into the education of children.

The question of whether sexual morality is something which government and legislation should regulate, or whether it is a personal and private matter, in which government should not interfere, other than to facilitate for those who want, was at issue fifty years ago in a debate over the Wolfenden Report on "Homosexual offences and Prostitution" in England. Then it had to do with legalization of both. Two sides were formed over the issue. One that sexual morality was not the State's business and it should allow consenting adults to do what they wanted in their private lives. That position was taken up by a prominent Oxford jurist H. L. A. Hart. The English Judge, Lord Patrick Devlin, espoused the other position, which I think most people of traditional faith uphold.

Devlin argued that the positions, which Governments and legislatures take up on matters of sexual morality, do *not* leave this as a merely personal and discretionary matter, which should not worry people who oppose them. Rather, when government legislates to legitimate, condone or support a position on some aspect of sexual morality, *society* is in fact making a statement about its values. Legislation, which endorses certain sexual behaviours, *effectively* teaches them and installs them as social mores. Society and law may not always be able to police morality. Devlin argued that adultery is an example: it is not feasible in our society to prosecute this. But by the same token, society does not have to facilitate, protect and reward adultery. The same applies to homosexual practice. It can either prosecute or tolerate or support a behaviour, and there are great differences between these, as we see in the case of homosexuality. Even those who, as our faith traditions teach us, believe homosexual conduct to be wrong, might agree that, under present circumstances — especially where spiritual literacy and awareness of universal values are weak — it should not be prosecuted. But there is a vast step from not prosecuting to supporting its practice. But that is where legislation and governmental practice is heading: the support of homosexual behaviour in education, legislation and IVF and adoption services effectively *promote it as a* social norm and a cultural value.

Interestingly, the claimed social norm and cultural value of homosexuality, is being pushed far more by heterosexuals than homosexuals. It is a credo of the politicized culture of the universities. Academics at professorial levels and university administrations are as frightened of a breach of political correctness in this area, as those further down the ladder who depend on the favour of their superiors for contracts, tenure and promotion. Intellectual conformity in the contemporary Western university is virtually as seamless as that of the academy under Stalin and Hitler. The difference is that the intellectual conformity of the universities of the West is not policed by secret agents (such as those of the KGB or the Gestapo) but is peer-marshalled by the culture of political correctness. From the universities come cadres of journalists, school teachers, bureaucrats, lawyers and health professionals all steeped in the same credo. They — the overwhelmingly heterosexually staffed professions and elites — promote the culture of homosexuality. Why? One reason is that it's part of a materialistic and hedonistic teaching about the nature of the human being (broached this in the first lecture). The second is an argument about "rights" and "equality", applied to this new concept of the human being. We shall return to these points.

The basic feature of this view of the human being is, as noted, a materialistic notion of humans as supremely entitled to pleasure and enjoyment. The secular ideal of human autonomy is now grasped, not merely as the European Enlightenment understood it as the autonomy of the mind (as the philosopher Kant said, "Have courage to use your own understanding!"), but also the autonomy of the body. This belief holds that the material flesh of humans should not be constrained in its gratification except where it stops another person's equally free enjoyment of pleasures (or where there is a power asymmetry in the pursuit of pleasure, such as in a sexual relationship of adults and children, or a non-consensual adult sexual relationship). According to this teaching, sexual morality is polymorphous. No one should dictate boundaries on personal and private conduct. On the contrary, it is the duty of the state to facilitate polymorphous self-gratification where the parties are equal and consenting.

Traditionally, in religious thinking, morality has been understood to operate in two dimensions: between person and person and between the person and G-d. In the realm between the person and G-d, obviously issues such as the belief in, and reverence for, G-d are present. But there is also another aspect of this dimension: human sexuality. Starkly put, matters of sexual morality and refraining from their breach (as in homosexuality) have to do with one's relationship with G-d and to one's innermost self, which is the spiritual self, made in the image of G-d. The sphere of one's relationship to G-d has to do with personal *identity*, who one *is*. Consequently, "consent" is irrelevant in validating a forbidden sexual relationship, because it is a personal matter affecting one's identity, as a human being created in the image of G-d. We shall return to explain this.

The interpersonal realm — the realm of interaction between person and person — on the other hand, is different. In that realm there is some room for individuals to negotiate their relationships — contract has a role in the market place and bargaining (such as plea-bargaining) and mediation has a role in the legal system. In the interpersonal realm, consent plays a role where one's property and entitlements are at stake. But in the personal sphere, including that of sexual morality, which has to do with personal identity, consent is irrelevant: the consent of two adult siblings to an incestuous relationship does not validate incest. The same is true of homosexuality. The problem is that the secular worldview of hedonistic materialism has little concept of G-d and consequently of the concept of a personal identity, constituted also by one's sexual unions, *before* G-d.

The doctrine, held and driven primarily by heterosexuals, which promotes homosexuality as part of its concept of the freely morphing human being already has its complete expression in Sweden. In Sweden, not only may homosexuals marry, but so also siblings with one common parent. That is to say, incestuous marriage exists in Sweden. In addition to this, Sweden has a new programme of gender neutrality in schools, whereby identification and rearing of children as male *or* female is suspended. Interestingly, the country is finally moving towards a ban on bestiality, which until now had been legal. But the ban comes not on the grounds that bestiality somehow confounds human identity but rather due to reports of suffering of animals in sexual acts with humans. The philosophical doctrine that promotes homosexuality as part of a polymorphous, hedonistic materialism has come to its logical conclusion in Sweden with the institutionalization of incest in "marriage". Sweden is also the most atheistic (non-formerly Communist) country in the world. Thus, it is ideologically consistent. Because human sexuality has to do with one's relationship to G-d, when G-d is abandoned so often — though not always — is the regulation of sexuality.

Body and soul: does "homosexuality" define the person?

One of the arguments used to legitimate homosexual conduct is that homosexuality is an inborn characteristic and, like any other characteristic, needs and deserves expression. There are two issues here. One is whether and to what extent homosexuality is an inborn characteristic. But even deeper than this is the issue of whether, if indeed homosexuality were an inborn characteristic and disposition, what difference that would make. Let us consider the more fundamental question.

One form of behaviour that justifiably receives universal condemnation is the behaviour of a paedophile acting on his or her predisposition. Yet the American *Diagnostic Statistical Manual*, the so called "bible" of American Psychiatry describes paedophilia as a *sexual orientation* (even though, realizing its consequences, there was a recent scramble to say that this word was a "typographical error"). The DSM describes paedophilia as an intense and recurrent sexual interest in prepubescent children, which becomes a disorder if it causes a person "marked distress or interpersonal difficulty" or if the person acts on his or her disposition.

There is a website for individuals who possess, but seek to control, this predisposition or orientation, entitled "Virtuous Pedophiles" (www.virped.org). On the website, a Professor of Psychiatry at the University of Toronto, Dr Ray Blanchard is quoted as saying:

> People do not choose to be attracted to children or adults any more than they choose to be attracted to males or females. Not all paedophiles are child molesters (or vice versa). Child molesters are defined by their acts; paedophiles are defined by their desires. There are paedophiles and hebephiles who never act on their sexual attraction towards children. They cannot be blamed for what they feel, and they should be supported for the constant self-restraint they must exercise in order to behave ethically.

In short, paedophiles are expected to do battle with a deep-seated predisposition towards sexual activity with children. Most people would not exonerate them were they to indulge that deep-seated — call it even "hard-wired" — drive. Indeed, our society seeks to punish them severely.

If possessing a deep-seated sexual orientation, paedophilia, does not justify the expression of that orientation in practice, why is the argument of "born that way" *per se* used to validate homosexual practice? One explanation is that the proponents of this argument have simply not thought of this contradiction. The second explanation used to explain their different societal treatment is: to follow a paedophiliac disposition involves a victim: the child; to follow a homosexual disposition in a consensual relationship between equals does not. That, however, is an *ethical argument* — not a psychophysical one of "orientation" — which raises the question of whether "consent" makes it acceptable (discussed above). Many would acknowledge that consent does not make an incestuous sexual relationship between adult siblings acceptable.

For those supporting homosexual practice, but who have not contemplated these contradictions, the argument continues that homosexuality is an "emergent characteristic" of certain persons and should be allowed expression in that it defines their "essential" being. Based on this view, much contemporary psychiatry and psychology went out to do battle with reparative therapies which sought to help individuals, who were distressed by their homosexual impulses, to function heterosexually. Several religiously backed therapeutic organizations were formed to help people with such problems such as the Christian group NARTH and the Jewish group JONAH. They and other non-affiliated practitioners of reparative therapy were attacked by mainstream psychology and psychiatry for seeking to cure behaviours the critics claimed are intrinsic and that attempts to help such individuals would only cause them "harm".

A politicized mainstream psychology and psychiatry chose to criticize the major proponents of reparative therapy who experienced successes with their clients, especially those identifying as religious persons with same-sex attraction. It was argued that this (religious) sample was unrepresentative of the general homosexual public, which they claimed did not want or seek therapy. The interesting question, however, is, why were those who sought out help from NARTH and JONAH often religious and did experience significant success in the therapies? The answer to this is that there was a *conscious* dimension of their being — a spiritual side — which wanted to do battle with their physical impulses. The physical side of their being was demonstrably *not* their whole or their essential being. In short, they manifested one of the deepest truths, namely that the human being possesses body *and* soul, and that these two can be in conflict with one another.

This should not come as a surprise. We all know that a child (and an adult too) may be tempted to steal something from a shop. But then something called conscience — if developed in the individual — enters to reject that impulse in the refined human being, based more on principle than fear of being caught. This is exactly the case of the religious person who seeks out therapy for homosexual inclinations. That person's soul or conscience believes that homosexual practice is wrong, and consequently seeks help to restrain or alter that physical impulse. Contemporary psychiatry and psychology, which for the most part is materialistic and physicalist in its assumptions, does not know what the soul is or irons it out of human personality. That is why it opposes reparative therapy: because it understands only a physical "emergent characteristic" and does not know that the human being also has a soul, the highest and the *essential* faculty of a person. So it is possible that the body might be homosexual; but the soul, imitating the Divine and the Divine prohibition on homosexual acts, is not.

Let us summarize this point. Homosexuality, whether it is due to biological or psychological factors, does not define any human being in his or her entirety. For the person also has a soul, which mirroring G-d and a Divine ethical template (that rules out homosexual practice), is *not* homosexual. The argument of inborn-ness of homosexual tendencies, even were it in some part true, brings no ethical justification for homosexual behaviour; just as it does not define the whole human being (body, mind *and* soul) and certainly not its highest faculty (the soul).

Beyond the wrongness of a politicized psychiatry and psychology (and the culture desiring to lock homosexuals into homosexuality) that wants to prohibit therapy, there is a deep danger and injustice to the homosexuals themselves.

In reality, there is a wide spectrum of homosexual tendencies: from very strong and deep-seated physical ones, through to less deep-seated tendencies which may have psychologically treatable causes, through to individuals who can and have had heterosexual relationships, but make a "lifestyle" choice to enter or experiment with a homosexual relationship. The attempted ban on reparative therapy tars all of these with one brush, where in fact — as documented by Robert Spitzer, Stanton Jones and others — reparative therapy can and does work successfully for a significant range of the spectrum.

But there is a more worrying consequence of the doctrine that homosexuality is an "emergent characteristic" which determines the identity of people with that characteristic. This is the application of the so-called homosexual anti-bullying programmes for schools. Whilst bullying of any kind and for any reason is cruel and must be stopped — and there is a variety of programmes to do this — a problematic programme, the "Victorian Safe Schools Coalition" (with different names in different States) has been introduced to schools. Its agenda is to win acceptance for homosexuality as a norm in childhood education, the best place to accomplish an overall cultural shift. The Labor Party, newly elected in Victoria, declared before the election an intention to impose this programme on every Government School. The programme invites young children to identify themselves sexually (heterosexual, homosexual etc) and thereby to lock themselves into a sexual identity. At an age when, according to some paediatric opinions, up to 26 per cent of children experience fluidity in their sexual identity, this is plainly dangerous. A girl's crush on another girl could be identified and confirmed as lesbianism. Quite apart from the ethical wrongness of this programme, significant psychological harm could be imposed by presenting a sexual choice to young children for their selection and identification. The programme not only uproots the moral culture of the Judeo-Christian or Abrahamic tradition, it also endangers children's normal development.

Homosexuality: "rights" and "equality"

One of the favourite arguments of the heterosexual lobby for the legitimation of homosexuality is the argument of "rights", with its concomitant slogan of "equality". Opposition to homosexual practice is made out as something akin to racism. This is a deep fallacy. A person can do nothing about the colour of his or her skin because it is something absolutely irrelevant to his or her personhood and conduct. Each human being stands on the merit of his or her conduct and is endowed with the Divine potential to choose and do good. On the other hand, homosexual practice is a behaviour, an act, which can be chosen or controlled. No person is exempted from responsibility merely due to a strong inclination, no matter how deep-seated. That point was previously made with regard to paedophiliac orientation. A person can refrain from homosexual practice, even if he or she cannot eliminate fantasy or the desire to perform these acts.

The equality of human beings derives from their shared possession of a soul or conscience, which innately resonates with the Divine, whether or not this potentiality has come into actuality in the individual's conduct. Mere elected feelings, perceptions – unadjudicated by the soul or conscience – on the other hand, are not morally equal. The same applies to "love". The love of a man and a woman may entitle them to marry; the love of a brother and sister does not. The naive, blanket formula of "marriage equality", being free marry equally whomever one "loves", finds its concrete (and barbarous) fulfilment in Sweden: in incestuous "marriage".

Homosexuality and human identity

At a forum my Institute organised before the last federal election, a number of candidates from across the political spectrum explained why they opposed homosexual marriage. I don't recall all the arguments that were made, but most of them are well-known. During question time, an individual stood up and stated, "I am a well-adjusted homosexual and I want you to know that

I agree with everything the speakers have said tonight". I got to know him later and he explained more.

He explained that everyone, including a homosexual, is entitled to a mother and a father. Let us unpack this a little. We know that it takes a mother and a father, a man and woman (or at least their gametes), to create a child. The Bible states, "Therefore a man shall leave his father and mother and cleave to his wife and they shall become one flesh". What this means is that man and woman (two different people) become one in their offspring. But don't animals also become united in their offspring? There is a difference. A medieval commentator, Nachmanides explains it that children identify with their parents, and parents with their children, long after the needs of nurture are over. Animals do not. Being born of man and woman has to do with human identity past, present and future. I was born of a man and woman, *my* parents. They are my past. I met my wife and married her and we became a unit: this union defines my present. My own and my wife's extension into the future are our biological children. They are our future. My past, present and future identity is bound up with a serious of biological unions of man and woman. This is not merely a biological fact. It is a matter of continuous *spiritual* intergenerational identity and self-concept. That is what a person is and the biological linkages of parents and children — with their psychological and spiritual significance — should not be removed from them. Homosexual unions are not biological unions and when they resort to artificial reproduction with donor gametes they create orphans. They have no biological extension in these children and depriving the children have no history or at best a partial history in these 'parents', who commissioned their production. This is a basic infringement of human identity, robbing both the homosexuals, who are taught that they cannot change and enter into a heterosexual reproductive marriage, of their future; and the children "commissioned" for them from the gametes of others, of their past.

Then there is another spiritual aspect of the identity afforded a human being by a mother and father. Despite the ideology of hedonistic materialism, men are different to women. This parallels a division of masculine and feminine in the Divine also. G-d creates transcendentally — that is masculine. G-d also nurtures the needs of all creatures immanently in their proximate particularity — that is feminine. The family division between father and mother is an analogue for these transcendent and immanent dimensions in the Divine. The father is a more remote moral authority figure for the child; the mother is much closer, nurturing individually the members of the family. A child needs both: a male role model (as we are finding out in this increasingly fatherless society) and a female role model. These combine to form and raise the whole human being further in the image and character of the Divine, which is both "masculine" and "feminine". Two men and two women cannot do this. At some level, this was what our homosexual friend in the audience meant.

If, as our tradition teaches us, "homosexual" can never define the spiritual essence of a person, but only a tendency within his or her body and/or mind, what favour have we done a person by endorsing and "boxing" him or her as a "homosexual" (and then barring him or her from access to therapy to modify bodily impulses and mental self-concepts)? Our homosexual friend in the audience told me that he finds much comfort in the religious life. He wants everyone, including homosexuals, to have a mother and a father, constituents of essential human identity. To block the freedom to change, and to impose another destiny, are a betrayal of the homosexuals themselves.

Third lecture
Life: Whose is It?

Euthanasia

In 2008, the Victorian Parliament passed a law in relation to abortion, which has been called one of the most radical, or alternatively, worst, abortion laws in the world. A bill allowing euthanasia was also presented to the Parliament that year. It was defeated, but new euthanasia and assisted suicide bills circle steadily above us. They are championed by elements of the mainstream media and are clearly part of the culture that produced the Victorian abortion law. The battle lines in debate on all these issues have traditionally been drawn with the words "pro-life" and "pro-choice". The wider public has only a fuzzy sense of what "life" means. In reality, we shall see that this issue too, fundamentally relates to the question: What is a human being?

The great faith traditions teach that a human being is a composite of body, mind and soul. The soul is the highest faculty in the human being. Some call it conscience, but whatever its name, it is that which welds the components of the human being into the one person and takes responsibility for the person. The soul or conscience is the primary person. To use a concept of Viktor Frankl, the soul has mind and body as its vehicles or instruments. When a person dies, that soul sheds these instruments and continues on as the essential person, the soul, without a physical body or mind. In this life, just as after life, vested in body and mind, the soul or conscience or spirit is the essential person too.

Another essential teaching found in the faith traditions, is that the soul is fashioned in the image of G-d. What that means is that it is a mirror of the Divine. In a lesser and reflected way, it possesses the attributes of the Divine: justice, mercy, kindness and so on. In a manner of speaking, it sees, knows and resonates with the Divine. We don't hear much about the soul in contemporary popular or contemporary high culture and correspondingly we don't hear much about G-d, because the two — the human soul and G-d — go together. One is the small G-d in the human being and the other is the great G-d of the cosmos.

The reason we don't hear much about the soul or G-d these days is because the strident contemporary culture is a culture of the body — with the mind existing merely to procure the objects of bodily needs and desires. Our culture is materialistic and pleasure-seeking. To reach the soul, on the other hand, you have to be able to set aside what you want — the demands of the psychophysical self — and ask instead what is wanted of you. You have to be able to transcend yourself. And when a person begins to transcend his or her own wishes, interests, stakes and pleasures, he or she is on a trajectory which will ultimately take oneself to discovery of one's own soul and of G-d. This is true for the so-called atheist and agnostic too. You don't have to pre-commit or sign up to religion. Just ask, "Is something wanted of me?" and you are *en route*, as Viktor Frankl said, to the terminus at which religious people have already arrived — the discovery of one's own soul and its intended object, G-d.

Now the point of this introduction, which is the traditional religious approach to the question of what a person is, is to apply it to the issue of euthanasia in the circumstance of, for example, an elderly bedridden person, in considerable pain needing a lot of help from other people. So, what is this person? Is it a body filled with pain? Is it a mind, which can no longer think fully rationally? Is it an entity making demands and placing strains on other people for its simple maintenance? Maybe this person is all of these: a pain-ridden body, a disturbed and distracted mind and a burden on others. But he or she is much more than this. Inside that pain-ridden body and behind the window of that disturbed mind is a soul, a mirror of G-d, with its unique personality. The essential person — the soul — is hemmed in, is trapped beneath the rubble of a broken body and/or a fractured mind. However, that essential person, the soul, despite its damaged instruments, is *healthy*, pure and whole. Euthanasia would remove not only a pained body and/or mind, but also this soul from this world. This is what Viktor Frankl had to say about euthanasia:

> Thus, the spiritual [dimension of the] person stands in... opposition to the psychophysical organism. The organism is an ensemble of organs, that is, of instrumentalities. The function of the organism — the task, which it has to achieve for the person whom it bears (and by whom it is borne) — is in the first place an instrumental one. ... As a tool, which in this sense it is, the organism is a means to an end, and as such has a utility. The counter-concept of utility is that of dignity. Dignity, however, pertains alone to a person and does so essentially independently of all living and social utility.

Only the person who overlooks and forgets this, can justify euthanasia. However, the one who knows about the unconditional dignity of every single person, has unqualified respect for the human person, including the sick person, whether incurably sick or incurably mentally ill.[149]

The faith traditions add a further insight: that the soul, with its accoutrements or instruments, body and mind, are the possession of G-d. What this means is that we do not have proprietorship over life and it is not for us to decide when our own or anyone else's life should end (other than when we kill in accordance with Divinely sanctioned principles, such as in self-defence). We do not necessarily have aggressively to pursue cures and treatments in circumstances, where there is no prospect of cure but only the prospect of continued pain. But by the same token we cannot intervene to terminate life. For apart from its intrinsic (spiritual) dignity, G-d has both ownership of and purpose with His property — the soul in the body — as long as that person lives.

What could that purpose be? We do not necessarily know. A soul in a body is capable of thought, even if it cannot speak or act through the body. And as Frankl pointed out, even the most hemmed-in human existence still possesses a crucial realm of freedom and responsibility: the ability to take up an *attitude* towards its own suffering and find meaning in its circumstances. Perhaps that expressed attitude alone could form a prayer that reverberates throughout and uplifts the universe. Perhaps that purpose is also to elicit care and compassion from others.

Euthanasia can be entertained only by a materialistic philosophy that recognises no soul and no G-d. For that philosophy, the human being is essentially sentient flesh, which has no owner other than itself. It can discard the body, its life, just as one discards a piece of one's material property. When the person, construed essentially as sentient flesh, ceases to have pleasure and instead experiences pain, this philosophy sees no remaining value to protect and no reason to live, because the flesh like the rest

---

[149] *The Rediscovery of the Human – Psychological Writings of Viktor E. Frankl on the Human in the Image of the Divine*, p. 120.

of the material world is "all there is". This attitude in fact fuels a culture of despair. Adults and youths who, not only on account of illness but also social breakdown, no longer have pleasure but only psychological pain, see increasingly little reason to live. The disappearance of meaning in their lives is attributable above all to the cultural suppression of that part of the human being *whose entire business is self-transcending meaning*: the human soul.

Abortion

Let us now take this debate over what essentially a person is, to the question of abortion. All the faith traditions agree that abortion is a very serious matter. The reason for this is that we are referring to an emergent person — body *and soul* — also. The foetus, like the terminally ill or comatose adult, is not able to make its own claims; it is a dependent existence. But it is a being that has received a soul. Its instruments of body and mind are not yet fully formed, but the highest faculty, the soul within that body and mind *is* fully formed — whole, pure and immensely significant. As such, the foetus has its essential human identity.

This does not mean that abortion is forbidden under all circumstances. Just as one can ward off an attacker in self-defence, where a mother's life is in danger, the foetus becomes that "pursuer", even though it does not mean to be, and abortion may be warranted. But the circumstances warranting abortion are rare. The concept of abortion on demand, that is, for no reason or any reason at all, as it applies under Victorian law for foetuses up to 24 weeks, is a licence for indiscriminate killing and is anathema to the culture and civilization our faiths have formed.

The Victorian Abortion Reform Act is extreme in many respects. However, one provision in it stands out over all others and darkens our civilisation more than any other. This is its provision in Section 8 that a doctor, who has a conscientious objection to performing a particular abortion, in circumstances of no threat to the mother's life, must refer this client to another doctor who the first doctor knows has no objection to performing the abortion. Refusal to do so may result in deregistration of the doctor.

Now this law mandates complicity — by referral — to an act of killing, to which the doctor's conscience and in most cases our faith traditions object. It has already happened in the case of a Victorian doctor refusing to refer for an abortion where the parents did not want the baby because it was female. The doctor was investigated by a tribunal under the new legislation. He believed — and indeed there are — no grounds for such an abortion. The response to this aspect of the legislation has been to call it a violation of freedom of conscience and freedom of religion: that is, of the doctor's practice of religion which prohibits him or her from complicity in an abortion on these spurious grounds. A survey of Victorian doctors found that over 80% found this clause in the Victorian abortion law to constitute a violation of their freedom of conscience.

In fact, the compulsion on the doctor to be complicit in such an abortion signifies something which includes but goes beyond a violation of religious freedom and freedom of conscience. It has to do with the invention of an absolute "right to abort". What does this mean? I was once sitting in my living room with a visiting American professor of law. He was telling me that in America there had been a debate as to whether a married woman should be required to get the consent of her husband to obtain an abortion. The professor put the argument against any such requirement in the following rhetorical terms: "Does a woman need to get her husband's consent to have a benign tumour removed from her body?" Well, of course, the answer to *that* question should be "no". But the problem is that the foetus is being compared to a "benign tumour".

The faith traditions say that the foetus posesses "life" (the unique composite of body, soul and mind), over which no one has sovereignty — not one's own life, nor another's life nor the life within one's body — to dispose of *at will*. The identification of the foetus with a tumour, the removal of which a doctor *must* facilitate, at least though referral as provided for in clause 8 of the Abortion Law, is the *absolute* negation of the value of the life of a foetus. This view corrodes our culture to the core.

Watch out for life

There is another deeply disturbing feature and erosion of civilization in the culture of state-enforceable abortion in the Victorian legislation. It is the idea of abortion as a sanitizing measure. Most abortions are performed on unmarried women — both teens and older unmarried women. Society reasons that pregnancies in these categories will occur and will be unwanted. Inevitably, therefore, we need abortions. So, we deal with the consequences but not with the causes. The curious thing is that teenagers are not encouraged to hold off having sex until they are married. Singles and people living together in uncommitted relationships are not urged to marry first and then have sex. The primary "right" is to be able to have unrestricted sexual activity at any age and circumstance, and if as a consequence of that girls or women get pregnant, then abortion is available as a sanitary solution to clean up the mess, the collateral damage.

As noted, our culture puts "sexual freedom" as one of its supreme principles, higher than personal responsibility and higher than foetal life. Compare this with driving a car. If a person kills another person through careless driving or through drunk driving they face severe punishment. Manslaughter in driver-caused deaths is by definition unintentional but nonetheless punished. Government spends a great deal of money on the policing and publicising of traffic laws and speeding offences. "If you drink and drive you are [an]...idiot", and further still, if you accidentally or carelessly kill someone you will be severely punished.

Now there is an activity other than driving which can also result in killing, as a result of irresponsibility, but there are no sanctions for it. This is the realm of unrestricted sexual activity. People who are married and have formal commitments can engage in this activity quite innocently, because if children are conceived, they can and generally will be cared for. Youth and adults who have sex outside marriage and conceive children in today's culture bear no consequences. The babies are often aborted. Unlike reckless or careless driving, it doesn't matter if lives are taken as a result of this activity. Abortion on demand, with its added-on compulsion on doctors, makes the world "safe" for unrestricted sexuality in uncommitted relationships. It supports and underpins a false principle: that the procreative act carries with it no responsibility. This undermines marriage, which, as the classic commentators write, has as one of its most fundamental purposes the care and raising of children. It promotes and sanitizes irresponsibility and non-commitment — and above all the disregard for life.

Children in schools are not taught the value of marriage and of the normative place of sexuality within marriage that exists largely for the protection and rearing of children. The most children are taught instead is "safe" sex (which in fact turns out to have a significant component of non-safety). There is no consideration of psychological harm done to girls through casual sexual relationships or the callousness which it breeds in boys and how it fuels the culture of titillation of which even the serious media have to provide a daily dose. Adults too encounter, at every supermarket checkout magazine stand, an endless parade of celebrity sexual antics.

Increasingly within our culture, people form uncommitted sexual liaisons. Today in Australia, one in three children is born out of wedlock. Only a crazy person would claim that children are unaffected. Statistically, it is de factos and singles that are major clients for abortions. So two principles seem to go hand in hand: an absolute principle of hedonism — of quantitatively and qualitatively unrestricted sexual activity — and a devaluation of foetal life to zero, expressed legally in the Victorian compulsion on doctors for abortion referrals.

Whom have we benefitted through all of this? Certainly not the 20,000 babies aborted annually in Victoria. But have we benefitted those living — the teenagers and the adults for whom abortion was the sanitary remedy in a culture of absolute hedonistic entitlement, without responsibility for relationships or life? They have been scarred and debased by the culture of abortion on demand.

Fourth lecture

Compassion and its corruption

Whose compassion?

Many of the worst features of hedonistic materialism present themselves as "compassion". Under this banner, human identity is reworked through allowing and institutionalizing boundary-less sexuality and an extraordinarily amount of killing, be it in abortion on demand in Australia and regimes of euthanasia overseas. The very expression "mercy-killing" is an oxymoron that sets the conscience of anyone, with a background in the world faiths and universal ethics, on edge. What then is compassion? What in "hard terms" assures its genuineness and morality and when does it tip over into the very opposite?

One of the commandments — albeit somewhat unusual — given to the Jewish people at Sinai is to shoo away a mother bird before taking its chicks or eggs. The reason for this seems to be that it would be compassionate not to let the mother bird watch its young (whether as eggs or newly hatched chicks) being taken away. This commandment does not apply to domesticated bird or fowl. One could take away the egg from a laying hen, i.e. one kept for laying eggs. Even though we learn this distinction from a scriptural verse, it is also understandable. A laying hen is accustomed to having the eggs removed and perhaps is not so distraught as an undomesticated bird would be.

Nevertheless, the Tradition from Sinai also teaches that one who, leading the communal prayers, declares before G-d (alluding to the commandment to send away the mother bird before taking its young), "Your mercies are extended to the nest of a bird..." is to be silenced. One reason given for this is that the public supplicant has "made the attributes [commandments] of G-d mercy, whereas in fact they are solely decrees". What does this mean? It means that the contours of Divinely mandated conduct, are not what *we* think are merciful, but what *G-d* in *His* compassion has decreed. G-d is surely merciful, but it is not for us to be the arbitrators and certifiers of mercy. When we follow G-d's instructions for merciful conduct we will be on track in our conduct.

This can be understood from the conduct of the archetype of evil, Hitler, and the so-called Third Reich. Under the Third Reich, Hitler enacted what may have been, even to this day, the most advanced legislation for the protection of animals. Section 2.1 of a law passed in 1934 made it forbidden, "to so neglect an animal in one's ownership, care or accommodation that it thereby experiences appreciable pain or appreciable damage", with an attendant punishment of 500,000 marks or imprisonment, and the same penalties were extended to failing to prevent children or other persons under their care from the same mistreatment of animals. This applied whether the act was intentional or negligent. It also applied to force-feeding fowl and shortening the tail of a horse without anaesthesia.

Now the question is, how can such an ostensible expression of "compassion" be understood in the person who murdered one-and-a-half million children amongst millions of others killed in the concentration camps? Even if, judged objectively, the laws enacted for the protection of animals by the Nazis were ethical, they originated from deeply perverted human beings. Hitler also took measures for the advancement of the natural environment ostensibly far ahead of his time. And the protection he took of the natural environment was not because of its benefit to human beings, but for the sake of nature itself. How is Hitler's enactment of these laws explicable in logic in the context of his world-view? The answer would appear to be that for Hitler a dog was loveable but not certain kinds of human beings. Hitler's "compassion" extended to animals but not to human beings.

Hitler was a man who most certainly did not reflect the Divine attribute of mercy. If some of his acts could objectively be described as merciful, such as the prevention of pain to an animal, it was essentially fortuitous. For G-d's law prohibits cruelty both to animals and to human beings. Today, we have the Greens who in their concern for the environment and the welfare of animals seem also to express compassion. Yet it is a movement that is on the front line of abortion on demand, with the destruction of foetuses in ways that cause it great pain to the foetus, alongside its advocacy for euthanasia and assisted suicide. The distorted logic of the Greens' "compassion" is that it extends to the flesh but not to the human soul.

Further biblical commentary states that, "Harshness against those who lead the people [… into evil] is compassion upon the world." The execution of Saddam Hussein, who sought not only to destroy other nations but an entire ethnic group under his own jurisdiction, is perhaps an example of harshness which in reality was "compassion upon the world".

Therefore, we should not assume that pity on an animal necessarily arises from a compassionate place and that destroying a tyrant does not. The bottom line is that we need to be tutored in our concepts of compassion or any other moral attribute for that matter. We need to be tutored in what G-d — that is to say the universal ethics carried forward from Sinai — calls compassion, and the actual hard lines, the specifications for conduct, with which we imitate G-d's compassion.

What is compassion?

Truly compassionate parents know very well that they have to apply "tough love" to children at times. Even though the day of the "rod" is over, the adage "spare the rod and spoil the child" still has a valid application. We have to know how to mix discipline with love, whether in regard to others or ourselves. The right mixture of the two is the essence of compassion.

To explain this further, kindness enters into compassion but kindness is not the same as compassion. Kindness tends to give unconditionally, or at least overlooks judgment of the worthiness of the recipient. Compassion — or pity or mercy, as it is also known — is giving while acknowledging that the other is not strictly worthy of it (that is, without surrendering judgment altogether). It harmonizes kindness and judgment. For compassion means "I feel for you and even though you have crossed a boundary you shouldn't have, I will make allowance for you". Both judgment, "you don't strictly deserve it" and kindness, "I want to give you" are brought together in compassion. That is, "You don't strictly deserve it, but I will give it to you anyway".

In compassion, therefore, we have both elements, kindness and judgment; though kindness is meant somewhat to prevail. Let us look at two cases of failure of compassion — where a proper mixture of kindness and judgment is absent. One is the case of the treatment of asylum-seekers coming on small boats to Australia. There is no doubt that the condition of simple folk who escape under very dangerous circumstances, where people smugglers may also have duped them, who arrive and are placed in detention centres, is an abject and pitiable one. That is the argument for *kindness* towards them.

On the other hand, the argument comes — the argument of strict judgment — that a nation is entitled to the integrity of its borders, that national security is not something to be trifled with. This is a true statement and stronger pre-emptive measures could and should be undertaken against people smugglers. However, by the same token, once people are on their way to our shores in an abject state, *and most probably are genuine refugees,* there should be room for kindness. That is to say, while they should not have come in this way, if they are fleeing and their condition is abject, we should show kindness. The idea of "processing" asylum-seekers though long detention is callous. As one politician said, "you process cheese, not people".

This is a case where grounds exist to alleviate a stern judgment with kindness, but the kindness has not been expressed and so there is a failure of compassion. Instead, it is all severity, where people arriving with good intentions or who are the genuine victims of persecution or genuine refugees deserve kindness despite their illicit crossing of a boundary. The refusal to grant it is about boundaries but it pushes boundaries too far.

The second case of a failure of compassion as a wrong mix of judgment and kindness is to be found in the concept of "mercy killing" or euthanasia. What is wrong with this? The proponents of euthanasia want to express kindness towards the suffering, for the travails of the body, but they violate the boundary and integrity of life: which is present as long as the soul is present in the body. If I were only flesh, one could argue that it is "my flesh" and I could deaden its pain permanently for my benefit. Since it serves a soul, made in the image of G-d, this brings it into a new category or boundary: it is something sacred, G-d's inviolable property, whose destruction He alone can authorize.

The stance that seeks to arbitrate everything in favour of the flesh and promotes the flight from pain and suffering through a host of forms of killing from abortion to euthanasia has no sense of boundaries, purpose and sanctity. It operates only on the "horizontal" (wholly earthly) dimension of the material world. It does not know the "vertical" dimension (relating things to the Divine intent, above, in their creation) that establishes boundaries, division and purposes of different entities within the creation. If we do not know the higher purpose for which a person lives, or that there is a purpose, and hold instead that the human being's existence is purely in order to escape from pain and to embrace "enjoyment", then this is a gross one-sidedness. It is not compassion, because compassion harmonizes judgment (the sense of boundaries and purpose) with kindness (the suffering which may exist within those boundaries). The advocacy for euthanasia is oriented to one dimension only — kindness towards the flesh — but tramples the boundary and purpose of life itself. Real compassion respects and protects life and cares for it in its suffering.

Another, related, false and corrupted compassion is in sexual permissiveness. It extends "kindness" towards children, approving and helping them to pursue sexual activity, when they are not ready for its psychological, physical and procreative consequences. For, in its view, the body is all. It extends full benefits towards a de facto couple where people can have all the benefits of marriage without any of its responsibilities, i.e. without boundaries. It follows the adage: "if you have the milk, who needs the cow?" And in Sweden, as we have noted, boundaryless "kindness" has led to incestuous marriage and the genderless (or gender-neutral) education of children.

Compassion has failed with the asylum seekers because the boundaries are too high. Compassion has failed in the euthanasia advocacy and permissive sexual ethic of contemporary Western society, because the boundaries are too low.

The respect for religion

What follows from the above two sections of this lecture is first, that G-d's — or universal ethics' — idea of compassion and contemporary cultural understanding of compassion do not necessarily align with one another. The task of a human being is to imitate and take instruction from the Divine, to model Divine compassion. Secondly, when the human being tries to apply compassion, he or she needs to know that compassion is a balance of kindness towards material suffering and respect for the boundaries and purposes of things, known by the spiritual compass within the person, informed by religious tradition. But for that, one must know and acknowledge the spiritual. "Compassion" which spurns and rejects the spiritual is headed towards barbarism, whether in the wholesale killing of abortion on demand and euthanasia or in the social breakdown caused by sexual dissolution and deregulation.

There is another aspect of the corruption of compassion, apart from the wrong mix of its components: where those who falsely deem themselves compassionate reach for compulsion. The organs of contemporary culture are not only significantly ignorant of religious tradition, they are also increasingly disrespectful of it. The media and academia make a carnival of denigration of religious tradition. Disrespect, of course, breeds a new generation of ignorance. Those who treat religious tradition lightly, will abandon its transmission and study. The blend of disrespect for and ignorance of religion can be seen in a policy which the new Government in Victoria espoused when it campaigned in the recent State elections.

The original Victorian Equal Opportunity Act, enacted by an earlier Labor government, sought to rule out discrimination in employment based on the beliefs, and sexual orientation and practice, of an applicant for a job. An exception was made for religious schools, but — under new proposed legislation — only where the school could provide a justification that these characteristics — belief, sexual activity and orientation, etc. — could be demonstrated to constitute an "inherent requirement" for the position in the school. Critics correctly understood this as a blow to religious freedom. Why shouldn't religious schools be able to employ staff, whom they judge to model in their own lives or at least not contradict the ethos of the school? What that legislation wanted to argue was that a Scripture teacher in a Christian, Islamic or Jewish school could justifiably be required to exhibit beliefs and a personal morality consistent with Christianity, Islam or Judaism. But it did not understand why the maths and English teacher, grounds staff, bursar and canteen manager should not be permitted openly to practice lifestyles at variance with the school's ethos. The Labor party could not or did not want to understand that a religious school does not make a distinction between teaching and practice and that children learn by example as much, if not more, than from books. Religious schools rightly wanted their environment to model the values of their tradition, conveyed as much by the maths and English teachers, canteen managers and the bursar as the Scripture teacher.

When the previous Liberal-National government (successor to the Labor Government which enacted that law) came into office, it appropriately removed this onus on the school to prove that each appointment warranted consistency with, or at least not a contradiction to, its values. It was presented very simply by the new Attorney General as a matter of religious freedom and freedom of association. Parents had a right to send their children to a school that consistently and throughout reflected their beliefs.

The present threat to reverse this freedom of religious schools and institutions in their staffing is symptomatic of a new imperialism in the supposedly but falsely "compassionate society". This version of "compassion" has suddenly become associated with compulsion: doctors are forced to refer, and so be complicit with abortions which are against their conscience, exposure to homosexuality is to be forced on all children in State schools and religious schools are to be forced to take teachers whose beliefs and lifestyles contradict their ethos. Why has contemporary "compassion" swung into compulsion?

True compassion is associated with a concept of harmony. As discussed, it balances judgment with kindness, bringing them into agreement with one another. The quality of harmony is associated with beauty, for beauty is harmonization, for example, in musical tones, or in colour and form in visual art. As a quality of action, it deals harmoniously in considerations of the other: it brings balance, or "beauty", of consideration to the circumstance of the other.

A narcissistic compassion, endemic to the culture of hedonistic materialism, is also drawn to beauty. The beauty it finds, however, is not in balanced consideration of the other but rather in itself. It is a self-, not an other-directed, beautification. It turns into personal vainglory and this is why the compassion of the hedonistic-materialistic culture is so imperious and intolerant of others. It is obsessed with the beauty of its own purported compassion. The narcissism of contemporary culture practises compulsion on the other, who resists the dictates of its self-imaged "compassion". It cannot tolerate an infraction of its own imperium, its own "beauty".

Authentic compassion is built on humility. For only humility can access the Divine attribute of compassion and seek to apply it to another. Narcissistic compassion inverts humility. Instead of being humbled before G-d and other people, it is humbled by its own grandeur and outraged by that which contradicts it. But of all the compulsion bred by a narcissistic and corrupted compassion — whether in forcing doctors with a conscientious objection to refer for abortion or forcing children to be exposed to homosexual lifestyles in violation of the right of parents to educate children in their own faith — the most serious compulsion is the attempt to dismantle religion, the teaching of G-d.

The proposed legislation (amendment of the Equal Opportunity Act of Victoria) would make a religious educational institution stand before a secular tribunal to justify why a particular member of their staff should have to be a practitioner of their faith and values, or at least not contradict them, on school grounds. How can a secular tribunal know better than a religious educational institution what is required of a staff member — in the area of beliefs, practices and values — to preserve the ethos of the school campus? It submits religion to a secular authority and a purely secular concept of what a "religious" education is. The very idea is imperious. It is beyond disrespect for religious tradition, of which secular authority has no or minimal understanding. It is an assault on religion and religious freedom. It is the negation of religion itself.

By attacking the freedom of religious schools to educate children in their faith and to transmit that faith and its principles, this secularist movement is doing something worse than weakening the transmission of religious tradition. It is attacking it and this is associated with blasphemy.

We began these lectures with the question of whether a religious person can sit down with a secularist — schooled in the contemporary hedonistic-materialistic culture — and try together to broach the most fundamental question: is there something more than the physical world and sentient flesh? But if the hardened secularist cannot yet come to *grapple* with this question, then let us at least ask of its proponents that this world-view not become a tyranny which destroys the freedoms which even secular democracy has historically vouchsafed.

Let us end on a good note — with an affirmation of the hope that compassion upon our common humanity will prevail, which means a compassion both for the human body *and* the human spirit.

Chapter 14

A Populism of the Spirit

Introduction

The word "populism" has been used to describe a variety of recent movements around the world, from Russia and Eastern Europe to Western Europe to the Anglosphere. It expresses a revolt against an imperious global liberalism which (until the election of Trump at least) has proceeded from the United States of America.

There is much talk about a rebellion against "elites": whether in the media, politics and industry, bureaucracy, the official arts and certainly in the universities and the professions, with their roof bodies, which were ideologically educated by the culture of the universities. I find it, however, more fruitful to speak of an *ideology* which has captured the elites rather than the phenomenon of elites, or centres of influence, *per se*. This ideology has, I would argue, eclipsed the human spirit or soul, with its moral compass and religious teaching that have guided civilization as we know it. Elites, with a world-outlook which embraced the human spirit and its tradition, would not have brought us to this.

At the same time there is something significant in the populist scepticism if not hostility towards the elites *as* elites. "Populism" proceeds from, or is driven by, "grass roots", ordinary people. Ordinary people are by nature humbler than the elite personnel, who are occupationally prone to hubris whether by virtue of intellectual prowess or power. In ordinary people, a residual humility — the consciousness that they are ordinary and not "tall poppies" — has allowed the soul or spirit to live with much better health than in the hubris-prone zones of the elites[150]. For the essential soul's spiritual knowledge is that it has a Creator and a purpose much greater than the self. From the soul (the likeness of G-d in the human being), and its natural resonance with its Creator, well up the values, which the populist revolt seeks to restore.

What is stated here is a spiritual reading of the significance and potential of the populist revolt. It does not claim that populist movements necessarily grasp themselves in this way. Populism may also have many other rough and objectionable manifestations. But in this essay, I would like to manifest the latent and potential spiritual content and affinity in this populist insurrection. I call this potential "a populism of the spirit".

The ideology against which populism rebels I have elsewhere called "hedonistic materialism".[151] It is based upon a model of the human being as a solely psychophysical being — that is to say, without a soul — with a variety of bodily and psychic impulses and interests, the fulfillment of which is to be brought about as a matter of "rights". These interests are largely ones having to do with pleasure and pain and the ideology employs a utilitarian calculus intended to minimize pain and maximize pleasure. All this is carried out under a much vaunted rubric of "compassion", but this compassion in fact overruns the traditional moral boundaries set by the moral review of the human soul, and the religious tradition which expresses it.

The code of universal ethics, which is found at the root of the great world religions and was renewed to all humanity at Mount Sinai, is known as the Noahide laws. Through the conduct of these laws, the human being "imitates" G-d, since Divine attributes translate into these forms of ethical conduct. I have written about these laws at length in my book, *The Theory and*

---

[150] Of course, this does not mean that intellectuals, leaders and professionals are incapable of humility. Indeed precisely that is demanded of them to be ultimately ethically *true* intellectuals, leaders and professionals. Humility and skills are *conjoint* requirements for them.
[151] S. D. Cowen, *Politics and Universal Ethics*, particularly Chapter 1.

Practice of Universal Ethics — the Noahide Laws. There are seven major Noahide laws and I have sought to correlate them in this essay with the major grievances and aspirations of the populist revolt — seen in its spiritual light — as follows.

The first object of grievance of the populist revolt is the atomization of the family and the destruction of its constituent member identities: male and female, husband and wife, parent and child. This is cured and the human being is actualized in the fullness of particular identity and relationships through the Noahide law of sexuality. This provides for the traditional, heterosexual family with clear identities of male and female, husband and wife, parent and child. The second object of grievance of the populist revolt is the aggressive secularization and repression of the culture of faith as the moral anchor of society and the individual. The application of three of the Noahide laws redress this secularization and reconnect society with the human spirit's consciousness of the Divine and its concomitant moral compass. They are the belief in G-d (or prohibition of idolatry), the respect for G-d (or prohibition of blasphemy) and the Noahide law of justice, which requires not only standards of objectivity and impartiality for law enforcement, but also keeps law in line with its universal ethical parameters. The third grievance has to do with societal "indifference" to the human impact on individuals of economic trends and technological processes. Here the Noahide law of theft and material harm insists that economic relationships are essentially human relationships and must forever and constantly be so regarded. The fourth grievance is against a "mythic" environmentalism expressed in doctrines of climate change which seem to reverse the traditional relationship of nature to the human being as something which can serve the human. This is corrected by the Noahide law relating to the treatment of nature which balances the legitimate expectation of the human being from nature, with constraints against wanton cruelty or waste. The fifth grievance is the indifference of hedonistic materialism towards the protection and value of life, which indifferently kills the vulnerable (abortion on demand and euthanasia) and fails properly to defend against violence practised internationally and within states.

The restoration of the family

The populist revolt resents the attempt of hedonistic materialism — the ideology of the liberal staffing of the elites — to rework human identity, as this is traditionally articulated in the fundamental unit of society, the family. Universal ethics, expressed in the Noahide laws, distinguishes male and female on the basis of their distinct biological forms and from these grow, or should grow, masculine and feminine personae or identities[152]. Roles within the family are predicated upon these biological distinctions. The most basic of them is the concept of heterosexual marriage, the stable sexual relationship of mand and woman, fortified by legal commitments and responsibilities. This relationship in turn allows children to be born, who have biological and thereby also full personal identity with their parents: these are my parents; this is our child. The family thereby also creates a sequence of generations, both caring and educative. Parents care for and educate their children and in turn children in some significant measure care for and respect their parents. The law of valid sexual union articulates the individual within the crystal of the family: as male or female, husband or wife, parent or child.

This ideology of hedonistic materialism wants to dissolve the crystal of the family and thereby the most basic human identities. It starts by negating the fact of biological difference between male and female as that upon which are predicated identities of masculinity and femininity. In fact it negates masculinity and femininity as concepts, and buttresses this by allowing individuals to assign their own sexual identities and to follow this through with the surgical sexual reconstruction of their bodies, even for children who wish it. Secondly it endorses all kinds of sexual unions other than heterosexual ones: homosexual unions, and in some countries incestuous and bestial unions. With this go also the distinctions of husband and wife. It then dissolves the relationship of parent and child. For homosexual humans which cannot reproduce, children are "commissioned" through artificial

---

[152] There is also the biological hermaphrodite, for which a distinct sexual ethics apply within the Noahide code.

reproductive technologies, never to be raised by both their biological parents. The identities of father and mother, parent and child are dissolved. Even where heterosexual relationships exist, the ideology removes the formal bonds of marriage, elevating simple cohabitation, in which no act of commitment or mutual designation has been made, to a status, identical with marriage, in terms of social benefits and rights. Every one of these phenomena is at variance with the prescriptions in universal ethics of the Creator of the human being.

A manifesto of traditional and eternal values, therefore, affirms first and foremost the complementarity of male and female, and the sole legitimate sexual union as a heterosexual one. With both moral clarity and compassion, it declares homosexuality and forms of gender dysphoria as irregularities and illnesses for which medical, psychological and spiritual counsel may be needed. It is integral to the created identity and spiritual purpose of the human being to be, as he or she was created, masculine or feminine. The sexual union of male and female is the sole sanctioned union. It may not be incestuous and it properly requires the formal commitment of marriage. Parents and children are defined through a biological relationship and from the generational relationship derive both obligations and entitlements from one another. Lawful sexuality and the family produced by it constitutes the basic prism of human identity.

Once a child has been born into a family, in which it has and can verify its biological parents, mother and father, it continues to need its parents for nurture and moral guidance, an education and formation in which a mother and father have unique and complementary roles. The idea of making children and youths into autonomous beings before they have completed their education and formation is also part of an ideology, which breaks up the organic unit of the family which raises the child in its values. The ideology of hedonistic materialism does this by sexualizing children and by incorporating into educational curriculum the sense of an entitlement to childhood sexual activity. Beyond this it models "sexual diversity" to children at an age (12 years) when 26% of children who would overwhelmingly settle into heterosexual roles, have as yet unconsolidated sexual identity. It seeks thereby to lock them into "diverse sexualities", at a time of high psycho-developmental vulnerability. It encourages children to undergo surgical sex-reassignment should they want it. Its outrage at pedophilia is not that sexual acts were performed with young children, for it encourages sexuality between children of the same age (often with psychologically and medically harmful consequences). Rather it is disturbed solely by the asymmetry of the pedophile relationship, where an adult takes advantage of a child. It upholds the "ideal" of persons as equal and autonomous pleasure centres, and children are not yet equal to adults in their practical autonomy. The Greens in Australia further want to turn children of 16 into voters. This is well before their secondary education is complete. But it is significant that 16 is the age of consent to sexual liaisons with any person. "Maturity" as a sexual pleasure centre confers for the Greens essential citizenship.

The culture of feminism, promoted by hedonistic materialism, is not about a very worthy topic — the respect due to women, as to men, seen in matters such as equal pay for equal work. Rather, it is about their intersubstitutability for men in all roles, starting from the family, and proceeding through every domain of society. Its goal is not to bring out women's unique strengths *per se,* but to make them identical to men. Through this it denigrates and denatures qualities of femininity, an approach which has played a significant role in the extraordinarily high divorce rate and the breakup of the family. This is stated without whitewashing male domestic violence or other failures on the part of men. The notion, furthermore, that they should work as much as men do, and that care-giver roles of men and women are interchangeable, leads next to a concept of universal child-care outside the home. This is also stated without ignoring the fact that economic pressures have also increasingly driven women to work. Here the objection is not to the notion that a woman may work, and indeed in traditional cultures women have been major workers and providers. Rather the point is that this should not come through a sacrifice of femininity — of the special nurture and care of their families and children — which women uniquely, and by the endowment of their Creator, possess. If working mothers need to find child care outside the home, then this is no more than an economic necessity, which should minimized as much as possible. It is not an ideal, which should be stretched to the maximum.

One of the areas of greatest concern for contemporary society is the phenomenon of aging and the care for the aged. In traditional societies, aged parents were largely cared for by their own adult children, whether in the children's homes or in proximity to them. One of the strongest reasons to fortify the traditional family is its capacity to care (or contribute in a variety of ways to the care) for aged parents. This is also a reason, why women should not be driven into full-time work force, since their caring capacity extends not only to children but also to parents and parents-in-law. Needless, to say, broken families are even more disadvantaged in the care that they can show for parents. The intact family, in which the wife and mother has a larger measure of work-free time, is good for the aged. So also, children who have been raised with a strong and unified family ethic will give not only physical, but psychological and spiritual sustenance to their aged parents. An elderly parent — even if for medical reasons, he or she has been placed in a nursing home, still needs to participate in a multi-generational context.

The breakdown of family is positively correlated with poverty. Family economies are lost and one-parent homes have to be supported. Contemporary social welfare policy tends to put cohabiting couples on a par with married ones. Cohabiting relationships break up at a significantly higher rate than do married ones, and the consequences for the children of those relationships and the instability is felt even without or prior to breakup. The fact that the State channels welfare equally to these cohabiting units as to married ones, only serves to compound the instability. People do not have to marry in order to have the benefits, and this encourages unstable frameworks for the raising of children. Government policy should motivate persons towards formal marriage.

Health in society is also related to the family. A human being's mental health — increasingly a problem in our society, aggravated by atomization of the family — and his or her physical health is significantly assisted by a strong family household. Higher mortality and morbidity is associated with the breakdown of the family. A drug culture feeds on disintegrated families. The combined cost of welfare and health in our society is a vast one, and it is directly related to the stability of families, aside from the actual suffering of individuals.

Community is an outgrowth of the family. It is spontaneously formed by the affinity of families with one another based on religion, culture and other values primarily fostered within the family. Where the family is atomized, so tends also to be community. Government programs become the universal substitute of the family's supportive and nurturing roles, its economic and health-stabilizing functions. That is why the Greens' platform is full of Government programmes: its world-view having atomized the unit which supports the individual and builds community, there remains only administered, bureaucratic welfare and care. Governments have found that community and faith-based organizations are the most efficient channels for welfare provision, and for that reason have sought to channel welfare funding through them. But for that one must have a community and its faith- or values basis.

Housing is also a basic human need. The breakdown of the family only compounds a crisis in housing, for more individuals need to be housed as a result of family breakup. Moreover, the phenomenon of crisis in accommodation, arising where individuals become homeless for a variety of social and mental-health reasons, be it drugs, psychological ill-health, family abuse and so forth — is also traceable often to family dysfunction and disintegration. The stable, traditional family is itself the best preventative against homelessness or housing crisis. After that comes the caring community, which can find accommodation for its members, when they are in crisis. But where the family falters so does the community. Again the State must step in and abstractly — and often inefficiently — seek to respond to what at root is a social and ultimately familial problem. The family grows into community — the "village" which, according to an African proverb "it takes to raise the child" — for the family is the seat of primary culture and transmission of values, and seeks its like in the community. The universal Noahide law which grants sole legitimacy to a heterosexual union fortified by the commitment of marriage is the foundation of family and the aggregation of families into community. The "sexual revolution" has first and foremost worked to dissolve the family, with its ultimate casualty — the individual who found identity and was nested within it. The family (and community) is replaced — at tremendous economic and human cost — with the bureaucratic provision of "human services": the atomization of the family replicates itself in the abstraction of administered care.

Religion and the culture of community

The "correctness" of political correctness comes from the authority of an ideology which has sought to establish itself against the sources of traditional morality: belief in G-d and the morality associated with religious belief. Above all the ideology of hedonistic materialism is aggressively secularist. The voices of this materialistic and anti-spiritual ideology come mostly from the universities and the media and also from the professions educated by the universities in hedonistic materialism. There is a constant derision of traditional religion. The most basic need and entitlement of a human being, who is ultimately and fundamentally a spiritual being, are to receive nurture and education in belief in G-d. This spiritual literacy includes knowledge of the core ethical religious tradition, that of the Noahide laws at the root of the world religions. Without an experiential education in belief and the morality which goes with it, to adapt a phrase ascribed to G. K. Chesterton, morally anything becomes possible. Populism — the voice and conscience of the ordinary person — values belief in G-d and religion in general. It resents the attempt to dismantle spiritual literacy in education and public life. The first (if we may so conceptually order it) of the Noahide laws is the belief in G-d, or at least the repudiation of idolatry, of which hedonistic materialism is a variety.

Signally, the Greens, in Australia, are opposed to public funding for private (which means, largely religious) schools. Their argument that the taxpayer should not have to a fund religious education overlooks the fact that some 70% of Australians in a recent census stated a religious affiliation. They are the taxpayers and for them religion is of value. The 2014 review of the National (Educational) Curriculum in Australia clearly stated a need to nurture spirituality. However, this has been perversely interpreted as a comparative study *of* spirituality, not an education *in* spirituality. Consequently, as the Government of Victoria excluded special religious instruction of the various faiths from their very small (one-hourly) weekly optional allotment from school hours in Government schools, it introduced a compulsory strand to the curriculum, which studies world faiths relativistically and includes with them secular humanism. This means that a child is not taught and strengthened in his or her family's or personal belief — i.e. in the *act* of belief. Instead, it is made into a formal and academic study which relativises world religions. This concept of "General Religious Education" comes from Sweden, one of the most atheistic societies in the world. Its real rationale is that religion is a "problem", which can only be solved by relativising it. Moreover, the subject includes in its smorgasbord of beliefs that of secular humanism, which is non-belief in G-d. That means, it is teaching children that belief is as good as non-belief. Whatever you call this, it is not a *religious* education. This negates the commitments of successive Governments, and most recently the Review of the National Curriculum, to nurture students' spirituality. This spiritual need — and its active suppression through an ideology entrenched in bureaucratic elites — touches the very soul of our civilization.

On the individual level, the dismantling of a religious education — which is of greater concern than ever before, since faith is less and less drawn from family and community in an internet saturated environment — has the consequence of deconstructing personal conscience. The child no longer situates values in the context of *belief*, and therefore does not internalize values in conscience.[153] All that could motivate a child to pay for a ticket on a public transport system is the fear of being caught by an inspector — not personal conscience.

The exclusion of religious education in public schools and ultimately, through relativization, the neutralization of religious belief (aside from the constant derision of religion in the media and universities) plays itself out in the undermining of public and personal morality. The preamble to the Australian Constitution uses the words "Humbly relying on the blessing of Al-mighty G-d". American currency has on it the words, "In G-d we trust". This — *default* — position of belief was the foundation of the morality which comes with it. The attempt to shake, relativize and remove this foundation of society has the gravest consequences. You cannot have it both ways, because the moralities predicated upon a belief in G-d and upon non-belief in G-d can become diametrically opposed. No contradiction to religious values is posed by constitutional doctrines of the separation of religion and state whether in Australia and in the US or elsewhere. All this doctrine requires is that no specific religion shall become the official religion of the state, and that its adherents can alone become office holders. Nowhere, however, does it imply that the common or shared beliefs of diverse religious groups, and indeed of our historical culture in general, cannot operate in public policy. The Noahide law setting forth belief in G-d (and prohibiting idolatry) needs to have basic expression in public life and its starting point is in education for all.

A further Noahide — universal — ethical law calls also for the respect of G-d and thereby also of religion. This is also couched as a prohibition of blasphemy. Populism rises up against the elite's — the media, university, bureaucracy and professions' — derision of religion. This is something carried out especially relentlessly by the media. The recent scandals relating to child sexual abuse in

---

[153] See "An education in a shared ethic", above, Chapter 6.

schools were pursued with almost exclusive attention to religious schools. The animus was at least as much against religion as against child abuse itself, which unfortunately occurred in schools across the spectrum. More recently, an invidious bill of the Victorian Government was defeated, which proposed to force religious schools to accept staff with values contrary to the ethos of the school. This Government was also successfully lobbied by an anti-religious group to exclude the optional special religious education hour from school hours, which we have mentioned above. The animus in all this is not indifference, but hostility to religious education and to religion in general.

"Multiculturalism" is a policy instrument of hedonistic materialism, which under the guise of preserving traditional cultures in their plurality, in fact works to destroy their organic structures and traditional values. The Greens state this quite clearly in their policy platform. It will accept the expression different cultures only within the framework of "universally accepted human rights." The ethics of traditional cultures are overwhelmingly opposed to same-sex marriage and to abortion on demand, and would like to see religious instruction made available to their children in Government Schools. All of these the Greens suppress as falling outside their categories of "universally accepted human rights." Thus, multi-culturalism does not seek to nourish the values of traditional cultures, but rather atomize them and bring their adherents into a secular universe of the Greens' materialistically conceived "universally accepte rights".

Not only does the populist revolt miss, and want to restore, G-d to our culture; it also resents the derision of religion in the public square. The Noahide law mandating respect for G-d, under a general rubric of a prohibition of blasphemy, is related also to the way in which religious institutions are treated by society. Religious institutions have always been privileged in moral societies. They have been non-taxable, donations to them have been tax-deductible and their students have been exempt from military service. Why is this so? It is because religious tradition is the guardian of ultimate social and personal values. It preserves the moral framework of society. Religious institutions are beyond society's mundane workings, but they are simultaneously supply the most comprehensive moral dimension within which social life proceeds. For this reason they were reverenced.

We see now how religion actually functions as the ultimate guardian of moral tradition in our own society: in times when the most basic values — such as the structure of the family and the protection of life, whether against abortion or euthanasia — are being attacked, and generally so by the liberal-relativistic media and the universities, it is *religious* bodies which are the primary source of resistance to these moves. It is religious bodies which know and remember and remind what the key and core values of the universal tradition are. Hence the attempts of radical-liberal and hedonistic-materialistic elites to strike at religious education, to remove protection from religious institutions and to apply all kinds of coercion to religious bodies, are essentially related to blasphemy. The attack on religion is blasphemy and in the words of an English Chief Justice in 1675, "the allegation that religion is a cheat tends to the dissolution of all Government". The populist revolt wants to restore respect for religion and its institutions.

Another of the Noahide laws also requires knowledge and respect for G-d and the ethics of religious tradition. This is the Noahide law of justice. The function of the justice system under Noahide law is to supervise society's conduct in accordance with Noahide law and all positive law (i.e. practical social legislation and regulation) consistent — or not inconsistent — with it. A judge must be beholden to G-d and to the Noahide laws. One of the greatest concerns of the present time is the personal belief systems of judges. Since they are not elected and are not recallable, except under the most unusual circumstances, and can influence the interpretation and application of law, it is essential that judges must first and foremost be beholden to the laws of G-d, that is to say to universal ethics. For it is universal ethics, the laws of G-d, which define the outer perimeter of the law. Judges, who give validity to same-sex marriage and abortion on demand — whether or not these have been previously enacted by Parliamentary statute — violate the Noahide law of justice.[154]

One of the greatest crises of our justice system today, is the growing incidence of crime, primarily associated with drugs, and family and social breakdown. We live in a time of unprecedented youth disaffection, depression and mental ill-health. Youth crime has also grown radically. Law and order, however, does not only require maintenance from above, from a judicial, corrections and police function. It also needs an anchoring in social values from below, which operate in the culture and in education.[155]

Certainly, there is a significant void in the teaching of basic ethics to emerging citizens. Beyond that, there is a disconnection between whatever ethics are taught and religious belief, which could fashion the effective authority *within* the human being for those values.[156] Traditionally this has been called *conscience*, and

---

[154] A former Chief Justice of the High Court of Australia, the Hon Murray Gleeson AC, writes (as quoted above in "The Courts and Universal Ethics"): "The idea of a level of justice over and above the positive law is widely accepted, but its practical implementation requires care. The enforcement of the law by courts is subject to an obligation of legitimacy. The law cannot rise above its source. The authority of judges cannot rise above the Constitution pursuant to which they are appointed. Problems in this regard come up from time to time. For example, in Fiji, to take a country in our region, as a result of activities in recent years, judges had to decide whether they would continue to sit in the courts and implement the law - and if so, what law? This was a society in which citizens were complaining that authority had been usurped. The judiciary in Pakistan, to take another example, has had to respond to changes in power raising questions as to the validity of the appointment of judges and the exercise of judicial authority.

I think the way most Australian judges would approach the question of universal ethics is not that there is some higher law, which authorizes judges to overthrow a positive law or to refuse to implement a positive law which they do not like, with which they disagree. Most judges would say that if they can't apply the law according to their consciences they ought to resign.

The approach of judges here is rather how universal ethics *inform the content and the practical application of positive law*. In our positive law, whether it is judge-made law or statute law enacted by Parliament, there are many values from the tradition of universal ethics, that inform the law and are taken into account by judges when they interpret and apply the law".

[155] As the Hon Murray Gleeson *(ibid.)* points out, a "hairy-chested" law-and-order rhetoric, with a multiplication of police officers and heavier jail sentences and reduced bail is not going to solve the law-and-order problem. As mentioned here, it is a question of how (a) we educate youth in values which make good social values and (b) how this can be internalized in personal conscience, i.e. anchored in *belief*.

[156] Professor Brian Hill remarks that *actually motivated* ethical conduct takes root in the context of belief systems and that education must accordingly situate ethics within a belief framework. See above Chapter 6, "An Education in a Shared Ethic".

the religious person relates this to the ethical knowledge of the soul, before and in the presence of G-d. The religious person calls it the soul. It is after all an education to civic values and the *internalization* of these values which gives children purpose, meaning and the internal monitoring of conscience to lead a moral life in society. A survey which I conducted with Professor Ramon Lewis demonstrated a positive correlation between a moral civic life — which eschews theft and respects justice. And a religious education (see "Why Should a Kid Pay for a Ride on a Train?", above Chapter 6).

The great crisis which faces us, today, however, is the vast sea of spiritual illiteracy. Religion is little more than an early childhood memory — if that — for most young people. It has received little or no support in Government schools. The youthful spiritually illiterate then enter college and university, ready for training into the secular world-view of hedonistic materialism. Populism, which rebels against lawlessness, senses the roots of lawlessness in a spiritual and ethical void. It welcomes religious belief and education back into society.

Mutuality in economic relations

One of the grievances of recent populism is that existing economic systems do not care for the integrity and security of economic relationships. We hear talk of a squeezed middle class and a deprived blue collar class. The phenomenon of economic restructuring and "dislocation" caused by constant technological innovation creates ongoing job insecurity. There is growing income inequality. Globalism leads to the outsourcing of jobs. Whether or not real earning power, house-purchasing power and employment has fallen, there is a strong sense of insecurity and flux in the economic life of individuals. Perhaps the strongest trend has been the relentless growth of huge corporations and the decline of small business, including the declining creation of new businesses, which were traditionally an important source of jobs.

As customers, people also find themselves as the fodder of vast corporations. Notwithstanding the action of regulatory bodies, banks, telecommunications companies and energy providers have a disproportionate leverage vis-a-vis the customer in an increasingly concentrated and oligopolistic market. Utility-prices rise, housing becomes increasingly unaffordable. The relationships between supplier, retailer or service-provider and customer become less personal; employment relationships within large firms similarly become more abstract and indifferent. The small intergenerational family business or farm is in decline. The technologically driven constant restructuring of business creates a feeling of insecurity and dislocation. Globalism and free trade contribute to the ever-present threat of annihilation of businesses which cannot stand up to them. Populism also has an anti-globalist streak which would seem to call for an element of protection and tariffs. But what is at the core of the populist discontent with economics is a crisis of the human relationships within economic relationships. Abstract, seemingly autonomous runaway processes — growing corporate agglomeration, technological restructuring, globalism — operate in a way seemingly independent of concern for the human being. No one cares if I lose my job; I am mere prey for the giant corporations — such as the banks — whose customer and client I am, but valued little or even cynically as such regarded; "innovation" proceeds, without any attempt to anticipate or control its consequences. The existence of a welfare safety net for those who fall by the wayside is only some solace for the loss of one's own economic and occupational identity.

Interestingly the populist upset with economics is not solved by the choice of a particular economic system. It does not find a panacea in some new economic model. Traditional and modern political-economic theories have looked for their answer to human economic wellbeing in specific models of ownership be they Capitalism, Communism, the Social-Democratic Welfare State and also a model of highly diffused private ownership called "Distributism" (or "Distributivism"). Each find their answers in different structures of ownership, which are supposed to guarantee the social goods of liberty and needs-satisfaction. Yet each model has been faulted. Laissez-faire capitalism was touted as a bulwark against the tyranny of the state, exemplified by Socialism. Such was the argument of Friedrich Hayek. But this system also has had its own major failings, where individual owners have been driven by rapacious greed. The Global Financial Crisis of 2008 put to rest the classic laissez-faire capitalist formulation of Adam Smith, that the universal pursuit of self-interest would enable an "invisible hand" to operate to guarantee prosperity for all. The experience of Communism, with the State ownership and management of the economy brought out all too vividly Lord Acton's maxim that power corrupts and absolute power corrupts absolutely. The mixed, welfare state might have been the best alternative to each of socialism and capitalism, but it operates at a huge social cost in terms of taxation and expenditure, plus the immense costs and inefficiencies of bureaucracy. Health and social services account for more than half the budget. Life on welfare is itself a subsistence existence. Welfare is not work, but a compensation for not working. Similarly, leisure does not compensate for unhappy work. The notion that we work in order to escape or end work and that work is attractive only because it gives the opportunity to "really live" during our holidays and leisure hours is a failure of the work relationship itself. The human being was "born" to work, as much as to enjoy leisure. Leisure does not therefore either quantitatively or qualitatively compensate for an unhappy work experience. Work *itself* must be a rewarding activity, both materially and humanly. The model of ownership, seeking the greatest possible distribution of ownership, called distributism, seeks to bolster small business, boost and multiply individual ownership, and to encourage cooperatives, trusting that this model avoids the evils of capitalism and socialism. Apart from the fact that franchises have been deemed not to meet the distributist model, because in fact the franchises are constrained into uniformity by the corporation that offers them (like MacDonalds), it does not seem politically or economically feasible to alter the existing structures of ownership on an economy-wide scale into a "cooperative commonwealth".

By revolting against the indifference of economic systems,

which seem to operate autonomously and automatically (*Selbstzweck*), instead of serving human beings, populism approaches a position of universal ethics. This is that universal economic ethics do not have to do with a particular system of economic relationships, but rather with ethical requirements upon any economic system. This has to do with the concept that *an economic relationship* — be it that of buyer and seller, employer and employee, manufacturer and distributor or distributor and retailer — *is a relationship between human beings*. Neither side should exploit the other and both are entitled to live and live decently, even if their prosperity is not equal.

The most basic requirement of the Noahide law of theft or material harm is that the property of one — be it goods, labour and bodily wellbeing or money — not be wrested without consent or be extracted through fraud and misled consent. But it goes beyond this and clearly we are not concerned only with this — the avoidance of theft and fraud — in ordinary economic relationships. These are matters of criminal theft. It is rather in the realm of civil law, and what is required *above* desisting from outright theft, that the Noahide law of theft and material harm is significant for the ethics of economic relationships. Here it does not only prohibit deprivation of the property and entitlements of others, but also requires *positive* expressions of human reciprocity. This relates to the avoidance of subtler forms of exploitation, to fairness, the negation of greed and to the regard for the wellbeing of others.

Accordingly, when the focus is upon the actual moral character of an economic exchange between two or more persons or groups, the structure of ownership, including its scale or size, becomes formally irrelevant. A huge firm in a capitalist economy may act ethically, whilst a tiny business could exhibit gross exploitation. A natural monopoly (such as a sole provider of water in a district) or a comprehensive socialist, managed economy could be run fairly or corruptly. A collective, made out of a large number of small owners, according to the distributist model, could also act, as a result of collusion, to exploit its suppliers or customers.

Whether one system is more or less prone to abuse, and whether such a system is politically, technically and socially more or less implementable is not our concern here. All can exhibit abuse; and all *could* function ethically: where seller and customer, employer and employee treat *one another* ethically.

The most fundamental consideration which must govern an economic relationship is that both sides of it deserve to make a living. This does not mean that their livelihoods have to be equal, but each needs to be able to live and satisfy basic needs. Predatory pricing, and the undercutting and eventual destruction of a competitor negates this principle. In this instance, a wealthier firm sells a product below cost for sufficient time to destroy the competitor, whose resources are not adequate to make a similar sacrifice. Once the competitor has been destroyed, the predatory firm then hikes its price and recovers its losses. The attitude of competition needs to be that the other is also entitled to a fair chance to make its living — not to be "destroyed". The exploitation of the consumer, through overcharging through price hiking or collusion, and similarly the exploitation of the supplier — for example the farmers, who are forced to accept less than subsistence prices for their goods by a supermarket duopoly are breaches of reciprocity. They constitute exploitation.

Greed is an attitude which is not only ethically reprehensible but can also be catastrophic in its consequences, as we saw in the Global Financial Crisis of 2008. The culture of huge CEO salaries carries the message of "profit at any cost you can get away with". In Australia this culture is seen in a highly concentrated banking market (controlled by four banking groups) extracting immense profits, for example, through inordinate fees for dishonoured cheques and slightly overdrawn accounts, something which can easily occur with delay in the processing of credit card orders. Technically, in a civil law relationship between individuals penalties cannot be unilaterally imposed (as distinct from the State's ability to punish), but banks in Australia were levying a $50 spot penalty every time a savings account was overdrawn by a dishonoured cheque or even through the late processing of a credit card order. The revenue from such fees and penalties levied against their own customers brought in millions to the banks, through the predation of their own client base. After an outcry, this particular fee ($50) was finally trimmed back to $9, based on assessment of "time-loss" and "harm" suffered by the banks through these micro-overdrawings.

The point has been made that companies which are listed on the stock exchange are particularly open to the pursuit of exploitative and non-reciprocal practices because they are driven by shareholders to make profits and profits alone. There is some solace for those whose superannuation funds are grown by the same firms that "rip them off" as customers. But this cannot provide an ultimate justification for all those customers who do not consent or are not party to this deal. It is precisely the large (indeed mega) family businesses like IKEA and ALDI which, being immune to the exclusive profit interest of publicly owned, share-holder driven companies, have significantly excelled in terms of their corporate ethics, relationships with suppliers and customers. A large firm can have a very good corporate ethos: it treats its workers thoughtfully, and its workers work hard and loyally for it. It considers its suppliers and customers as persons, entitled to livelihood and value.

The fact that a privately owned company has a greater potential to act ethically does not morally permit a publicly owned company — answerable to its stockholders — to act unethically. And here we must remember that unethically does not only mean "criminally" but also "inconsiderately" and "callously". There are various ways ethically to "audit" and regulate the conduct of business. But regulation and legislation to achieve this first requires a culture which recognizes the partner of our economic exchange as a human being like ourselves, with whom we should deal with regard, reciprocity and care. This is actually a spiritually informed ethics, and under Noahide law translates into concrete requirements. In the populist ferment it means that, above our commitment to any one existing economic, trade or financial system, the primary consideration is the actual (quantitative and qualitative) livelihoods (not wholly replaceable by welfare handouts) of the people party to it. If necessary, modifications and mixes must be made to our existing systems to implement these *concrete* moral objectives. The two sides of an economic relationship should be driven not by mere *envy*, which breeds conflict and confrontation, nor solely by *competitiveness* for an ever larger stake, which drives exploitation. The ruling ethic needs to be one of reciprocity, which grasps that each side of the relationship needs and deserves to live. Populism, as its name suggests, is about *people*.

Restoring a true perspective on nature

The populist grievance against the world-view of hedonistic materialism with regard to the environment has both theoretical and practical sides. The Greens' philosophy is one which makes nature an "Absolute". It is a fundamentally materialist world-view which sees physical nature as "all there is" and human beings as a form of animal life which inhabits it. Consequently, human survival and well-being depends on the maintenance and service — to the extent that the human being can carry this out — of the body of nature. Nature, in their view is finite and combustible. It is worn down by human industry and human needs. The dominant concern is the theory of "global warming". The future of the planet — as an inhabitable place for human beings at least — depends, according to their view, on human management, especially of carbon emissions, which can, they think, eventually destroy the planet.

The consequences of this doctrine are twofold — practical and ideological. In practical terms, it means that human industry and energy production (and farming, since animals are also emitters) must be transformed and cut back, in order to maintain the mechanism of creation. Consequently, industry must be penalized through carbon credit and emissions trading schemes until it gives up using fossil fuels. Consumers of energy must be prepared right away to pay higher prices for renewable energy. So too they must be ready for price-increases on all commodities, as the penalties on commodities produced through high carbon industries are passed on to them. Above all industry and jobs which depend on high carbon emissions must be cut back. Many in the populist revolt perceive this as a direct threat to the economic wellbeing of industry and of ordinary citizens as workers and consumers.

If, the ideology of global warming continues, humanity does not go this way, then arctic ice-caps will melt, landmasses will sink into the water, and a whole host of disasters will come upon nature and of course, as a consequence, humanity. There are two things about this global theory which irk the populist revolt. One is its mythic quality: a view of nature as a vast, wounded beast, which must be helped back on to its feet. Others have termed it, less delicately, "witchcraft" and "neo-Paganism", according to which the human being must "serve" nature.

The traditional religious view, with which populism has a much stronger affinity than hedonistic materialism (which in fact repudiates it) is that nature was given by G-d to serve the human being. This does not mean that the human being may willfully abuse animals or heedlessly destroy natural resources. On the contrary: in the use which the human being has been permitted to make of animals and vegetative or mineral parts of nature, one is restricted not in the amount of one's use but in the constructiveness of one's use. That is to say, the material incorporated or used, should be done purposefully and with a minimum of pain to animals and wastefulness to non-animal resources. If our actions directly affect another person, i.e. we draw heavily on a finite water supply, or we pollute a stream and thereby kill fish which others need to consume, that is directly calculable harm to other people and for that reason is forbidden. Similarly, if I wish my own fields to produce next year, I must be careful to let the land rest at intervals and to fertilize it. But all of this is in the calculable and foreseeable short term. On a "cosmic" scale, however, I am not bound to make calculations of remote places and time frames about the state of the cosmos.

In short, I must do what is demonstrably and foreseeably beneficial to myself and avoid what is demonstrably and foreseeably harmful to others, including inflicting unnecessary pain on animals and heedless waste in material resources. Yet as far as knowing the macro-conditions and inputs, these have always been beyond me. How the soil will yield, what the rains will be — these have always been things for which people of traditional faith have prayed. They sowed seed in the earth, and prayed to G-d for its success. They have been careful of what they have done, to sow the land properly, but they have not made the macro-calculations, they have not calculated the weather. And this is because this is in the lap of G-d. Nature is not a big machine. It is the glove of G-d's providence. Its bounty is not calculable. We have to do ours and G-d His. Cosmic calculations are therefore idolatrous: they make nature into a huge self-subsistent animal or machine, for which human beings are veterinarians or mechanics. That is not the posture of the ordinary, prudent but praying person. It is not about servicing or appeasing the "great one", "the all that is there", the "mythic beast" — "nature".

The second grievance of populism in regard to this environmentalism is a more practical one: human beings' livelihoods (in industries which rely on fossil fuels) and the affordability of their goods and services (raised by costs for carbon emissions) should not be sacrificed out of fear for the health of the "great beast" of nature. It has rebelled against the practical economics and impact upon human livelihood of the doctrine of "global warming".

Those who reject the "theory" of global warming are not anti-science. They are sceptical of its grand-theoretical vision and its evidence. Many top scientists share this scepticism. So it is with all dominant scientific paradigms. The fact that a majority of the world's scientists might support historically one paradigm over another does not make it more true. History and the transformation of scientific paradigms attests to this. Rather, we have instead the ideological dominance of a particular grand theory and way of looking at the world. What irks grass roots is the mythic cast of this particular grand theory — its metaphysic which changes nature from the glove of G-d, into a huge machine or beast, to be serviced by humanity.

It is worth finally considering traditional religious doctrine concerning nature. In the biblical Garden of Eden, the human being did not have to work at all. One of the curses handed out to the human being after the sin of the tree of knowledge was the phenomenon of work: that nature became an opponent and that the human being had to toil to eke out a living from it. This curse, however, is not an eternal punishment for the human being. Rather work, as taught by mystical religious doctrine, is the process by which nature, tainted and corrupted by human sin, is restored to its pristine state, as a instrument for the manifold blessings of G-d. Thus, Maimonides writes, that in the times of the Redemption of humanity, material abundance will be readily available and the human being will be lifted out of the struggle with nature, and the occupation of all humanity will be "to know G-d", to study, pray and behold G-dliness.

What this signifies is that "nature" is in fact an instrument of G-d's bounty. Its relationship to the human depends not only one's circumspect use of it in the immediate present and place, but also upon one's personal merit and prayer before G-d. It is not for us to take over G-d's work, and to predict and produce nature's responses. As someone once said about global warming, "Let's get tomorrow's weather right first". The weather was always something which a human being *prayed* for.

One could educate populism not to be afraid of various trends which point towards the end of work. The spectre of robotics might be viewed with some anxiety, but it can also be grasped as the actual freeing from work. There is no doubt that technology is available to endow humanity with abundance, the only question being how the management and distribution of that abundance is to proceed. The spiritual — redemptive — concept that nature can in fact be a source of great bounty, and that this bounty can be extracted without bitter toil is even anticipated in the writings of Karl Marx in his *Grundrisse*, where it is envisaged that human beings will be primarily occupied with the management of things

— the developed instruments of production — not people. Unfortunately, the materialistic philosophy which underpinned Marxism saw to it that the struggle of human interests perverted the socialization of industry. A *spiritual* humanity — given that souls work together better than bodies — might well manage the economy of abundance much better.

Work — the original biblical "curse" upon humanity — is often viewed anxiously as an existential need of humanity. Unemployment per se is a fear. Does that fear proceed from the equation of employment with livelihood or because people *do not know* what to do with leisure and see it as existential abyss? Certainly, the phenomenon of longevity and an aging population, creates this issue potentially for all individuals: what are they to do with decades of retirement? The answer to this from a religious point of view, is that as people get older, their spiritual sensitivities mature: the growing weakness of the body is associated with the growing strength of the soul. But this can only properly be when humans are spiritually literate, when they have developed spiritual consciousness and have a spiritual education, to deploy in their leisure and old age. Indeed it has been — rightly — suggested, that older people should not be seen as an economic problem (unproductive and expensive to maintain) but as a spiritual resource for society. So too, with humanity: in its old age — the times of redemption — it comes into its spiritual maturity: in the words of Maimonides, quoted above, "at that time, all the material luxuries will be as abundant as the dust of the earth, and the occupation of humanity will be to know G-d alone". Spirituality comes into its own amongst the bounty of nature.

What unlocks the bounty of nature is not only technology, but also spirituality. This is because nature is not a mythic beast, but the glove of G-d, Who both dwells within, and transcends, it. The populist revolt — the revolt of ordinary people, who believe in G-d more consciously than the elites — resents turning nature into an idol, and making humans its servants. Without dispensing with prudence, care, holding back from cruelty to animals and wastefulness with resources, ordinary people know or are ready to hear that nature was created to serve the human being in the ethical project of civilizing the world. The farmer and the worker — and all those who have not been overtaken by hubris — know that the weather (and all other material abundance) will be brought to them by a G-d *beyond* nature, through the circumspect preparations which they make *within* nature.

The protection of life

Populism is unnerved by, and responds strongly, to violence to, and the removal of protection from, life. The greatest attack on G-d, is the attack on the human spirit, made in G-d's likeness, in a living body. The attack on life is an attack on Divine property. This attack comes from two directions, pre-eminently, in our time. On the one hand there is violent killing perpetrated by international terrorism of which ISIS and its related bodies are the major exemplar. The other is from the (until now) hegemonic liberalism which installed across the world regimes of unlimited killing of human babies prior to (and sometimes right up to) birth, and which toys constantly with euthanasia and "assisted suicide". Most, if not all, the populists are against the regime of abortion on demand. The connection which Noahide law places between killing of the vulnerable and the failure to stand up to violence within and against societies is that both constitute a failure to protect and defend life.

The liberal left — consistent with its hedonistic materialism — tolerates killing in the advancement of interests. Around the world it supports insurgent movements. It speaks about the so-called right to self-determination of movements which are not states. One example of this is the so-called Palestinian liberation organization and its sister organization, Hamas. Instead of granting Governments prima facie sovereignty and authority in their own lands, they endorse insurgent or "liberation" movements around the world.

When, however, it comes to national *self*-defence, the Greens, the flag-bearers of hedonistic materialism, are very soft. They want Australia to renounce any development of nuclear power, whether with or without military applications. In addition to that, they want to remove Australia from an alliance with America, as that would implicate Australia in American conflicts. An extraordinary naïveté comes at the price of high vulnerability. Another aspect of the Greens' foreign policy is an extension of what President Obama called multilateralism, and the reliance on international organizations, including the United Nations and the International Court of Justice. The defect in these organizations is that they have no real power and subscription to them in fact weakens the traditional role of deterrence in favour of toothless diplomacy. The nuclear deal with Teheran is a classic case of the renunciation of the threat of force (and sanctions) in favour of mere diplomatic assurances. This is effectively a renunciation of self-defence in real, military terms. Yet another downplaying of self-defence is the Greens' call for a minimal defence force, and a substantial removal of filtering on refugees and border protection. In this they are typical of the left-liberal regimes against which populism has arisen.

The supposed "idealism" which postures amidst the disavowal of real military self-defence (including pursuit of the pursuer) in fact fosters global extremism and terrorism, for which the United Nations General Assembly has been a cover, as we see in the vast number of motions supporting a non-state "liberation" movement, namely the PLO. It has allowed for Iranian adventurism. On the other hand, this movement uses international aid as a weapon for disseminating abortion on demand to third world countries (by making it conditional on abortion). This is also a Greens' policy: to tie this string to all Australian aid, and it was a string of American policy under Obama. It promotes this form of killing, — of the unborn, forbidden by Noahide law — internationally.

Within our own society the policy of left liberalism and of the Greens in particular, unleashes killing on a grand scale. It has defined prenatal life totally out of the realm of life deserving of any protection at all. This however is not what biblical and universal ethics state. Under Noahide law, full culpability exists for killing an unborn child. Even though its existence has a quality of latency, it is still endowed with a soul (from after 40 days from conception), and this makes such a life Divine property, which no person has the right to dispose of, other than under grounds of self-defence, i.e. threat to the life of the mother or possibly radical non-viability of its own life in the event of extreme deformity. Within 40 days of conception, in extreme circumstances such as rape or incest, there may also be permission to abort. However, the child is not the property of its mother — anymore than her own life is her property — to dispose of at will. Human life is sacred, it is a Divine possession, and can only be disposed of under circumstances which G-d Himself has prescribed.

Abortion has become an anchor of the permissive society, in which sexuality is pursued without commitment or responsibility. A person knows that he or she may face extremely serious consequences for killing someone as a result of careless driving. However, this society does not import that seriousness or responsibility to life which can be engendered through sexual activity outside the framework of marital commitment. The idea that one can do what one likes and the state will kill (and medically rebate the cost of the abortion of) any children born from such activities underwrites a culture of indifference to life. Open-slather killing of babies up to birth is the mark of society which has repressed its spirituality to a high degree. The even more ghoulish spectre of euthanasia is also ever present in this society, and also constitutes murder under Noahide law. Apart from that, it destroys the ethic of care, whereby the family of a terminally ill person could conceivably pressure the dying person to exit, and the dying person must then find the inner strength to defend his or her own existence. It poses as compassion, but it has no compassion at all for the true person, the living soul. In euthanasia, it corners the vulnerable, who are losing speech, to defend themselves, and in abortion on demand kills outright those who have no speech. For the ideology of hedonistic materialism, life is the calculus of pleasure and pain of sentient flesh. In euthanasia, it is the flight from one's own (the suffering person's) pain; and in abortion on demand, from the pain (or burden) caused by others (the unborn). The attack on life, and so upon the human spirit (and Divine likeness within it), casts upon the wider society the long shadow of depression and suicide, which has grown steadily. The populism of the spirit, by definition, values life.

It is under G-d, that the "anarchy" of international society becomes a society with a common law. What will make peace and put an end to violence is not diplomacy and treaties, but as John F. Kennedy stated, those values which resonate in the hearts and minds of ordinary men and women. Populist leaders around the world are drawn to one another on the basis of shared values, and there is, above all, a commonality between leaders who publicly acknowledge G-d, and the set of shared values anchored in religious tradition. Such leaders, in finding their commonly affirmed code in the Noahide laws and common authority in G-d, will come together by virtue of that authority alone. Neither ISIS (a pseudo-religious organization which speaks about "G-d" but means itself), with its associated terrorist groups, on the one hand, nor hedonistic materialism, on the other, hand believe authentically in G-d or universal morality. The violence which haunts international relations can only be turned into a peaceful international society by the acknowledgment of a common authority, G-d, and His laws, the Noahide laws. This is the promise of a true populism of the human spirit.

A Populism of the Spirit

www.ingramcontent.com/pod-product-compliance
Lightning Source LLC
Chambersburg PA
CBHW052055300426
44117CB00013B/2141